D1519025

A Study of Cyril Tourneur

A Study of Cyril Tourneur

by

Peter B. Murray

UNIVERSITY OF PENNSYLVANIA PRESS
Philadelphia

Published in Great Britain, India, and Pakistan

by the Oxford University Press

London, Bombay, and Karachi

Library of Congress Catalog Card Number: 64–10898

Printed in the United States of America

Preface

CYRIL TOURNEUR IS COMMONLY MENTIONED IN THE NEXT breath after Shakespeare and Webster as one of the important poet-dramatists of the Jacobean era, yet he has never received the attention his stature would seem to deserve. Lamb and Swinburne praised his work, but neither they nor later scholars and critics such as T. S. Eliot and Una Ellis-Fermor have fully understood him. His writing has too often been regarded as neurotic self-expression rather than art, and since little is known of his life, critics have hesitated to undertake a full-scale interpretation of his works. And there are other problems. The allegory of his *Transformed Metamorphosis* seems as lost and dim as the facts of its author's life, and the murky controversy over the authorship of *The Revenger's Tragedy* must give pause to any would-be student.

For my attempt to dispel the darkness surrounding Tourneur, I have sought light from the literature and thought of his time, especially from his works themselves and their sources and analogues. My study of *The Revenger's Tragedy* has turned up new and I think conclusive internal evidence that Thomas Middleton is the author, and I have therefore interpreted *The Transformed Metamorphosis* and *The Atheist's Tragedy* apart from that play. *The Revenger's Tragedy* has so greatly affected most critics that they have been able to see Tourneur's other works only as leading up to or away from it —a critical approach that has seriously distorted *The Trans-*

7

formed Metamorphosis and has made *The Atheist's Tragedy* appear confused. The exclusion of *The Revenger's Tragedy* from Tourneur's works seems to clarify his art and thought and to explain the place of creative writing in his life.

In quoting Renaissance writers I have exactly reproduced the texts cited, with the exception that I have used modern *s, u, v, i,* and *j,* and have substituted *n* for the tilde.

I owe a great debt to Professor Allan G. Chester, who guided me through this study, and to Professors Matthias A. Shaaber, Matthew W. Black, and Maurice Johnson, whose helpful criticism of my work on this and other projects has been of great value to me. I also thank my colleagues John Bernstein and J. M. LaSala for their helpful suggestions, and William E. Miller of the Horace Howard Furness Memorial Library at the University of Pennsylvania and Mrs. Delphine O. Richardson of the University of Pennsylvania Library for their kind advice and assistance in my research.

Further, I owe an obvious debt to those who have studied Tourneur and his contemporaries before me. I wish to mention here those who have graciously given permission to quote copyrighted works : Allardyce Nicoll, for his edition of *The Works of Cyril Tourneur,* Fanfrolico Press (London, 1929); Basil Blackwell and Mott, Ltd., for *The Works of Thomas Nashe,* edited by R. B. McKerrow (Oxford, 1958); Cambridge University Press for Muriel C. Bradbrook's *Themes and Conventions of Elizabethan Tragedy* (Cambridge, 1935); Mrs. Gerald R. Owst for Professor Owst's *Preaching in Medieval England* (Cambridge University Press, 1926); Methuen & Co., Ltd., for Una Ellis-Fermor's *The Jacobean Drama,* fourth edition (London, 1958); the Henry E. Huntington Library for Paul H. Kocher's *Science and Religion in Elizabethan England* (San Marino, 1953); Harcourt, Brace, & World, Inc., for T. S. Eliot's *Selected Essays, 1917–1932* (New York, 1950); the

Indiana University Press for *The Novels of Thomas Deloney,* edited by Merritt E. Lawlis (Bloomington, 1961); and Phyllis B. Bartlett and the Modern Language Association of America for Professor Bartlett's edition of *The Poems of George Chapman* (New York, 1941). I am grateful to Robert F. Metzdorf, editor of the *Papers of the Bibliographical Society of America,* for permission to reprint my study of the authorship of *The Revenger's Tragedy,* which was published in the *Papers* for the second quarter of 1962. And lastly I am grateful to my wife, without whose encouragement this project would not have been possible.

PETER B. MURRAY

Swarthmore, 1962

For Grace Pearson

Contents

I

Life and Works

VERY LITTLE IS KNOWN ABOUT THE LIFE OF CYRIL TOURNEUR. We have only a handful of documents that attest to his having ever existed at all, and so we can only speculate about the general shape of his career, suggesting when and why he wrote and so getting some idea of the place of writing in his life. Nothing is known of his family or education. He may have been related to Richard Turnor of Canons, Essex, since both of them were associated with Sir Francis Vere and the Cecils, but no documentary evidence has been found to support this possibility.[1]

We have a letter of 1613 telling us that Tourneur had served as secretary to Sir Francis Vere "in former times,"[2]—a relationship that leaves a mark on most of his signed works. Of these the earliest, *The Transformed Metamorphosis*,[3] printed by Valentine Sims in 1600, was dedicated to Sir Christopher Heydon, who had been with Vere on the expedition of Essex

---

[1] See the introduction by Allardyce Nicoll to his edition of *The Works of Cyril Tourneur* (London, 1929), pp. 2–5. My account of documents concerning Tourneur is mostly drawn from this source.

[2] See below, p. 18.

[3] S.T.C. 24152.

15

and Drake to Cadiz in 1596. In view of Tourneur's later association with both Heydon and Vere, there is a chance that he went on this voyage, probably in an humbler berth than as secretary to Vere : quite possibly in service to Heydon, whom he regards as his patron in the dedication of *The Transformed Metamorphosis*. Perhaps the fruit of that appeal for Heydon's help was the appointment as Vere's secretary. In any event, his later works indicate that it cannot have been many years after the voyage of 1596 that Tourneur went to work for Vere.

Tourneur's next signed work was *A Funerall Poeme. Upon the Death of the Most Worthie and True Souldier, Sir Francis Vere, Knight,*[4] printed for Eleazar Edgar late in 1609, a few months after Vere's death. The three hundred or so iambic pentameter couplets of this poem describe in plain terms the virtues of character and intellect that made Vere a great commander and a true subject of the realm. The poem is important chiefly as it shows Tourneur's considerable familiarity with Vere's military career and with his methods as a commander, but it also has literary merit in its unadorned and straightforward manner, which is appropriate to the manly, honest character of its subject.[5]

The Atheist's Tragedy,[6] printed by Thomas Snodham at the end of 1611, has as its hero a young soldier who, like Vere, served at the siege of Ostend in 1601–02 and wore a scarlet garment by which he could be recognized on the field of battle.[7] Judging by its apparent imitation and criticism of

---

[4] S.T.C. 24148. Entered in the Stationers' books on October 16, 1609. *A Transcript of the Registers of the Company of Stationers of London, 1554–1640,* ed. Edward Arber (London, 1875–77), III, 419.

[5] See Ruth Wallerstein, *Studies in Seventeenth-Century Poetic* (Madison, 1950), p. 84.

[6] S.T.C. 24146. Entered in the Stationers' books on September 14, 1611. Ed. Arber, III, 467.

[7] *Cf. Funerall Poeme,* l. 517, with *The Atheist's Tragedy,* I.ii.244–245, and II.i.115–121. All citations of Tourneur are to the edition of Nicoll.

George Chapman's *Revenge of Bussy D'Ambois,* usually assigned to 1610, *The Atheist's Tragedy* must have been written within the period 1610–11.

On February 15, 1611/12, "A play booke beinge a Trage-comedye called, *The Noble man* written by Cyrill Tourneur" was entered on the Stationers' books for publication by Edward Blount.[8] This play was never printed, however, and its manuscript was one of those destroyed over a century later by Warburton's infamous cook.[9] It is ironic that for this lost play we can cite some seventeenth-century stage history, though we cannot do so for either Tourneur's *Atheist's Tragedy* or the anonymous *Revenger's Tragedy*[10] (published 1607). *The Nobleman* is recorded in the Revels' list as having been performed at court by the King's Men on February 23, 1611/12, and again at the end of 1612.[11]

Some time in 1612 Tourneur wrote a "character" of Robert Cecil, Earl of Salisbury, who died in May of that year.[12] This character ticks off Cecil's virtues and accomplishments with no attempt at wit or art, and Tourneur's purpose seems to be simply to demonstrate appreciation of the great statesman as an appeal for assistance from succeeding members of the powerful Cecil family.

The final surviving work bearing Tourneur's name is *A*

---

[8] Ed. Arber, III, 478.

[9] Nicoll, *op. cit.,* p. 24.

[10] S.T.C. 24149. Entered in the Stationers' Register October 7, 1607. Ed. Arber, III, 360.

[11] E. K. Chambers, *The Elizabethan Stage, 1558–1616* (Oxford, 1923), III, 500; IV, 126–127.

[12] Nicoll, *op. cit.,* pp. 25–27. Though the "character" exists in several manuscript copies, the attribution to Tourneur was based upon the interpretation of the "Jerrill" or "Sevill" of the manuscripts as mistranscriptions of *Cyril* until Bernard M. Wagner reported a manuscript having "Cyrill Tourneur" at the end. See "Cyril Tourneur," *TLS,* April 23, 1931, p. 327. Samuel A. Tannenbaum is not convinced by Wagner's evidence of Tourneur's claim to the character, however. See "A Tourneur Mystification," *MLN,* XLVII (1932), 141–143.

Griefe On the Death of Prince Henrie . . . ,[13] printed by
Nicholas Okes and published both separately and in a volume
containing *Three Elegies on the Most Lamented Death of
Prince Henrie,* the other two written by John Webster and
Thomas Heywood (1613). In the elegy on Henry, as Miss
Wallerstein notes, Tourneur moves beyond the simple eulogy
and character analysis that sufficed for his treatment of Vere.
He now sets his lines in a dramatic context, and broadens his
contemplation to include the metaphysical implications of
Henry's death. These features of the poem, and also its
rhetoric and the rhythm of its couplet, suggest familiarity
with Donne's *Anniversaries.* Tourneur is still, however, as in
the elegy on Vere, more plain in diction and straightforwardly
rational in approach than is Donne.[14]

The only other contemporary record of Tourneur as a
writer is in a June 1613 letter by Robert Daborne, one of
Henslowe's hack playwrights. Writing to Henslowe to request
an advance of forty shillings for his work, Daborne stated that
he had "given Cyrill Tourneur an act of ye Arreignment of
London to write."[15] This play, if it was ever actually written,
has left no traces discernible in our time.

Later records of Tourneur's life chiefly relate to his career
as a public servant. In December of 1613 he carried official
letters from London to Brussels.[16] From Nimuegen on August
14, 1614, James Bathurst wrote to William Trumbull:

> The party whose letter I enclosed to you, and whose name you
> could not decipher, is one Mr. Cirrill Turner, that belongs
> to General Cecil and was in former times Secretary to Sir

---

[13] S.T.C. 24151. Entered in the Stationers' Register December 25, 1612.
Ed. Arber, III, 510.

[14] Ruth Wallerstein, *op. cit.,* pp. 84–86.

[15] Quoted from *The Alleyn Papers,* ed. John P. Collier, in *Shakespeare
Society,* IX (London, 1843), 58.

[16] Nicoll, *op. cit.,* p. 29.

Francis Vere. He told me at his first coming to this town he
had been at Brussels and received many courtesies from you.
He is now gone to the army with his Colonel; otherwise he
had written a second letter to you that you might have better
known him.[17]

In 1617 Tourneur was arrested on the order of the Privy
Council for reasons unknown to us, but was soon released upon
the bond of Sir Edward Cecil, nephew of Robert Cecil.[18] At
some time during these years Tourneur held a position under
the States of Holland, for at the end of his life he had a pension
from them of sixty pounds a year.[19]

Sir Edward Cecil took Tourneur along with him as Secretary of the Council of War and the Marshal's Court on the
voyage to seize Spanish treasure ships at Cadiz in October
1625. Tourneur lost the better position when Charles I
appointed Sir John Glanville Secretary of the Council of War
as a punishment for criticizing the expense of the royal court.
The Spanish fleet eluded the English, and Cecil's ships turned
north on November 16. Before they could reach England,
however, disease ravaged many crews. Cecil's flagship, the
Royal Anne, put ashore 160 sick men at Kinsale, Ireland, on
December 11, 1625. Among them was Cyril Tourneur, who
died at Kinsale on February 28, 1625/26.[20]

This concludes what is known with certainty of the life and
works of Cyril Tourneur. What remains is conjecture. In 1656
Edward Archer attributed *The Revenger's Tragedy*—mistakenly, as I believe—to "Tournour." This attribution stood
without recorded question until the end of the nineteenth
century, but since then it has been much debated. Most

[17] In Trumbull Papers, Misc. Vol. VI, No. 99, quoted from James R.
Sutherland, "Cyril Tourneur," *TLS,* April 16, 1931, p. 307.
[18] Nicoll, *op. cit.,* p. 29.
[19] *Ibid.,* p. 31.
[20] *Ibid.,* pp. 29–32.

twentieth-century scholarship, including my own, favors instead the claim of Thomas Middleton to the play.[21] Even before I became convinced that Middleton was the author, I had concluded that, contrary to many earlier interpreters, the play does not reveal its author to be, like Vindici, neurotically obsessed with evil. Since this supposed obsession of the author has been the chief consideration barring the play from a place among Middleton's works, I have included a detailed explication demonstrating the playwright's psychological objectivity and his controlled artistry in symbol, character and structure.

Allardyce Nicoll believes that Tourneur may have written the prose satire *Laugh and lie Downe: or, The worldes Folly,* printed in 1605 by Jeffrey Charlton. The dedication bears the initials C.T., but no other evidence, internal or external, attaches Tourneur to this dreary pamphlet under a delightful title.[22] Scholars have also argued that Tourneur may have written Act I and the first and perhaps the third scenes of Act II of *The Honest Mans Fortune,* a "Beaumont and Fletcher" play believed to date from 1613.[23] Evidence from style, especially meter, is used to divide this dull tragicomedy among five writers, Tourneur being given at least his due share of the total. The portion assigned him is well beneath his range of work.[24]

---

[21] See my discussion of this question in Chapter IV. *The Revenger's Tragedy,* printed in 1607 (S.T.C. 24149), was doubtless written after Marston's *Malcontent* (1604). Let us note in passing that there was no second printing of any of Tourneur's works or of *The Revenger's Tragedy* in the seventeenth century, excepting the reprint of *The Revenger's Tragedy* in 1608, which differs from the text of 1607 only in the date on the title page (S.T.C. 24150).

[22] Nicoll, *op. cit.,* pp. 16–18.

[23] See E. H. C. Oliphant, *The Plays of Beaumont and Fletcher* (New Haven, 1927), pp. 385ff., 514 and 516; and J. Gerritsen, *The Honest Mans Fortune,* Groningen Studies in English No. 3 (Djakarta, 1952).

[24] The candidacy of Tourneur as author of the anonymous manuscript play, the *Second Maiden's Tragedy,* is based almost entirely on its similarities to *The Revenger's Tragedy.* If we discount *The Revenger's Tragedy,*

Tourneur's career seems to be divided into three fairly distinct parts. From about 1600 to 1609 he was Sir Francis Vere's secretary. After the death of Vere in 1609, he began to devote more of his energies to creative writing, developing the talent he had shown in *The Transformed Metamorphosis*. For 1609–July 1613 there is no record of his service in any official capacity. In this period falls virtually his entire literary production: all of his signed works except *The Transformed Metamorphosis* date from this period, and there is record of his work on two lost plays. From his employment as one of Henslowe's hack playwrights in 1613, we may guess that he was trying to earn a major portion of his livelihood from his writing, and was having a hard time doing so. Before the end of that year he returned to government service, and we hear no more of him as a writer. As his bid for patronage in *The Transformed Metamorphosis* perhaps won him the appointment as Vere's secretary, so it is possible that the elegy on Henry and the character of Cecil won him later posts.

The figure emerging from these scant facts is a man whose fine hand as a secretary would never permit time to give full development to a quite correspondingly fine ability as poet and dramatist. Evidence of genius there is, to be sure, in *The Atheist's Tragedy* and *The Transformed Metamorphosis,* but in what we know of his life there is also evidence that his work as a writer was not of paramount interest to him : he wrote only when he was unemployed, and in what he wrote his effort was often directed more to the pursuit of patronage than of what we understand as literary excellence. *The Transformed*

---

and study the play only in relation to Tourneur and Middleton's undisputed works, we can see only similarities to Middleton. See Richard H. Barker, "The Authorship of the *Second Maiden's Tragedy* and *The Revenger's Tragedy,*" *SAB*, XX (1945), 51–62, 121–133; and Harold Stenger's critical edition entitled *The Second Maiden's Tragedy*, a 1954 University of Pennsylvania dissertation.

Metamorphosis and *The Atheist's Tragedy,* however, stand apart from the general mediocrity of Tourneur's career, and deserve attention as striking achievements of poetic imagination.

II

The Transformed Metamorphosis

1 THE CORRUPTION AND RENEWAL OF THE WORLD

TOURNEUR'S DEDICATION OF *The Transformed Metamorphosis*, after describing Sir Christopher Heydon as an adorner of Parnassus and as "Artes Patron, Champion to the highest,/ That givest the Sunne a fairer radiance,"[1] goes on in a series of metaphors to provide an obscure key for the interpretation of the poem :

> To thee Musophilus, *that still appliest*
> *Thy sacred soule, to be Trueths esperance.*
> To thee (*this Epinyctall register,*
> *Rasde out by* Eos *rayes) I write to thee.*
> To thee (*this hoarie* Hiems, *kill'd by* Ver :)
> To thee (*this metamorphosde Tragoedie*)
> To thee, *I write my Apotheosie:*
> Moecenas, *strengthen my Tyrocinie.*

These lines tell us the poem is a dark or nocturnal (Epinyctall)

---

[1] All quotations of Tourneur follow the text of *The Works of Cyril Tourneur,* ed. Allardyce Nicoll (London, 1929).

register in which the darkness is dispelled by the light of dawn
(Eos). The work is to be "Epinyctall" in three senses : it
concerns a period of darkness in the world, it reflects a possible darkness of soul or outlook, and it is darkly obscure. The
poem is also a greyed winter (Hiems) overcome by spring
(Ver), and, similarly, a tragedy "metamorphosde" by a happy
ending. For the poet it is a spiritual rebirth or glorification, a
new beginning in his life.

According to each of these metaphors, the poem tells a story
of death and rebirth. In every instance Tourneur implicitly or
explicitly employs the sun as his central symbol. In the first
instance it is the coming of the dawn that drives away the
night. In the second it is the return of the sun from the south
that ushers in the spring. Finally, the rebirth of the sun at the
winter solstice and the triumph of sunlight over darkness at the
vernal equinox have long been mythic archetypes for human
"apotheosie," for the triumph over the "tragoedie" of death.

Sun-fall and sun-rise compose the plot of the poem, its
structural soul, fulfilling the promises of the dedicatory sonnet.
The action begins with the rebellion of the powers of disorder
and darkness against the sun. They drive Phoebus from his
chariot and replace his clear light with smoking and hellishly
flaring torches. In the darkness that follows, the scorched and
sooted world is metamorphosed into a monstrous inversion of
its proper, ordered state. At the end mankind is redeemed and
the atmosphere purged of clouds in a glorious new sunrise
brought about by a Unicorn who turns out to be "Eliza."

The central episode of the poem concerns the heroic knight,
Mavortio, described as the Phoebus of his land, and his battle
against an evil monster. This monster has been devouring the
lambs in the herds of an island called Delta, but Mavortio's
sword destroys her and the brood that rises from her blood.
Shortly after this triumph Mavortio suffers a "sun-fall," fol-

lowing which his spirit ascends into the heavens. The poem then gives an account of his early upbringing by the Muses, and of their degradation after his ascension. The sunrise concluding the poem purifies the Muses as it purifies church and state.

Interpreters of *The Transformed Metamorphosis* have chiefly concentrated on efforts to decide which of England's heroes is meant by Mavortio. Scholars have suggested that this military darling of the Muses might be the Earl of Essex,[2] Henry VIII,[3] Sir Christopher Heydon,[4] or Edmund Spenser.[5] Others who might plausibly be added to the list are Sir Francis Vere and the two favorite Elizabethan poet-soldiers, Sir Philip Sidney and the Earl of Leicester.

But each of these candidates fails to match some aspect of the character, exploits or fate of Mavortio. The description of Mavortio is generalized; he is a composite person having the attributes of many historical figures, and the monster he fights, called a "hyenna," is another composite, representing the power of Rome and the many monstrous deformities born in the darkness of a world transformed into hell, or chaos. To Tourneur, as to other Elizabethans, the danger that order might give way to chaos stemmed from violation of degree within the ordered hierarchy of nature, man and God, and especially from the disruption of that hierarchy introduced by the new science, which drove the sun from its ordered course

---

[2] John Churton Collins, *The Plays and Poems of Cyril Tourneur* (London, 1878), II, 178–184.

[3] John D. Peter, "The Identity of Mavortio in Tourneur's 'Transformed Metamorphosis,' " *NQ*, 193 (1948), 408–412.

[4] Kenneth N. Cameron, "Cyril Tourneur and *The Transformed Metamorphosis*," *RES*, XVI (1940), 18–24.

[5] Dorothy Pym, "A Theory on the Identification of Cyril Tourneur's 'Mavortio,' " *NQ*, 174 (1938), 201–204. *Cf.* A. C. Hamilton's broader thesis regarding Spenser in "Spenser and Tourneur's *Transformed Metamorphosis*," *RES*, VIII (1957), 127–136.

about the earth and permitted mutability above the moon. Throughout the poem Tourneur alludes to the effects of this impulse toward dissolution—effects evident in political and religious turmoil throughout Europe, and in seemingly unprecedented numbers of new stars, comets and eclipses.[6]

This interpretation of Mavortio, of the "hyenna" and of the context of their battle enables us to make a good deal of sense of the poem, but it still leads only to a partial reading, for in any historical interpretation the description of Mavortio as a Phoebus-Apollo must be virtually ignored, leaving large areas of the poem in total darkness. However, many of the passages that have been so "Epinyctall" to readers seeking an historical allegory begin to seem not quite so obscure when we consider the possibility that they refer to Mavortio as an embodiment of the Phoebus-Apollo of the first half of the poem.

Mavortio is first related directly to the sun after his battle with the monster, when his "sun-fall" and deification occur (ll. 461–469). In lines 470–504, Mavortio is *"Elizium's* melody," incarnated and nursed by the Muses. He is related to Mars as one trained or "apt" to sing "coelestially" of war :

Downe he descended, and no whit disdaines

---

[6] For a general discussion of Elizabethan thought related to "mutability," see E. M. W. Tillyard, *The Elizabethan World Picture* (London, 1943). For historical background consult John B. Black, *The Reign of Elizabeth, 1558–1603*, 2nd ed. (Oxford, 1959), Vol. VIII of The Oxford History of England, ed. Sir George Clark. See also Wilbur K. Jordan, *Philanthropy in England, 1480–1660* (New York, 1959). For the relationship of cosmic and social disorder see John Norden, *Vicissitudo Rerum* (1600), ed. D. C. Collins, in Shakespeare Association Facsimiles, No. 4 (Oxford, 1931), especially stanzas 32–40, and Collins' introduction, pp. xiv–xviii; Lynn Thorndike, *A History of Magic and Experimental Science*, V and VI, "The Sixteenth Century" (New York, 1941); and Johnstone Parr, *Tamburlaine's Malady and Other Essays on Astrology in Elizabethan Drama* (U. of Ala., 1953).

To live on earth, leaving the sacred skies,
Only the muses deare to Martialize.

(ll. 501–504)

But Tourneur makes clear that even in this close relation to Mars, Mavortio retains his relation to Apollo, because "For *Mars* his knights, are 'squires to'th muses first" is true to traditional myth only if *"Mars* his knights" are also regarded as servants of Apollo (l. 497).

Then follow lines in which the obscurity of the poem reaches a climax, in which nearly all the symbols of the poem appear in apparently confused concatenation :

> But (O) when *Delta's* hope, the muses wonder,
>   Foes feare, feares foe, *Joves* martialist,
>   On *Thetis* gan like to a fearefull thunder
>   Make *Hydra* shake with a *Dodonian* fist;
>   When *Delta* deem'd her selfe in him thus blest,
> Then *Delta* of her hope was quite bereaved :
> See how the world is by the world deceived!
>
> The *Phoebus* of his soile, scarce shewd his sheen,
>   And fac'd the West with smiling Aurory,
>   When fatall *Neptune* with his trident keene,
>   (Behind him) hal'd him to his *Thetisie*, . . .

(ll. 505–515)

If we remember that in the earlier part of the poem Hydra has been a symbol of corrupted Rome, and the hostile Neptune a bringer of corrupting wealth or an enemy maritime power, we may seek to find here an explicit reference to some naval action in which England lost her heroic Mavortio through enemy fire or drowning. The lines become clearer, however, when we realize that Tourneur is not referring to any historical individual or event, but is using Mavortio as a representative of Phoebus; for what he describes is the sun's daily rise, short career and setting in the sea.

In the stanzas that follow, *"Mars* himselfe goes wandring up and downe" with the Muses, and "A pitchie night encurtained with clowdes/ . . . / Is the sole *Theater* that them enshrowdes" (ll. 526–527, 533, 535). The heroic Mavortian spirit has given way to the ugly god of war, and darkness has replaced the sunlight still present during Mavortio's fight with the monster—which ended, the poem tells us, just before sunset. Indeed, the lines may be taken to link the setting of the sun on Mavortio's victory with the sun-fall and deification of his spirit. Mavortio, seeing that every drop of the monster's blood he spills is only transformed into a new monster, knows that he and his squire will not be able "To take our leaves of this thiefe-harb'ring ground/ Before *Apollo Thetis* lap hath found" (ll. 431–432). And at the end of the battle we learn of the monsters that "Ere *Sol* with *Neptune* sleeped, slept their harmes;/ All beeing shooke with deaths all deadly charmes" (ll. 445–446). Almost immediately after this "happy houre" (l. 447) we have the first announcement of Mavortio's "sun-fall" and deification (ll. 461–469).

The entire Mavortio episode, beginning under the light of the sun and ending with a description of the "pitchie night" following his "sun-fall," can be interpreted, then, as a parallel to the opening of the poem where Phoebus' fall is described. Speaking generally, whereas Phoebus' fall brings the darkness of corruption to church and state, Mavortio's brings corruption to the Muses.

This explains the apparent confusion of symbols in the account of Mavortio's rebirth. The Muses are told not to lament the lost Mavortio:

Your wombe may bring forth such another sonne.
And as thy Sunne not still could face the north,
  But by his falling reaved thee of day;
  (Because the day light's by the night put forth)
  Nor can thy nights blacke hew endure alway :
Then hope sweet *Delta* hope, from murmure stay,
Thy *Phoebus* slumbreth but in *Thetis* lap :
Hee'l rise before thou thinkst of such a hap.

                                    (ll. 574–581)

Here the desire of Collins and others to find an historical allegory has leapt the context to see an allusion to King James VI of the northern kingdom of Scotland. Rather, however, Tourneur here fuses the figure of Mavortio with the figure of Phoebus-Apollo so that their parallel stories may end in a common sunrise. Beginning with a play on "sonne" and "sunne," Tourneur first implies that what is to follow is a *"hoarie* Hiems *kill'd by* Ver." The sun had approached its seasonal death when it turned from the north toward its southern nadir, but this was to be followed by its seasonal rebirth at the winter solstice, and then by the victory of day over night at the vernal equinox. This reference to a seasonal triumph of the sun is repeated in the first stanza of the Epilogue, where Tourneur tells us, after Eliza has retransformed the world and put Apollo back in the heavens, that "now the Sunne doth face the frosty north" (l. 7).

Having fused the narratives of Phoebus and Mavortio and established the happy ending to his poem as a seasonal transformation, Tourneur returns to the figure of sun-fall as sunset, describing the rebirth itself as a dramatic sunrise :

   Thy *Phoebus* slumbreth but in *Thetis* lap :
   Hee'l rise before thou thinkst of such a hap.

                                    (ll. 580–581)

The Unicorn-Eliza purifies the springs of the Muses, clears "the world of her blacke vironries," and frees Apollo from the treachery of the stars, placing him "in his former dignitie" (ll. 587–595).[7]

In the Epilogue we are told how all the lights of day and night are restored to their proper duties and courses, and that Tourneur's "subject was a heav'nly tapers death," which is why his "wittes light did waine" in writing it, since "but with night, I could with none conferre/ In this my Epinyctall register" (ll. 24–28). This stanza has usually been interpreted to mean that Tourneur wrote of some hero's death, but it must now be clear that no specific person's death need have occurred at all : Tourneur has written of the death of the sun at sunset and in winter, and the figure behind this Phoebus-Apollo might be a mythic figure undergoing death and resurrection, or a man or group of men, some dead and some living, who share key features and aims of the mythic figure.

There are many indications in the poem that the myth of the sun's fall and rebirth is being used as a symbol for Christ. The mixture of Christian and classical terms has often been trounced by the critics. But the mixture is in fact functional; a Christian framework is established to govern the interpretation of the classical mythology.

Early in the poem, just after Tourneur calls on his readers to "marke the transformation,/Wrought by the charmes of this rebellion" of the stars against Phoebus, he introduces

> That sacred female (which appear'd to him,
> Who was inspir'd with heav'ns intelligence;
> Who was the last that drunke upon the brim,

---

[7] Collins, and Peter after him, misread the end of the poem, believing Tourneur says Eliza is *successor* to Mavortio. Actually lines 579–595 say that the Mavortio-Phoebus-Apollo figure is *restored* by Eliza. See works cited, II, 183, and p. 411, respectively.

Of deepe divining sacred influence)
That heav'nly one, of glorious eminence.
She, whom *Apollo* clothed with his robe :
And plac'd hir feet upon th'inconstant globe.

(ll. 113–119)

This is the sacred woman of the Revelation of St. John the Divine :

And there appeared a great wonder in heaven, a woman clothed with the Sunne, and the Moone under her feete, and upon her heade a crowne of twelve starres. (Rev. XII : 1)[8]

Throughout the Book of Revelation the sun is compared with the light of God, and when we first meet Christ He is described as a sun-god :

His head and his heares were whyte, as white wooll, & as snowe : and his eyes were as a flame of fyre. And his feete like unto fine brasse, as though they burnt in a furnace : and his voyce as the sounde of many waters. And he had in his ryght hand seven starres : and out of his mouth went a sharpe two edged swoorde : and his face shone even as the sunne in his strength.

(Rev. I : 14–16)[9]

The readers of Tourneur's day were familiar with the sun as a symbol for Christ, for elements of sun-worship were completely integrated with medieval Christianity. In the early centuries of the Christian era, when Christianity was competing with other religions for dominance in the Roman Empire,

---

[8] All quotations of the Bible are from the Bishops' Bible (*The holie Bible,* London, 1572).
[9] See also Matt. XVII : 2 : at Jesus' transfiguration, "his face dyd shine as the sunne, and his clothes were as whyte as the lyght."

there was a long period of syncretism during which it absorbed elements of Mithraism and other sun religions.[10] In the fourth century, Christians began to celebrate Jesus' birthday at the winter solstice, when the sun turns north, because this enabled the church to subsume the pagan celebrations of the birth of the sun-god.[11] "O Oriens" is the fifth of the seven Great Antiphons for Vespers from December 17 to 23 : "O Orient, Splendor of the Eternal Light, and Sun of Justice, come and enlighten them that sit in darkness and in the shadow of death."[12] In Catholic churches the congregation faces east, toward the cross and the rising sun.[13]

The elements common to the sun myths that entered the medieval religious and poetic tradition are these : a glorious hero, destroyer of monsters, is fated to suffer an early death. He makes a journey of rescue into the nether world, and after his death he rises again.[14] He is venerated because he is a transforming god, controlling the seasons and the life of vegetation and all creatures, including man.[15]

The myth of Apollo, prophet and healer, the brilliant god of the sunlight, is central in *The Transformed Metamorphosis*. Hera, jealous of Leto for consorting with Zeus, sent the dragon, Python, to destroy her. Poseidon saved Leto by hiding her in the eastern waves, and there Apollo was born. He immediately acquired the strength of a man and pursued the serpent to its lair on the side of Parnassus, where he slew it. Compare this with the following from Revelation :

---

[10] Helen Flanders Dunbar, *Symbolism in Medieval Thought and its Consummation in the Divine Comedy* (New Haven, 1929), p. 138ff.

[11] *Ibid.*, p. 412.

[12] *Ibid.*, p. 411.

[13] *Ibid.*, p. 400.

[14] *Ibid.*, pp. 108–115. Analyses by more recent comparative mythologists yield similar results. *Cf.* Joseph Campbell, *The Hero with a Thousand Faces* (New York, 1949), pp. 245–246.

[15] Dunbar, *op. cit.*, p. 234.

And there appeared a great wonder in heaven, a woman clothed with the Sunne, and the Moone under her feete, and upon her heade a crowne of twelve starres : And she beyng with childe, cryeth travaylyng in byrth, and payned redy to be delivered. And there appeared another wonder in heaven, for beholde a great red Dragon, having seven heads, and ten hornes, & seven crownes uppon his heades. And his tayle draweth the thirde part of the starres of heaven, and he cast them to the earth : And the Dragon stoode before the woman whiche was redy to be delyvered, for to devoure her chylde assoone as it were borne. And she brought foorth a man childe, whiche shal rule al nations with a rod of iron : and her sonne was taken up unto God, and [to] his throne. And the woman fled into the wyldernesse, where she hath a place prepared of GOD, that they shoulde feede her there a thousand, two hundred, and threescore dayes. And there was a battaile in heaven, Michael and his angels fought with the Dragon, and the Dragon fought and his angels, And prevayled not, neither was their place founde any more in heaven.

(Rev. XII : 1–8)

These myths are echoed and re-echoed in *The Transformed Metamorphosis*. The rebelling stars which drive Tourneur's Phoebus-Apollo from the heavens and begin a hellish reign of darkness on earth are suggested by Satan and his followers, the stars who rebelled and were ultimately defeated in the War in Heaven :

And I sawe a starre fal from heaven unto the earth : and to him was geven the keye of the bottomlesse pit. And he opened the bottomlesse pit, and the smoke of the pit arose, as the smoke of a great fornace, and the Sunne and the ayre were darkened, by the reason of the smoke of the pit.

(Rev. IX : 1–2)

The serpent opposed to Apollo and Christ is related to the various evil serpents opposed to Tourneur's Phoebus-Apollo-Mavortio. In the Book of Revelation the glorious woman clothed with the sun is soon replaced by a woman sitting on a scarlet beast with seven heads (Rev. XVII : 3). This woman is a Hydra of sin, the mother of harlots and all evils (Rev. XVII : 3–5). We are told that the beast is he of the bottomless pit, and that his seven heads are seven hills the woman sits on, presumably the hills of Rome (Rev. XVII : 8, 9, 18). These verses seemed especially prophetic at the time of the Reformation, and Tourneur draws upon them for his account of the transformation of the woman clothed with the sun into an evil woman associated with "the stately Pyramis of glorious price;/ Whose seav'n hill'd head did over all aspire," which "Is now transform'd to Hydra-headed vice" (ll.58–60).

Tourneur's serpent "in female shape" (l. 184) whose "Leucrocutanized" voice entices men to sin in the allegorical mansion rising out of fiery Phlegeton, is described in John Florio's *A Worlde of Wordes:*

> *Leucrocuta, a beast that hath all his teeth of one piece, as big as an asse, with neck, taile, and breast like a lyon, and head like a cammell, and counterfeits the voice of a man.*[16]

This creature, in its composite nature, is similar to the beast in Revelation XIII : 2 :

> And the beast whiche I sawe was lyke a Leoparde, and his feete were as [the feete] of a Beare, and his mouth as the mouth of a Lion : and the Dragon gave hym his power . . .

---

[16] London, 1598, p. 203, *Cf.* Abraham Fraunce, *The Third Part of The Countesse of Pembrokes Yvychurch, Entituled, Amintas Dale* (London, 1592), ff. 22r–22v, where "Leucosia" is one of the three mermaids who by their singing entice sailors to the dangerous rocks.

The "hyenna," like Spenser's monster Error in Book I of *The Faerie Queene,* was half woman and half serpent, not the animal we know : she is described as a mermaid in line 397. In ancient Egyptian religions, the hyena was a symbol of Typhon, the devil.[17] Typhon was nursed by Python, the serpent later slain by Apollo.[18]

There is further specifically Christian symbolism in the "rock" of Tourneur's refuge (ll. 92–98). This rock, rising literally between the devilish fires of hell and the deep blue sea, is a conventional Christian symbol of the truth about Christ, that He is the saving Son of God. The symbol is a common one in Elizabethan emblem literature :

> Let Boreas' blasts and Neptune's waves be join'd,
> Thy Æolus commands the waves, the wind :
> Fear not the rocks, or world's imperious waves;
> Thou climb'st a Rock, my soul! a Rock that saves.[19]

At the end of the poem, when "Phoebus" is about to rise again and be restored to his rightful place, this "same rocke, the rocke of my defence,/ Is metamorphosde to an Unicorne" (ll. 582–583). This is the Unicorn that purifies the springs of the Muses and generally retransforms the world. In the tradition derived from medieval bestiaries, the unicorn is a creature that associates with virgins. It usually symbolizes Christ, and its single horn, like the rock from which it is transformed in

---

[17] Manly P. Hall, *An Encyclopedic Outline of Masonic, Hermetic, qabbalistic, and Rosicrucian symbolical Philosophy* (San Francisco, 1928), p. xcii.

[18] It is just possible that at its most "mythic" level the "Delta" of the poem is not some particular island, but the classical "three-nook'd world" (*Antony and Cleopatra* IV. vi. 7).

[19] Francis Quarles, *Emblems, Divine and Moral,* ed. Augustus Toplady and John Ryland (London, 1839), Book IV, p. 63. In Geffrey Whitney, *A Choice of Emblemes* (Leyden, 1586), ed. Henry Green (London, 1866), p. 129, a similar emblem makes clear that "By raging Sea, is ment our ghostlie foe."

Tourneur's poem, represents the gospel of the truth about Christ.[20] The intense purity of the unicorn repels all evil, and its horn has the power to purify water. In emblems the unicorn is often pictured "with a virgin holding a dove," and may have for a motto such phrases as "Faith undefiled victorious."[21] The unicorn's constant association with virgins caused it sometimes to be feminine, to be regarded as a "creature of maiden modesty protectress pure."[22] From this it is easy to see why the English should come to link the unicorn with Eliza, their virgin queen, as Tourneur does here.

Throughout *The Transformed Metamorphosis,* then, Tourneur uses Christian symbolism and apocalyptic-Christian material to make it clear that Phoebus-Apollo-Mavortio is to be related to the figure of Christ as he appears in the Book of Revelation. This is especially clear in the details of the battle with the "hyenna." From Mavortio's[23] introduction, "pricking on the plaine," to the end of his fight with the monster, Tourneur bases his account on the exploits of Spenser's Red Cross Knight. It is a commonplace that the Red Cross Knight's battle with the dragon has as its source the legendary fight of St. George and its medieval analogues, and that these in turn are ultimately related to the battles with the dragon in the Revelation of St. John,[24] especially to the account in Revela-

---

[20] Ebenezer Cobham Brewer, *Brewer's Dictionary of Phrase and Fable* (New York, 1952), *s.v.* unicorn. I cite Brewer and some other general authorities to stress the fact that this symbolism was very common.

[21] Harold Bayley, *A New Light on the Renaissance Displayed in Contemporary Emblems* (London, 1909), p. 16.

[22] Henry Green, *Shakespeare and the Emblem Writers* (London, 1870), pp. 371–372.

[23] In Christian symbolism, Mars (Mavors) is the personification of Divine Fortitude, the defender of Christianity. Brewer, *op. cit., s.v.* Mars.

[24] *E.g.,* Variorum Ed. of *The Works of Edmund Spenser,* ed. Edwin Greenlaw, Charles G. Osgood and Frederick M. Padelford (Balt., 1932), I, 176, where a note on the armor of the Red Cross Knight described in the opening stanzas of *The Faerie Queene* relates it immediately to St. George and the Archangel Michael.

tion XII, already quoted, in which Michael[25] and his angels
overcome the dragon, Satan, and to Revelation XIX:

And I sawe heaven open, & beholde a white horse : and he
that sate upon hym, was called faythful and true, and in
ryghteousnesse [he] dooth judge and make batayle. His eyes
[were] as a flame of fyre, and on his head were many crownes.
. . . And he was clothed with a vesture dipt in blood : and his
name is called the woorde of God. And the armies whiche
were in heaven folowed him upon white horses, clothed with
white and pure raynes. And out of his mouth goeth a sharpe
sword, that with it he shoulde smite the heathen. . . . And he
hath on his vesture, and on his thigh a name written, Kyng of
kynges, and Lord of Lordes. . . . And I sawe the beast, and
the kyngs of the earth, and their armies geathered togeather, to
make batayle agaynst hym that sate on the horse, and agaynst
his armie. And the beast was taken, and with hym that false
prophete that wrought myracles before hym, with whiche he
deceyved them that receyved the beastes mark, and them that
woorshipped his image. These both were cast quicke into a
pond of fire, burning with brimstone : And the remnant were
slayne with the swoorde of hym that sate upon the horse,
whiche sword proceeded out of his mouth : & all the fowles
were filled with their fleashe.

(Rev. XIX : 11–16, 19–21)

Tourneur's readers were familiar with the interpretation of
St. George as a symbol of Christ. Selden comments on the St.
George legend :

Your more neat judgments, finding no such matter in true
antiquity, rather make it symbolical than truly proper. So

---

[25] Michael was regarded as patron of knighthood in the Middle Ages.
The Catholic Encyclopedia (New York, 1907–12), ed. Charles G. Herbermann *et al*, X, 275–276.

that some account him an allegory of our Saviour Christ, and our admir'd *Spenser* hath made him an emblem of Religion.[26]

In Richard Vennard's *The Right Way to Heaven . . .*[27] is "St. George for England," describing English efforts to quell the Irish rebellion under Tyrone at the end of Elizabeth's reign. Compare the following lines with *The Transformed Metamorphosis* :

> A Virgin Pricesse and a gentile Lambe
> Doomb'd to death to gorge this ugly beast :
> This valiant victor like a Souldier came,
> . . .   (ll. 1–3)
> Saint George, the figure of our Saviour's force,
> Within the Dragon's jawes his speare hath entred.
> . . .   (ll. 7–8)
> Saint George's Knight, goe noble Mountjoy on,
> Bearing thy Saviour's badge within thy breast :
> Quell that Hell's shape of divellish proud tirone.
>   (ll. 19–21)

And in another work nearly contemporary with *The Transformed Metamorphosis*, Gerard Malynes' *Saint George for England, allegorically described,* St. George is interpreted as Christ and the dragon as Satan.[28] In Malynes' work, Elizabeth, patroness of the fraternity of St. George, the Order of the Garter, delivers England from peril.

This combination of the legendary St. George with the apocalyptic vision of the world and the myth of Apollo makes it doubly evident that the gallant knight of the poem has his archetype in the figure of Christ and His analogues in myth-

---

[26] Quoted from Ray Heffner, "Spenser's Allegory in Book I of the *Faerie Queene,*" *SP,* XXVII (1930), 153.

[27] London, 1601. Also quoted from Heffner, *ibid.*

[28] London, 1601. Cited from Heffner, p. 154.

ology. The Mavortio episode in isolation might be considered purely "historical," and the apocalyptic sun-fall might be considered merely a satirical convention, but the two have only this Christian interpretation in common, and their fusion in the poem serves to reinforce their common interpretation.

But this is not to declare the historical interpretations of the poem to be irrelevant. As we have just seen, St. George's knight could be Mountjoy, Elizabeth's general, and the dragon could be Tyrone, the Irish rebel. The significance of Mavortio-St. George extends in one direction toward the Archangel Michael and Christ, in the other toward the ideal human Defender of the Faith: toward Henry VIII, Leicester, Sidney, Spenser, Essex, Vere, any Knight of the Garter (the Fraternity of St. George), or even Sir Christopher Heydon, who is flattered as a Mavortian in the dedication.

The combination of Phoebus and St. George would, in the absence of the great amount of Christian apocalyptic material, and in the presence of a closer historical parallel, argue for the unambiguous identification of Phoebus-Mavortio with the English ruler. The king, as Defender of the Faith, chief of the Order of the Garter, and Christ's vicegerent in the kingdom, was often referred to in Elizabethan poetry under the names of St. George and Phoebus. Richard Niccols writes in *England's Eliza* (London, 1610) that

> When England's Phoebus *Henrie's* hopeful sonne
> The world's rare Phoenix, princely *Edward* hight,
> To death did yeeld, his glasse outrun,
> And Phoebus-like no more could lend his light:
> Then men did walk in shades of darksome night.[29]

---

[29] Quoted from Ray Heffner, *op. cit.,* p.154. Edward, like Mavortio in the poem, suffered an early sun-fall, and would be as good a Mavortio as Henry.

Joseph Hall, in part III of "Cearten veerses written by Doctor Hall upon the kings coming into Scotland," asks James I to return to England :

> Turne the agayne o phebus fayre
> Earths sole delight and heavens care
> O turne thee to ye soutth o turne
> Lest wee doe freeze whilest others burne

—making a paradoxical point of the seasonal turns of the sun to north and south.[30] The astrological condition of the sun at a king's nativity was thought to be especially important. In the "geniture" of Henry VIII, "the Sun is Hyleg, or Giver of Life."[31] But it is because he rules for Christ and defends Christ's Faith that the king stands closest to the Mavortio-Phoebus figure, and the brilliance of Christ's sword is also reflected, however dimly, by the swords of His humbler knights.

2   SOUL-SICKNESS AND SPIRITUAL REBIRTH

For Tourneur, this vision of the world transformed into hell and retransformed in a glorious sunrise has personal as well as religious and historical meaning. The poem may be read as an allegory of an experience analogous to a "dark night of the soul" for Tourneur, a period of spiritual darkness culminating in his "apotheosie." In this reading the events in the cosmos would be seen as events taking place in the poet's mind. Tourneur's Elizabethan readers could quickly grasp this sig-

---

[30] *The Collected Poems of Joseph Hall,* ed. Arnold Davenport (Liverpool, 1949), p. 152.

[31] E. Sibley, *A New and Complete Illustration of the Occult Sciences* (London, n.d.: late 18th century), p. 853.

nificance of the poem because they were familiar with the
theory of correspondence between the microcosm of man and
the macrocosm of nature, which taught that "In all points our
brains are like the firmament, and exhale in everie respect the
like grose mistempred vapors and meteors; of the more foecu-
lent combustible ayrie matter whereof, afrighting formes and
monstrous images innumerable are created; but of the slymie
unweeldier drossie part, dull melancholy or drousiness."[32]

The theory of correspondence went beyond proposing
merely parallel workings of mind and cosmos, for it suggested
that events in the one could directly affect events in the other.
Similar to Tourneur's poem is George Chapman's *The Shadow
of Night*, "Hymnus in Noctem," in which social and mental
chaos are meshed with cosmic chaos. All things

> Are turnd to chaos, and confound the time.
> A stepdame Night of minde about us clings,
> Who broodes beneath her hell obscuring wings,
> Worlds of confusion, where the soule defamde,
> The bodie had bene better never framde.
>   . . .   (ll. 60–64)
> But in the blind borne shadow of this hell,
> This horrid stepdame, blindnesse of the minde,
> Nought worth the sight, no sight, but worse then blind,
> A Gorgon that with brasse, and snakie brows,
> (Most harlot-like) her naked secrets shows :
> For in th'expansure, and distinct attire,
> Of light, and darcknesse, of the sea, and fire,
> Of ayre, and earth, and all, all these create,
> First set and rulde, in most harmonious state,
> Disjunction showes, in all things now amisse,
> By that first order, what confusion is :

---

[32] Thomas Nashe, *The Terrors of the Night* (London, 1594), in *The
Works of Thomas Nashe*, ed. R. B. McKerrow (Oxford, 1958), I, 377.

Religious curb, that manadgd men in bounds,
Of publique wellfare; lothing private grounds,
(Now cast away, by self-lov's paramores)
All are transformd to Calydonian bores,
That kill our bleeding vines, displow our fields.[33]

(ll. 70–85)

According to the principles of order of the pre-Copernican universe, man could strive toward correspondence with the immutable order that lay beyond the moon. But the new science was showing that mutability holds sway even above the moon, and the principle of correspondence came to imply that chaos is inevitable in human affairs—an implication that could well be terrifying.

But Tourneur is not terrified. At the same time that he wants to integrate his own experience into the allegory so that he can conclude the poem with a personal "apotheosie," he also wants to make it clear that he is not overwhelmed by the apocalyptic darkness. I shall consider the degree of his involvement in some detail in order to counter the usual critical exaggerations of his pessimism. *The Transformed Metamorphosis* is often read as an obsessed vision of the world abandoned to hell-fire, as an outpouring of Tourneur's despair. Una Ellis-Fermor relates what she calls the "evil universe" of *The Revenger's Tragedy,* a "world vibrant with imaginative horror," to this poem. She thinks that in Tourneur's world, as in de Sade's, nature is "a ravening and dominating force, destroying and urging on the destroyer."[34] Thomas M. Parrott and Robert H. Ball describe the "vision obscurely appre-

---

[33] *The Shadow of Night,* "Hymnus in Noctem" (1594), quoted from *The Poems of George Chapman,* ed. Phyllis Brooks Bartlett (New York, 1941), p. 21.
[34] *The Jacobean Drama,* 4th ed. (London, 1958), pp. 155–156.

hended" in the poem as a "fiercely unhappy poet's outlook on life."[35] Henri Fluchère goes further, concluding that in both *The Revenger's Tragedy* and *The Transformed Metamorphosis* "le monde que voit Tourneur est un monde irrémédiablement perdu."[36]

These readers regard the restoration of order and light at the end of the poem as purely conventional flattery of Elizabeth. It is partly to combat this error that I have developed the evidence showing that the ending is not "stuck on." The triumph of Phoebus-Apollo, and all it signifies, is an organic part of the poem, implicit in the title, the dedication, and the prologue, in the mythic metaphor of the daily and seasonal death and rebirth of the sun, in the account in Revelation, and in general throughout the Christian-classical myth informing the poem.

Most unaccountably, the same readers overlook the purely conventional and impersonal representation of evil in the poem. Tourneur puts himself at two removes from "sin" and "vice." First, he treats them as abstractions, and then he allegorizes them. Who can feel obsession in his attack on drunkenness, sloth, gluttony, hypocrisy and greed:

> The vines *Ædonides;* dead *Murcianie;*
> Smooth *Philoxenus;* murders ground;
> Disquiet *Eriphila;* hel's Syrenie;
> *Philocrematos;* the soules deepe wound;
> And whatso els in *Hydra's* head is found.
>
> ((ll. 148–152)

There is nothing "personal" in the poem. The vision is apocalyptic not so much in quality as in source; virtually every

---

[35] *A Short View of Elizabethan Drama* (New York, 1943), p. 218.
[36] In the introduction to his translation of *The Revenger's Tragedy*, *La Tragédie du Vengeur* (Paris, 1958), p. 131.

"intense" detail is drawn from Spenser or the Bible, and Tourneur writes not *of* an experience of hell in life but *through* a conventional medium representing the darkness of life as hell. Here, as in the Book of Revelation, the vision of hell could not be so impressive if it were not written from a desire to reveal the glorious transfiguration of the New Jerusalem or the new sunrise.

Tourneur establishes the precise degree of his detachment from the visionary material by describing himself as "chorus" and by questioning the reality of the apocalyptic horrors. He is involved in the horror because the darkness of cosmos and society has caused his spiritual vision to darken, but his questioning and his controlled, artificial style suggest his awareness that the apocalyptic tradition has provided him with material that, improperly understood, might imply a deep personal obsession with evil which he does not suffer. The "obsession" and the "vibrant horror" of the poem belong to the convention, not to the poet.

The style is determined by the principle of decorum, through which manner is adapted to matter. In the dedication Tourneur describes the poem as an *"Epinyctall register,/ Rasde out by* Eos *rayes,"* and in the epilogue, when "Sacred *Apollo*, cheeres the lightsome day," he concludes:

> But when my heart was urged forth to breath,
> Fell accents of soule-terrifying paine;
> My subject was a heav'nly tapers death;
> Night was my lampe; my inke, hell's pitchy maine :
> Then blame me not, if my wittes light did waine,
> Since but with night, I could with none conferre
> In this my Epinyctall register.

(ll. 22–28)

I interpret this to mean that he has intentionally made the diction and the form of the poem to follow the movement from darkness to light in its *plot*. The bulk of the poem is obscure and "chaoized" as a result, but at the end, after Apollo is restored, there is greater light; the mysterious unicorn yields to the obvious Eliza, and the obscure style eases off toward a more conventional one. Also in accord with the principle of decorum, Tourneur naturally uses the rhyme royal stanza, a form said by both Gascoigne and King James to be proper for complaints and other tragic matter.[37]

Tourneur repeatedly suggests his detachment by telling us that he doubts the reality of what he sees, sometimes describing the events he reports as taking place on a stage. In the dedication he calls the poem a metamorphosed *tragedy,* and in the "The Author to His Booke" he suggests a theatrical image in saying the poem pulls "the curtaines backe, that closde vice in" (l. 5). In the lines "To the Reader" he shows his detachment from "up-heaped sinne" by discussing its supposed effect upon him, according to the apocalyptic convention :

> For as the troubled mind, whose sad complaint
> Still tumbles forth, halfe breathed accenties,
> Th' *Idea* doth confuse and chaoize :
> So will the *Chaos* of up-heaped sinne
> Confound his braine, that takes in hand to lay
> A platforme plainly forth, of all (that in
> This *Pluto*-visag'd-world) hell doth bewray . . .
>
> (ll. 8–14)

The opening of the prologue suggests a birth-into-death as the poet enters into night's dark womb. Blinded and wandering,

---

[37] Hallett Smith, *Elizabethan Poetry: A Study in Conventions, Meaning, and Expression* (Cambridge, Mass., 1952), p. 113.

he gropes for his bearings, asking for the reason why he has been born *thus:*

> O Who perswades my willing errorie,
>   Into this blacke Cymerianized night?
> Who leades me into this concavitie,
>   This huge concavitie, defect of light,
>   To feele the smart of *Phlegetontike* sight?
> O who, I say, perswades mine infant eie,
> To gaze upon my youths obscuritie?
>
>   (ll. 1–7)

He wonders "What chaoizd conceit doth forme my feares?/ What object is't that thus my quiet teares?" (ll. 11–12). In the final stanza of the prologue Tourneur doubts his own vision and calls on the reader to act as judge of its clarity: "Looke on my sight . . ./ And tell me whether it be blear'd or no" (ll. 36–37).

Then, in the body of the poem, after the sun and the stars have been driven from the sky and replaced by torches of hell, the poet recoils from what is to follow on earth. Here, and each time afterward when he introduces a new sequence, he uses a theatrical metaphor to define his relation to the material:

> Where shall I stand, that I may freely view,
>   Earths stage compleate with tragick sceans of wo?
> No meade, no grove, whose comfortizing hew
>   Might make sad Terror my sad minde forgoe?
>   (ll. 50–53)

When heaven directs him to stand on the symbolic rock, he rejoices in its sanctuary (ll. 85–91), but continues to fear his conceits will be "chaoized" by the apocalyptic smoke:

Now eies prepare, and be your sight as cleare,
  As is the Skie, when none but *Phaetons* sire
  Inhabites it : for O (alas) I feare
  They will be dazled with smoake and fier,
  That with repulse of heav'n doth downe retire,
Heart, teach my tongue directed by mine eie,
To be the *Chorus* to this tragedie.

Marke, you spectators of this tragicke act,
  (If any rest unmetamorphosed)
  O you whose soules with hel are not contract
  Whose sacred light is not extinguished;
  Whose intellectual tapers are not fed
With Hells flame : marke the transformation,
Wrought by the charmes of this rebellion.

                         (ll. 99–112)

Here for the first time Tourneur explicitly declares that he
is to be *chorus* to the tragedy. He is the interpreter of the
action whose own mental state is *analogous* to what he
describes, but not to be read directly out of that description
itself. He is not directly involved in the events of the poem,
but feels his vision to be darkened as the world is darkened,
and so enters into the scene far enough to convey to us the
emotions appropriate to the events. Through Tourneur's eyes
the reader is to receive an impression *not* of events objectively
observed and "reported," but of events as, according to the
apocalyptic convention, they "burn" their story through his
"darkened" soul into his "Epinyctall register." Tourneur is
careful to maintain this relation of a witnessing chorus to the
action, with its dual emphasis on vision and on the artifice of
the stage, and he keeps before the reader the possibility that
his vision is distorted by stressing how difficult it is to see
properly in the evilly metamorphosed world. He laments the

blindness of enchanted sinners (ll. 183–189), of corrupted age
(ll. 239–245) and of Pan (ll. 281–285). In his treatment of the
enchanted sinners and their blindness he differentiates his own
reaction to the metamorphosed world from that of those whose
souls are smothered by the "slime" of bodily pleasures (l. 182).
Whereas the sinners are *tempted* through their senses in a
Palace of Sin (ll. 183–217), Tourneur's senses are *appalled* by
the sights and sounds of hell; he feels "the smart of *Phlegeton-
tike* sight" and asks, "Who fills my nosthrills with thicke foggy
sents?/ Who feedes my taste with hony-smacking gall?" (ll.
5, 15–16). He grieves that he cannot hear his wonted
"Symphonie harmonical," and concludes, "O who, O who
hath metamorphosed/My sence?" (ll. 22–23).

The introduction of the Mavortio episode is prefaced by a
restatement of Tourneur's relation to the action :

> Is't possible the world should yet affoord,
>> More cause of woe, then yet mine eies have seene?
> Can *Pluto* in his horrors cave yet hoord,
>> More woe then in this tragicke sceane hath beene?
> Is't true I see? Or do I overweene?
> O, O, I see more then I can expresse,
> Amaz'd with sense-confounding wretchednesse.
>> (ll. 323–329)

And after Mavortio has suffered his sun-fall and been replaced
by the sinister figure of Mars himself, Tourneur says of the
Muses :

> A pitchie night encurtained with clowdes
>> (That kept from it heav'ns star-bright comforture)
> Is the sole *Theater* that them enshrowdes.
>> (ll. 533–535)

This is the last of the theatrical metaphors, for only six stanzas later come the first gleamings of that glorious sunrise which is to restore Phoebus, the "star-crown'd female" and, indeed, "all the world," including the poet (ll. 598–599). His soul partakes of the mysterious regeneration :

> My very soule with heav'nly pleasure's fed,
> To see th'transform'd remetamorphosed.
>
> (ll. 601–602)

But in the Epilogue, perhaps dazzled by the restored lights of heaven and earth, the poet still questions his own vision, and suggests that the restoration of light to the world may be an illusion, even if the deprivation of light was not. His reaction to the light of day parallels that of men suddenly exposed to the light of reality in Plato's allegory of the cave :

> Now is the Moone not blemisht with a cloud,
> Nor any lampe (that should illuminate
> And lighten ev'ry thing that heav'n doth shrowd)
> Darkned; or else my sight gin's to abate,
> And s'reaved of it intellectuate.
> Each obscure cave is lightned by the day :
> Or else mine eyes are forced to estray.
>
> (ll. 15–21)

3   LIGHTS METAMORPHOSED AND THE MUSES DEFILED

Tourneur relates his eyes to the sun and moon as one more way of paralleling the cosmic sun-fall and sunrise with the inner experience of darkness and spiritual renewal. The conception of the sun as the eye of God must be as old as Western culture, and symbolic relationships between men's eyes and the macrocosm of sun, moon and stars were common in Elizabethan writing.[38] Sometimes eyes were contrasted with stars, the eyes representing the active life, the stars the contemplative. Or the sun and moon symbolised the eyes of the soul.

Clear vision is to Tourneur "lycophosed" or sun-clear in *The Transformed Metamorphosis,* and elsewhere he refers to "the cleare and uneclipsed *eye*" of Sir Francis Vere's "strong *intellectuall* faculty."[39] These very ordinary metaphors link the cosmic darkness depriving the outward eye of proper light with the darkness of soul that may dim man's vision of life until he stands fast upon the truth of Christ and witnesses to the glorious resurrection, the coming of the new day after the long night of despair, the seasonal return of the sun with new life.

The sun-fall does not result in total darkness, however. The world transformed into hell is "defect of light" only until a "flaming torch" is put into the poet's hand (Prologue, ll. 4, 13). In the questioning of the Prologue Tourneur asks what has happened to the heavenly lights appointed by God to guide man and the world (ll. 29–35), and in the body of the poem he describes how, when Phoebus is driven from the sky by the rebellious stars, all heavenly light is replaced by the light from hellish torches.

Other false lights also symbolize the corrupting agents that oppose God's lights, paradoxically blinding men. When the cosmos is in order,

> Sacred *Apollo,* cheeres the lightsome day,
> And swan-plum'd *Phoebe* gards the star-faire night,
> Lest *Pluto's* forester, should cause estray.
>
> (Epilogue, ll. 8–10)

---

[38] Muriel C. Bradbrook, *The School of Night* (Cambridge, 1936), pp. 70–71, 113–114, 160.

[39] *A Funerall Poeme Upon the Death of the Most Worthy and True Souldier, Sir Francis Vere, Knight . . .* , ll. 371–372.

But when the sky is "pitchie . . . at noone," it is "As though the day were govern'd by the Moone" (Prologue, ll. 34–35). The moon, when it usurps the place of the sun, may symbolize the false light of secular concerns usurping the place of the spiritual. Thus the stars, the "lights that should truth animate," submit "unto th'unstedfast moones controle," and, fed with *"Phlegetonticke* flame," extinguish "Celestiall light" (ll. 22–28). The sacred female, clothed by Apollo so that "she might to heav'n her minde applie," loses "Her twelve starr'd glorious coronet" because "her high rebellious starres,/ (Their minds ambitioniz'd) do seeke her fall," after having "dim'd the Sun with smoaky warres" (ll. 113–147).[40] Her robe is transformed to gold "because she did combine/ Affection with the Moon" (ll. 136–137).

The wisdom of age, that should lead youth "with heedie doctrine and celestiall light;/ Hath bin conversing with hells taper, night," and has been metamorphosed into an evil guide (ll. 155–161). The morning star, *"Apolloe's* herauld, that was wont to cheare,/ Night-wounded soules with bright celest'all raies," is "metamorphosde to a torch of hell" (ll. 162–168). True gentry, which "shines in them to heav'n their minde that give," yields to a status bought with gold (ll. 218–231). The enticing shimmer of pearls and gold, "Hell's twinckling instrument that never sleepes," is also the light that makes Pan unable to see "but in a minery" (ll. 272–287).

The spirit of evil corrupting the world is, then, represented

---

[40] The dark clouds of smoke from the stars transformed into torches are perhaps to be understood as the physical agents causing the unnatural darkness at noon the poem describes, for it is when their smoke "gathers to a cloud;/ And like blacke *Orcus* vault the earth doth shrowde," that the daylight world gives way to "blacke *Plutoe's* hall" (ll. 29–35, 43–49). And the restoration of Phoebus is figured not only as a dawn but as a purgation of clouds from the sky by the virtue of the burning rays of light from the Unicorn's eyes (ll. 589–595. *Cf.* also Epilogue, ll. 1–7).

by the false lights of torches, of celestially proud minds, of gold, and of the "sence-bereaving" illusion of the palace of sensual sin, made "al pleasing to earth's sight" (ll. 186, 211, 207). Opposed to these false lights are the true lights of the sun, moon and stars when Order prevails, the light of the Unicorn's eyes, of the human spirit when not corrupted by pride, greed or sensuality—the human spirit as a "heavenly taper" which has not fallen or which, as here, suffers death only to be resurrected. The "heav'nly tapers death" that Tourneur describes as his "subject" in the Epilogue is therefore not only a *sun*-fall but is also the *star*-fall of Satan and any human spirits of whom it may be said that "With *Phlegetonticke* flame these tapers fed,/ Celestiall light have quite extinguished" (ll. 27–28).

The symbolism of true and false lights and the general contrast of the true and the evilly metamorphosed worlds can be applied to the corruption of the Muses at the end of the Mavortio episode. The name "Mavortio" poses a problem at the outset : why not call him Mars, a medieval symbol of the Defender, and be done? Apparently Tourneur uses here the common astrological notion that a single planet might exert different influences depending on its association with other heavenly bodies. "Mavortio," associated with symbols of the Trinity in Jupiter, the Sun and Mercury, was surely intended by Tourneur to be favorably regarded. Sir Christopher Heydon has this to say of people favorably "signified" by Mars :

> When he is well dignified, the person signified by him will inherit a courageous, invincible disposition, careless of danger, hazarding his life on all occasions, so that he can but triumph over his enemy or antagonist.[41]

---

[41] Sir Christopher Heydon, *The New Astrology* . . . 2nd ed. (London, 1786), p. 27. A later edition of *An Astrological Discourse* (London, 1650).

On the other hand, the figure who replaces Mavortio in the dark world following his sun-fall is *"Mars* himselfe" (l. 526):

. . . a masculine, nocturnal planet; in nature hot, and dry; choleric, and fiery; the lesser in fortune; author of quarrels, dissensions, strife, war, and battle.[42]

Whereas Mavortio was *"Elizium's* melody" whose work brought glory to the Muses, now, under the malign influence of Mars, "the sacred Muses are infected" (l. 560), and only Urania remains undefiled:

> Ayde (mighty *Jove*) for *Nilus Crocodiles*
> Are bathing in the pure *Castalian* head.
> Pure horse-foot *Helicon,* their filth defiles,
> Art, like Ægyptian dogs, must scape their wiles.
> O dreary woe! the Muses did but sup,
> And are infected with that pois'nous cup.
>
> (ll. 548–553)

Tourneur, adhering to the Spenserian-Mavortian literary conventions and attitudes, is critical of the new literary trends of the fin-de-siècle. Recalling Mavortio's possible identification with Edmund Spenser, we are immediately struck by the aptness of Theodore Spencer's suggestion that "Spenser's death in the last year of the century—as a result, it was said, of starvation—can be seen by the symbolically-minded as a microcosmic reflection of what had happened to the ideals of the early Renaissance which had originally inspired him." Writers were turning away from Spenser's allegory and idealism to the realism of satire.[43] And heroic poetry was also giving way to what Tourneur evidently regarded even more unfavorably, to Martial's witty obscenity and the amatory or scurrilous

---

[42] *Ibid.*
[43] *Shakespeare and the Nature of Man* (New York, 1942), pp. 47–48.

poetry in the "metamorphic" tradition. Tourneur rejects realistic satire here by employing the allegorical method,[44] and he
attacks the others *through* the allegory, playing on the idea
that the world of his day is evilly "metamorphosde" and on
the ambiguity of the word *Martial*.

Thus Mavortio is associated with truly heroic "martial"
poetry, and perhaps we are to infer that *"Mars* himselfe" and
the "infected" poetry associated with him refer to the amatory
works of Marlowe, to the works of Marston, "the Elizabethan
Martial" (especially his *Metamorphosis of Pygmalion's Image*),
and to such things as John Harington's "foul book entitled *A
New Discourse of a Stale Subject called the Metamorphosis of
Ajax,* treating of a new way to make a jakes that shall be rid of
stink; but intermixed with many other unsavoury matters."[45]

It is possible that Tourneur also looks critically at Chapman's *Shadow of Night* (1594), listed by C. S. Lewis along
with *The Transformed Metamorphosis* as one of the surviving
"monuments" of what he says "might be called poetry of the
cryptic school." Chapman's poem, quoted earlier, is a multiple
allegory in which Night is the world's chaos, ignorance, the

---

[44] Oddly enough, *The Transformed Metamorphosis* has actually been
classed with Marston's formal satires, chiefly because it affects something
like Marston's obscure manner. See Collins, *ed. cit.,* I, xxi, and Douglas
Bush, *Mythology and the Renaissance Tradition in English Poetry* (Minneapolis, 1932), p. 313. But as Raymond MacDonald Alden points out,
the poem is not at all like Marston's imitations of Roman classical models:
The Rise of Formal Satire in England under Classical Influence (Philadelphia, 1899), p. 162. Some critics who see that *The Transformed
Metamorphosis* differs from Marston's work still regard it as primarily
a satire. C. S. Lewis relates it to the "cryptographic obscurity of *The
Spider and the Fly* or *Speak Parrot,"* and Hallett Smith thinks it derives
from *Mother Hubberds Tale.* See *English Literature in the Sixteenth
Century* (Oxford, 1954), p. 476, and *Elizabethan Poetry,* p. 252.

[45] G. B. Harrison, ed., *The Elizabethan Journals* (New York, 1939),
II, 119. It should be observed that *The Transformed Metamorphosis*
appeared in the next year after the edict of 1 June, 1599 banning the
satires and calling in those of Marston, Hall and others to be burnt.

darkness of obscurity and actual night.[46] The theme and its treatment afford a reasonably close parallel to *The Transformed Metamorphosis,* and it is likely that Tourneur knew the poem and was influenced by it. Lewis points out that in Chapman's poem the multiple significances of Night conflict with one another, unlike the mutual enrichment of the levels of symbolic meaning we have seen in Tourneur's poem. But Tourneur does not presume to say to Chapman, "This is how it is done." He is far too self-critical to do anything so naïve, and I think he says instead, "See! this monster is the sort of thing the befoulments of our time force one to write." Having no ink but hell's pitchy main, no light but guttering Phlegetontic torches, his "troubled mind" can only produce "halfe breathed accenties," in which "Th'Idea doth confuse and chaoize" (ll. 9–10 of "To the Reader"). Tourneur, who elsewhere is a model of lucidity, here adopts the obscurity of Chapman's *Night* and of Marston's satires to express his protest against the extremes of their work. He imitates Spenser and he imitates and *criticizes* Chapman and Marston, assuming a stance toward these last two that is, incidentally, maintained in his later work. Thus *The Atheist's Tragedy* rejects the bloody-handed revenger of Marston's early tragedies, and imitates and looks critically at the combined revenge-overreacher tradition as it was developed by Chapman.

It may be that through *The Shadow of Night, The Transformed Metamorphosis* is related to *The Atheist's Tragedy* in another way, too. Chapman was a member of the supposed "School of Night," which included also Marlowe, Ralegh and the astronomer Harriot. The group was suspected of atheism and was known to have an interest in science and occult lore.[47] Robert Ornstein has suggested that the death of D'Amville, at

---

[46] Lewis, *op. cit.,* pp. 510–511.
[47] M. C. Bradbrook, *The School of Night,* p. 111 *et passim.*

the end of *The Atheist's Tragedy,* is based on a published
account of the death of Marlowe,[48] and so it is tempting to
speculate that both *The Transformed Metamorphosis* and
The Atheist's Tragedy might have part of their source in their
author's interest in the Chapman-Marlowe-Ralegh group.

[48] See below, p. 83, note 15.

III

The Atheist's Tragedy, or The Honest Man's Revenge

1 THE DOUBLE TITLE AND THE UNITY OF ACTION

As THE TITLE INDICATES, *The Atheist's Tragedy, or The Honest Man's Revenge* is akin to Aristotle's second and inferior sort of tragedy in which there is a happy outcome for the good characters and an unhappy for the bad. The tragic story dramatizes the rise and fall of the atheist, D'Amville, in his conflict with God, and determines the structure of the play as a whole. Linked with this story in a single unified plot is the fall and rise of the Christian, Charlemont, who occupies a position roughly corresponding to that of Hamlet in his play, but who is commanded by his murdered father's ghost to leave to Heaven his revenge against his uncle D'Amville.

If we view *The Atheist's Tragedy* for a moment as a revenge play, we immediately see a problem Tourneur had to solve in order to dramatize successfully the thesis that "Patience is the honest man's revenge," his acceptance of the Christian *Vindicta Mihi.* Somehow he had to find ways to make the non-avenger a person with whom the audience could sympathize. Londoners, if not bloody avengers themselves, had become accustomed to heroes who accepted revenge as a natural duty. There was a widely held assumption that the law barred from inheritance a son who refused to avenge a wrong done to his father.[1] And it can be argued that Charlemont, the lawful successor in his father's estate, could act as the agent of the law in seeking vengeance.[2] In any event, though he might not stab, garrote or poison D'Amville, Charlemont might be expected at least to take some *legal* steps against his father's murderer.

Tourneur's solution of the problem is to have Charlemont forget the ghost's command in a moment of passion and attack D'Amville and his son, Sebastian (III.ii). D'Amville runs for the guard, and Charlemont is about to kill Sebastian when the ghost enters to repeat his command to "Let him revenge my murder, and thy wrongs,/ To whom the Justice of Revenge belongs" (III. ii. 46–47). This scene shows Charlemont to be a true-hearted son, and at the same time reestablishes the essential command restraining him from action —a command he thereafter obeys. For a while after this scene Charlemont loses the opportunity to act because D'Amville returns with the guard and sends him off to prison. When Charlemont is later released, it is under circumstances leading him to believe he has been mistaken about his uncle, and they are reconciled, so that when Charlemont again has an opportunity for revenge, he no longer has a motive (III. iii–iv). Later, in the graveyard scene (IV. iii), when he sees for himself that D'Amville is a villain, the experience of imprisonment has strengthened his Christian fortitude, reinforcing his determina-

---

[1] Fredson T. Bowers, *Elizabethan Revenge Tragedy, 1587–1642* (Princeton, 1940), p. 38.

[2] Lily Bess Campbell, "Theories of Revenge in Renaissance England," *MP*, XXVIII (1931), 293.

tion to obey his father's ghost. At the end of the graveyard scene he is returned to prison, this time for killing Borachio in self-defense, and there he remains during the brief scenes before the trial that closes the play. Thus Charlemont's almost constant imprisonment after his return from the war enables him to remain a sympathetic character at the same time that he is kept inactive in order to leave the stage clear for the direct vengeance of God against the atheist.

And this is as it should be, for the play is, after all, primarily *The Atheist's Tragedy,* and only secondarily *The Honest Man's Revenge.* The central question of the play is whether the atheist is right in his belief that nature is mercly a mechanism to be manipulated by human reason. Tourneur answers this question, appropriately enough, through action that is natural, yet so improbable as to be clearly of God's doing. The improbability of the divine vengeance he tries to save from dramatic absurdity by giving it clearly *symbolic* meaning in its clearly symbolic dramatic context.[3] The dramatization of D'Amville's "career" is in the allegorical and symbolic medieval tradition of metrical tragedies and of morality, miracle and saints' plays.[4] The pyramidal structure of the metrical tragedies is paralleled in the rise, triumph and fall of the protagonist atheist. As in the typical morality play,

---

[3] I reserve judgment on Tourneur's handling of the divine vengeance until the closing section of this chapter, after the whole play has been reviewed. Most critics have thought he failed to handle it well. See, for example, Bradbrook, *Themes and Conventions of Elizabethan Tragedy* (Cambridge, 1935), p. 184; Clarence Valentine Boyer, *The Villain as Hero in Elizabethan Tragedy* (New York, 1914), p. 170; Robert Ornstein, *The Moral Vision of Jacobean Tragedy* (Madison, 1960), pp. 118–120.

[4] For good discussions of the general influence of medieval culture on Elizabethan drama, see Willard Farnham, *The Medieval Heritage of Elizabethan Tragedy* (Berkeley, 1936); Howard Baker, *Induction to Tragedy* (University, La., 1939); Theodore Spencer, *Shakespeare and the Nature of Man;* A. P. Rossiter, *English Drama from Early Times to the Elizabethans* (London, 1950); and John Peter, *Complaint and Satire in Early English Literature* (Oxford, 1956).

we at first are given a glimpse of man as he should be, in the orderly society controlled by Montferrers and Belforest; then we see man being led away from God, in the career of D'Amville; and finally we see the restoration of the Christian order as men return to the proper relation to God.

The unifying action of the play is to find fulfillment of the human potential.[5] Toward this end each character pursues a course of action consistent with his view of man and nature. D'Amville, regarding nature as a mechanism to be understood and exploited by human reason, sees man as ultimately but a part of the mechanism:

[D'AM.] *Borachio,* thou art read
          In Nature and her large Philosophie.
          Observ'st thou not the very selfe same course
          Of revolution both in Man and Beast?
BOR.   The same. For birth, growth, state, decay and death:
          Onely, a Man's beholding to his Nature
          For th' better composition o' the two.
                                              (I.i.6–12)

Though they reject the idea of an immortal soul, this view of nature makes D'Amville and Borachio conscious of the full potential of physical life, including the processes of generation through which a creature may in a sense have life and a kind of fulfillment in its offspring. D'Amville repudiates in so many words the mere "minutes pleasure" that is the goal of sensualists; he attempts rape and he steals not to gratify his own physical appetites but to insure that he will have descendants and that they will be wealthy.

Tourneur contrasts the rationalist atheists D'Amville and

---

[5] Here I want to acknowledge my great debt to Francis Fergusson's interpretation of the unity of action in drama. See *The Idea of a Theater* (Princeton, 1949).

Borachio with two other groups of people seeking fulfillment.
The sensual atheists Levidulcia and Sebastian seek pleasure in
sexual gratification, and in them the reason is entirely at the
service of the appetites. Opposed to both sorts of atheists are
the play's Christians, Castabella, Montferrers, and his son
Charlemont, who seek fulfillment in the life of the spirit. Tourneur did not need to state in full their view of man for his
seventeenth-century audience, but he did give Charlemont
lines implying a belief in the immortality of the soul, thereby
making clear the fundamental distinction between the Christian and the atheist. Death, the end of everything for the
atheist, is for the Christian a way to a higher existence:

> [CHARL.] . . . O
>   That Man, with so much labour should aspire
>   To worldly height; when in the humble earth,
>   The world's condition's at the best! Or scorne
>   Inferiour men; since to be lower then
>   A worme, is to be higher then a King!
>   (IV.iii.18–23)

Charlemont can face death

>   In expectation of the victorie,
>   Whose honour lies beyond this exigent.
>   (V.ii.141–142)

Montferrers, like his brother D'Amville, seeks continuance in
his posterity, but he and Charlemont, having an orthodox
faith, are unwilling to undertake evil action in order to find
fulfillment in worldly life. Charlemont does not reject the
world, but he is willing to forgo it rather than substitute conclusions reached by his reason for heavenly truth revealed
through the ghost of Montferrers and the Christian tradition.
  The events growing out of the unifying search for fulfill-

ment form the structure of the plot in such a way that the views of D'Amville and Charlemont lead them directly to their respective fates. The atheist's estate is born, grows, reaches a peak, and then decays and dies. His career follows the "selfe same course of revolution" as lower forms of life. Charlemont, on the other hand, falls but to rise. He is symbolically killed and buried, but returns to life. He is imprisoned and condemned to die, but God saves him from destruction, and he becomes possessor of all D'Amville wanted, and more. Thus Tourneur gives vitality to Aristotle's "inferior" sort of tragic plot having a good outcome for the good characters and a bad outcome for the bad. The double outcome is unified by the theme of the play, and is therefore artistically justified.

The *quest* for fulfillment takes many forms in action and language. In the opening scene there is a mental quest as the atheist uses logic to move from point to point in his search for the true basis of human happiness. He decides "Wealth is Lord/ Of all felicitie" and proceeds to use his riches to pursue his initial ends: the absence of Charlemont and the assistance of Snuffe (I.i.35–36). Later, as he plunges deeper and deeper into his effort to wrench nature into the forms he desires, D'Amville employs ritual and conjuration, and searches among tombstones for worldly security and a posterity.

Charlemont's quests take the form of journeys. When honor in war is his chief end, he goes to the siege of Ostend. Later, when he can perhaps see that the honor he bought with D'Amville's gold had evil results, he renounces the honor he might gain if he should make active war on D'Amville, and prepares himself for a spiritual journey. Facing death, he thinks of himself as a "warlike Navie on the Sea,/ Bound for the conquest of some wealthie land" (V.ii.137–138). Charlemont, in contrast to D'Amville, never relies on reason alone to guide his actions. When he bases his action on a form of *un-*

reason, the "force of reputation," he goes a fool's journey; when he accepts the words of the ghost as a divine revelation he is led to his justification.

Of the many Elizabethan and Jacobean plays continuing the tradition of *de casibus* tragedy, *The Atheist's Tragedy* most successfully combines new forms and ideas with the medieval religious conception of a tragedy of Fortune.[6] In many earlier poems and plays of this tradition Fortune seems to be mere chance, and in most of the later plays the secular has gone far toward eliminating the religious view of the world. In *The Atheist's Tragedy*, however, as in the medieval tradition, Fortune and the stars are finally seen to be divine providence,[7] and the all-important distinction is made between the man who lashes himself to Fortune's wheel and the man who does not. D'Amville is not destroyed by chance, but by what the medieval mind regarded as the most serious spiritual error : his senses delude his reason into believing that what they report is all of reality, and so he stakes his whole being on the things of the material world, making himself subject to Fortune. Her massy wheel, though it may raise him up, must as surely bring him down to ruin. But man need not be the victim of Fortune : if—as in the medieval view he should, and as Charlemont ultimately does—he accepts divine guidance and refuses to stake his eternal felicity on transient material things, he is beyond the power of Fortune to harm.

In *The Atheist's Tragedy*, as in *The Transformed Metamorphosis*, mythic analogy and traditional symbolism are fundamental to Tourneur's thought and art. The analysis of the play that follows will show that at every stage of the dramatic conflict the events, characters and language are arranged into

---

[6] See D. W. Robertson, Jr., "Chaucerian Tragedy," *ELH*, XIX (1952), 1–37.

[7] See Farnham, *The Medieval Heritage*, p. 104; Baker, *Induction to Tragedy*, p. 185.

symbolic patterns that are given significance by their relation to Christian ritual and legend.

2   THE STRUCTURE OF THE PLAY

At the beginning of the play, the manorial world of *The Atheist's Tragedy* is in its normal order, controlled by the patriarchs Montferrers and Belforest; but this order is threatened by the apostate D'Amville, younger brother of Montferrers, who plots to substitute himself for Charlemont as his brother's heir. D'Amville's atheistic denial of the father-hood of God is thus fittingly coupled with an asocial attack on patriarchy and primogeniture. The atheist's tragedy is that his reason, of which he is so very proud, fails to inform him that his denial of patriarchy is for all time: he succeeds in diverting the estate of Montferrers from Charlemont to himself, only to find it impossible to make either of his own sons heir to it.

D'Amville is, in fact, blind to all the realities of the father-son-relationship. He even misunderstands the immediate physical and emotional relationship of a father to his son, and this failure of understanding leads to his destruction. At the end of the first scene he says:

> Here are my Sonnes.—
> There's my eternitie. My life in them;
> And their succession shall for ever live.
> And in my reason dwels the providence,
> To adde to life as much of happinesse.
> Let all men lose, so I increase my gaine,
> I have no feeling of anothers paine.

> (I.i.139–145)

Here he asserts the dependence of his whole "eternity" on the continuance of his line through his sons, and then in the next breath says he has no feeling of another's pain! In his egoism he forgets that his sons are "others" rather than mere extensions of himself. Later, when they both die, he is maddened and reduced to the folly that destroys him.

Contrasting with D'Amville's blindness is the perception of Montferrers:

> *Enter old* MONTFERRERS *and* CHARLEMONT
> MONT. I prithee let this current of my teares,
>   Divert thy inclination from the warre.
>   For of my children thou art onely left,
>   To promise a succession to my house.
>   (I.ii.1–5)

Montferrers has lived long enough to see sons die before, and to suffer in their suffering, and he knows that he will be hurt again if anything happens to Charlemont. In the few scenes in which he appears, Montferrers affords a perspective from which to judge D'Amville. Montferrers, too, is concerned for his succession; but, not being an atheist, he perceives the truth of the father-son relationship and accepts the normal order of society.

The normal order of Montferrer's society is faulty, though, and therefore vulnerable. The society accepts the war in the Low Countries as part of its order; wealthy men can buy power; and parental authority may be overcome by the force of reputation. D'Amville, the naturalist manipulating phenomena, is quick to exploit these weaknesses to create the social disorder that is his primary goal: the dislocation of Charlemont from his inherited place in society. Once Charlemont is out of the way, D'Amville has a second goal, to marry Rousard to Castabella. To bring this about, he bribes Snuffe, and he and Belforest assert their parental authority. Whereas in the elimination of Charlemont from the scene, wealth and "honor" overcame parental authority, the forced marriage is effected only when wealth and parental authority overcome honor.

Charlemont is linked to the unprincipled Snuffe by his willingness to accept D'Amville's wealth (I.i.97–103; I.ii.177–197). Unlike Snuffe, Charlemont himself is not corrupted by receiving D'Amville's gold, for it is a loan, not a bribe, yet dependence on D'Amville's bounty seriously undercuts the value of the "honor" Charlemont allows to outweigh the solid arguments of Montferrers and Castabella that he should remain at home. Though Charlemont is aware of the weakness of his stand, he feels *compelled* to go to war:

> Something within me would perswade my stay,
> But Reputation will not yeeld unto't.
>
> (I.ii.142–143)

An awareness that they are being compelled to act against their will, coupled with a sense of foreboding, weighs heavily on Montferrers and Castabella throughout the first act. Thus when Montferrers finally gives his permission for Charlemont to go to war, he says:

> Your importunities have overcome.
> Pray God my forc'd graunt prove not ominous.
>
> (I.i.45–46)

And when Castabella is commanded to marry Rousard by Belforest's authority to "claim th' obedience," she thinks:

> Now *Charlemont!* O my presaging teares!
> This sad event hath follow'd my sad feares.
>
> (I.iv.135–136)

This consciousness that actions are determined not by the free will of individuals but by compulsion of some sort is interpreted hypocritically by D'Amville as evidence that there is an unalterable destiny controlling the affairs of men :

> And I am of a confident beliefe,
> That ev'n the time, place, manner of our deathes,
> Doe follow Fate with that necessitie;
> That makes us sure to dye. And in a thing
> Ordain'd so certainly unalterable,
> What can the use of providence prevaile?
>
> (I.ii.49–54)

Later, when he is alone with Borachio, D'Amville shows that he really believes the providence of his reason has determined all that has happened (II.iv). Through these statements of D'Amville on fate and providence, and through the feeling of his victims that their actions are compelled, Tourneur creates the general impression that *some* power is interested in the destinies of men. This prepares the audience for the active role to be played by divine providence, setting up an expectation of divine vengeance for the murder of Montferrers even before his ghost announces it.

In the first act we see D'Amville developing and deploying the instruments he is to use in his conflict with society and with God. Most of these instruments are already in action by the end of the first scene. In the opening lines of the play we see him use his reasoning power in a debate with Borachio, and it is not long before his wealth goes into action. Borachio himself is to be the chief human agent of his villainy, killing Montferrers and attempting to kill Charlemont. "Borachio" serves as an instrument in another way, too. This word, in the Spanish from which it comes, is associated with drunkenness, and the drunkenness of the servants is D'Amville's instrument in the murder of Montferrers. Ironically, drink is also instrumental in D'Amville's self-murder in the last scene of the play, when the wine he drinks, working on his already distracted mind, leads him to attempt the execution of Charlemont and then to stagger fatally in the performance of it.

But the atheist's most powerful instrument is his pretended piety. The first act closes on a penetrating line: Sebastian's "The nearer the Church; the further from God" (I.iv.150–151). We shall return to this line later in treating the crimes of D'Amville, Snuffe and Borachio in the churchyard in Act IV, but here let us note that it brands the forced wedding of Castabella as a false rite and aptly describes the hypocritical piety of both Snuffe and D'Amville. From the middle of the first scene, when Charlemont joins Borachio and D'Amville, we see that when others are present it is the atheist's policy to pretend he is a pious Christian. D'Amville works through the established social and religious forms to subvert society and religion themselves.

Through hypocritical exploitation of social and religious rituals D'Amville masks his crimes and attempts to insure his gains. By means of this combination of crime and hypocrisy he gains increasing control of the machinery of society, but the murder of the father, the cornerstone of his plot as of his blasphemous theology, brings attacks by the son and by the spirit of the Father, so that the more D'Amville tries to establish his new order, the worse his real situation becomes. He is driven to ever greater desperation in his effort to *exorcise* "spirits" by means properly employed to *invoke* the spirit. To rise in worldly power D'Amville conducts a series of increasingly potent and self-damning rituals in which he moves from the position of lay participant to high priesthood and finally to self-deification.

Each act after the first begins with an on-stage or off-stage ritual, and in each case D'Amville's inversion of the normal basis for religious ritual is repaid in an inversion of the result he intends. The first scene of Act II is the wedding feast of Castabella and Rousard, ostensibly a celebration of the perpetuation of life. D'Amville directs the affair, proposing healths to Castabella and Charlemont, and presiding as master of ceremonies over Borachio's false narrative of Charlemont's death at Ostend.[8] In D'Amville's hands the wedding rites produce results exactly opposite to those expected. Rousard, instead of beginning to generate new life, becomes impotent. As he says later :

> A gen'rall weaknesse did surprise my health
> The very day I married *Castabella*.
>
> (III.iv.73–74)

The forced ceremony of the perpetuation of life is followed through the rest of Act II by scenes of violence and real or symbolic death : Borachio's tale of siege and war, more truly descriptive of the scene in D'Amville's mansion than of Charlemont's fate, comes in II,i; the servants fight in II,ii; the impotence which foreshadows the actual death of Rousard is revealed in II,iii; Borachio and D'Amville murder Montferrers in II,iv; and we finally reach the stormy and dark warfront itself in II,vi, the last scene of the act. Ironically parallel-

---

[8] Borachio's story is based on the famous stratagem of Sir Francis Vere in the repulse of the Spanish assault at Ostend on January 7, 1602. Henry Hexham, Vere's page, recounts how "General Vere perceiving the enemy to fall off, commanded me to run, as fast as ever I could" with the order to "open the West Sluice : out of which there ran such a stream and torrent, through the channel of the West Haven, that, upon their retreat, it carried away many of their sound and hurt men into the sea. And besides, our men fell down our walls after them, and slew a great many of their men as they retreated." *Account of the Assault on Ostend, 7th January, 1602,* in *An English Garner,* ed. Edward Arber (Birmingham, 1883), VII, 181.

ing the events of the rest of Act II is the sex war of Levidulcia
with Fresco, Sebastian, and Belforest, which reaches a climax
in II,v. Here the lust of Levidulcia and Sebastian is balanced
against the earlier scenes showing the chastity of Castabella
and the impotence of Rousard. Violent action ensues when
Belforest enters while Sebastian is with Levidulcia and Fresco
is hiding behind the arras, and the invented tale of pursuit and
siege told by Fresco at the prompting of Levidulcia parallels
Borachio's story of the siege of Ostend.[9]

After the murder of Montferrers, D'Amville and Borachio
rejoice together over the success of their plot thus far, and
D'Amville thinks of himself as an evil priest performing
black masses. Whereas the Christian Church has as its cornerstone the divinity of Christ, the cornerstone of the mansion
D'Amville will build is to be the stone that has killed Montferrers :

> Upon this ground Ile build my Manour-house;
> And this shall be the chiefest corner stone.
>
> (II.iv.118–119)

And of the wedding healths they say :

> BOR. Then your healths.
> Though seeming but the ordinarie rites,
> And ceremonies due to festivals :—
> D'AM. Yet us'd by me to make the servants drunke.
> An instrument the plot could not have miss'd.
>
> (II.iv.142–146)

---

[9] "The Conveyance away of *Sebastian* and *Fresco*, on her Husband's
approach, is taken from *Boccace's Novels, Day 7. Nov. 6.*" *The Lives and
Characters of the English Dramatick Poets,* (First begun by Mr. [Gerard]
Langbain[e], improv'd and continued down to this Time, by a Careful
Hand [Charles Gildon] (London, [1699?]), p. 142. Jackson I. Cope
suggests that Tourneur's actual source for this episode may have been a
stage piece, the jig of "Singing Simpkin," which is itself based on
Boccaccio and is the only version of the story in which Fresco is a clown
used for ironic commentary. "Tourneur's *Atheist's Tragedy* and the Jig
of 'Singing Simpkin,'" *MLN*, LXX (1955), 571–573.

At the end of the scene they are already planning the next perverted ritual, the funeral they hope will lay the spirit of Charlemont.

As the wedding feast opening Act II leads to impotence and death for Rousard, so the funeral of Charlemont at the beginning of Act III is followed immediately by his return from death. None of society's symbols of regeneration avail for the atheist, whereas for the Christian, a funeral is a prelude to resurrection. If in the wedding D'Amville only seconded the evil performance of Snuffe, in the funeral he wears black robes and plays the evil priest himself. D'Amville's eulogy of Montferrers and Charlemont contains phrases suggesting the resurrection to come, though not so intended by D'Amville. He refers to Montferrers as a phoenix, the mythical Arabian bird reborn from its own ashes, a traditional Christian symbol of the Resurrection (III.i.43). He says that "Non ultra" might be inscribed on their monuments, intending to imply that nothing lies beyond their lives, but ironically suggesting the Renaissance, post-Columbian retort to the ancient belief that no land lay beyond the straits of Gibraltar: "Plus ultra!"[10] The third volley is fired, concluding the funeral, and D'Amville, in an aside, speaks of the purpose of the ritual and invokes Charlemont to "come" again:

> T'is done. Thus faire accomplements, make foule
> Deedes gratious. *Charlemont!* come now when t'wut.
> I've buryed under these two marble stones
> Thy living hopes; And thy dead fathers bones. *Exeunt.*
>
> (III.i.57–60)

---

[10] Charles V of Spain had as his device the Pillars of Hercules and the words "Plus ultra," to indicate the expansion of empire into the new world. This icon was also associated with Elizabeth. Frances A. Yates, "Queen Elizabeth as Astraea," *Journal of the Warburg and Courtauld Institutes,* X (1947), 52.

Castabella enters, and she has no sooner wept over Charlemont's "blasted Spring" than he appears (III.i.70). At first she
takes him for a spirit, but he hastens to assure her of his
corporeal reality.

The atheist's rejection of the immortality of the spirit is
answered in this "resurrection" of Charlemont and in the
return of the ghost of Montferrers. These returns from death
are set in a context of general concern for the question of what
"spirits" are and whether they are real. The sensualists Levidulcia and Snuffe think of the spirits chiefly in terms of the
spirits in the blood that raise the spirit of lust :

> [Levi.] Lust is a Spirit, which whosoe'er doth raise;
> The next man that encounters boldly, layes.
> > (II.iii.80–81)

> Lang. Your hand Gentlewoman.—
> The flesh is humble till the Spirit move it;
> But when t'is rais'd it will command above it.
> > (IV.i.90–92)

D'Amville, on the other hand, believes that a spirit inhabits the
mind and will, as well as the body, but he will not grant
immortality to it. He fears for Sebastian's life because "His
spirit is so boldly dangerous" (IV.ii.44), and he thinks of
Sebastian's spirit as something that he, god-like, may control
through gold :

> D'Am. *Borachio!* fetch me a thousand Crownes. I am
> Content to countenance the freedome of
> Your spirit when t'is worthily imployed.
> A Gods name give behaviour the full scope
> Of gen'rous libertie; but let it not
> Disperse and spend it selfe in courses of
> Unbounded licence. Here, pay for your hurts.
> > (III.ii.72–78)

The Christians, on the other hand, think of the human spirit in relation to God :

> CAST.   O thou that knowest me justly *Charlemonts,*
> Though in the forc'd possession of another;
> Since from thine owne free spirit wee receive it,
> That our affections cannot be compel'd,
> Though our actions may. . . .
>
> (III.i.62–66)

This is the beginning of Castabella's lament at the tomb of Charlemont, which his appearance interrupts.

Repeatedly, as here, the characters are confronted with a "ghostly" apparition that they must accept or reject as part of reality. Sometimes what they see is a human being pretending to be a ghost, sometimes it is a hallucination and sometimes it may really be the ghost of Montferrers. The first reaction of most of the characters to these apparitions is incredulity; but the impact of repeated visitations forces at least an unconscious acceptance of the reality of the spirit, which leaves the subject inwardly shaken.

When first confronted by the ghost of Montferrers at the battlefront in II,vi, Charlemont is skeptical, and tries to give a natural explanation for what has happened, as a good Protestant should.[11] After all, the fatigue of his mind and the dark and stormy night create precisely those conditions which are conducive to delusion. But the ghost appears again when Charlemont knows himself awake, and he can no longer disbelieve it :

---

[11] The "orthodox" Protestant position was that all ghosts are either feignings of the devil or an optical illusion. Catholics believed souls in purgatory could return as ghosts to ask prayers and masses. These ghosts might also be agents of God's justice against their murderers, but not by asking revenge. See Robert Hunter West, *The Invisible World* (Athens, Ga., 1939), pp. 20, 48, 187, 194.

O pardon me ! my doubtfull heart was slow
To credit that which I did feare to know.

(II.vi.78–79)

Since what this ghost speaks is proved true, and since it never urges evil action, Charlemont has no reason to associate it with an evil origin. He comes to regard its words as divine revelation.

The return of Montferrers from beyond the grave to tell Charlemont what has happened leads to the return of Charlemont from the war and from his supposed death, and throughout the rest of the play the sense that Charlemont has returned from death is maintained by having him be taken for a ghost. After he appears to Castabella at the end of the joint funeral of father and son, he goes to see D'Amville, who *"counterfaites to take him for a ghoast"* and flees for the guard (III.ii.22–23). The precise Protestant Snuffe denies the reality of reality :

No. T'is prophane. Spirits are invisible. T'is the fiend i' the likenesse of *Charlemont.* I will have no conversation with Sathan.

(III.ii.30–32)

Sebastian's approach to the problem is more empirical :

The Spirit of *Charlemont?* I'le try that.
    Strike, and the blow return'd.
'Fore God thou sayest true, th'art all Spirit.

(III.ii.34–36)

The "spirited" fight that follows is interrupted by the entrance of the ghost of Montferrers, which tells Charlemont to leave revenge to God.

Charlemont appears as a ghost again in the graveyard scene in Act IV. He rises from a grave to frighten off D'Amville, who ironically has himself invoked "the dead" in trying to tell Castabella no one can rescue her from being raped:

> . . . Crie to the graves;
> The dead can heare thee; invocate their helpe.
> (IV.iii.184–185)

D'Amville takes Charlemont for the ghost of Montferrers, and the belief that he has seen the ghost of the brother he murdered turns his mind toward un-reason, and through un-reason to a partial vision of the truth that lies beyond the power of unaided reason to perceive. From the middle of IV,iii, D'Amville is susceptible to ghosts: he starts at the sight of death's-heads (IV.iii.238–239), sees the image of Montferrers in a cloud (IV.iii.258–263), and finally sees and hears the ghost itself in a dream (V.i). Each of these apparitions drives D'Amville further toward distraction. Thus while Montferrers' ghost opposes human revenge, the real or imaginary ghosts are themselves instrumental in God's overthrow of the atheist's proud reason.

The "resurrected" Charlemont is also regarded by D'Amville as a "spirit" in his own person. Charlemont disguised as a ghost attacks D'Amville's mind at a point where his reason cannot defend him, and he is there defeated, but D'Amville thinks he knows how to deal with the spirit of Charlemont himself:

> . . . I tooke
> You for a Spirit; and Ile conjure you
> Before I ha' done.
> (III.ii.60–62)

The mock funeral has not entirely succeeded in exorcising the threat Charlemont represents to the legality of D'Amville's estate. Charlemont has returned, and now D'Amville has a new trick to bury him : he will have him coffined in a prison, where he hopes he will die and rot. He speaks the incantation three times :

> . . . *Charlemont*
> Shall die and rot in prison; and t'is just.
>   (III.iv.3–4)
> . . . He shal rot.
>   (III.iv.14)
> I tell thee hee shall starve, and dye, and rot.
>   (III.iv.31)

But in this, too, D'Amville fails. He gives a thousand crowns to Sebastian, enabling him to thwart his father's will, as the earlier loan of an identical amount to Charlemont enabled him to thwart the will of Montferrers. Sebastian uses the money to free Charlemont, who once more returns from what was to have been a tomb, forcing D'Amville to invent new means for dealing with his enemy. He now decides to murder Charlemont, to put him in an actual grave. To neutralize and disarm his victim he pretends piety again, declaring that all he has done has been misunderstood. The gullible Charlemont accepts his fatherly advances and they depart to seal their reconciliation with a sacramental supper :

> D'AM. Come, let's to supper. There we will confirme
>   The eternall bond of our concluded love.
>   (III.iv.84–85)

At the opening of Act III, D'Amville has assumed the role of priest, but as the act proceeds and he endeavors to consoli-

date his power, he tends increasingly to make a god of himself
—a movement consummated in the ritual of self-deification
which opens Act V. He is becoming a Satan, and is, indeed,
exorcised by Charlemont as such (III.ii.63–66). But Castabella
tries to rescue Charlemont from prison by urging D'Amville
to imitate God, not Satan:

> CASTA. O Father! Mercie is an attribute
> As high as Justice; an essentiall part
> Of his unbounded goodnesse, whose divine
> Impression, forme, and image man should beare.
> And (me thinks) Man should love to imitate
> His Mercie; since the onely countenance
> Of Justice, were destruction; if the sweet
> And loving favour of his mercie did
> Not mediate betweene it and our weakenesse.
>
> D'AM,   Forbeare. You will displease me. He shal rot.
>
> CASTA. Deare Sir! Since by your greatnesse, you
> Are nearer heav'n in place; be nearer it
> In goodnesse. Rich men should transcend the poore,
> As clouds the earth; rais'd by the comfort of
> The Sunne, to water dry and barren grounds.
>
> (III.iv.5–19)

Almost immediately after Castabella speaks these lines, Charlemont and Sebastian enter, and D'Amville decides to "tem-
porize." Significantly, he adopts Castabella's metaphor of the
sun for the position of God, and applies it to himself in proposing his pretended new relationship to Charlemont:

> [D'AM.] Nephew, had not his open freedome made
> My disposition knowne; I would ha' borne
> The course and inclination of my love
> According to the motion of the Sunne,
> Invisibly injoyed and understood.
>
> (III.iv.39–43)

I will supply your Fathers vacant place,
To guide your greene improvidence of youth;
And make you ripe for your inheritance.

(III.iv.58–60)

The first scene of Act IV takes place in the house of Cata-plasma, but at the same time the supper is in progress which is to "confirme / The eternall bond" of the love of D'Amville and Charlemont—the third in the series of act-opening rites through which D'Amville seeks his ends. As the second scene begins, Charlemont takes leave of D'Amville, having con-cluded the meal that the atheist intends shall be his last supper. As the Christian meditates in the churchyard, he is betrayed by D'Amville to Borachio, who goes to murder him. Earlier, in the murder of Montferrers, D'Amville has assumed the role of Cain. Now he becomes a Judas.

Through the rituals of wedding and funeral D'Amville has tried indirectly to provide himself with a posterity and to lay the spirit of Charlemont. These rituals have failed, and D'Amville is now prepared to use more direct means to gain his ends. His new means reveal the true character of the earlier rituals: the funeral is to be followed by the murder of Charle-mont, and the wedding that was a rape is to be consummated in the actual rape of Castabella by D'Amville. He takes her for the purpose into the same graveyard where Borachio is to murder Charlemont, and here the lustful and the macabre meet and are fused. Tourneur rings all the bizarre variations on this theme, ludicrously paralleling D'Amville's unnatural attempts at rape and murder with Snuffe's pursuit of Soquette among the tombstones. First Snuffe dresses himself in a macabre disguise, and so Soquette embraces a "ghost." Later the situation is reversed, and we see Snuffe embrace the actual corpse of Borachio, mistaking it for Soquette:

Verily thou lyest in a fine premeditate readinesse for the
purpose. Come kisse me sweet *Soquette*.—Now puritie defend
me from the sinne of Sodom.—This is a creature of the
masculine gender.—Verily the Man is blasted.—Yea? cold and
stiffe?—Murder, murder, murder.   (IV.iii.233–237)

As these grotesque displays of graveyard lust draw to a close,
and we see how true Sebastian's aphorism—"The nearer the
Church; the further from God"—is to be, D'Amville recalls
the beginning of his plot and characterizes his evil employment
of funerals to guarantee the results of weddings as a fornication
with death, an unnatural relation which must ever be as fruit-
less as the wedding of the impotent Rousard has been. In the
murder of Montferrers, says D'Amville, "that same Strumpet
Murder & my selfe/ Committed sin together" (IV.iii.249–250).
And in the final scene of the tragedy, when for D'Amville the
wheel has come full circle, he cries : "O!/ The lust of Death
commits a Rape upon me/ As I would ha' done on *Castabella*" (V.ii.291–293).

Meanwhile, surrounding the action in the graveyard, the
opening and closing scenes of Act IV reveal the final consequences of the lust of Levidulcia for Sebastian. The emblematic interpretations of the patterns in the sewing of Soquette
that open the act also interpret the action to follow. The moral
of each pattern is that a creature that lusts "stands as if it were
readie to fall and perish by that whereon it spent all the
substance it had" (IV.i.41–42). Nevertheless, Levidulcia and
Sebastian "goe up into the Closet" together (IV.i.67). At the
end of the act Belforest, becoming suspicious, bursts into Cataplasma's house. Once again lust unites with death : Belforest
and Sebastian kill each other, and Levidulcia cries out before
taking her own life :

> Their bloud runnes out in rivers; and my lust
> The fountaine whence it flowes . . .

(IV.v.66–67)

As the divine counteraction against the atheists gains
momentum, Tourneur draws upon ancient and medieval
myths of saintly martyrdom and divine vengeance. The basis
for some of the central events of Acts IV and V would seem
to be the legend of St. Winifred, whose shrine at Holywell was
famous in the seventeenth century.[12] Snuffe suggests that this
legend might be relevant when he identifies as St. Winifred's
the church in whose yard D'Amville attempts to rape Castabella (IV.iii.57).

Winifred, a chaste virgin like Castabella, was being tutored
by her uncle, St. Beuno, in preparation for consecrating herself
to God. Caradoc, son of a neighboring prince, came to call on
her at a time when her parents were at church with Beuno,
who was celebrating the mass. Caradoc took advantage of their
absence to attempt to make love to Winifred. When she re-
pulsed his advances and fled, he pursued her to the brow of
a hill next to the church. There he caught her and told her she
must yield or die. When she refused to yield, he cut off her
head with his sword. The head rolled down the hill to the
church door, and immediately a miraculous spring gushed
forth on the spot where it came to rest. St. Beuno rushed forth
from the church and invoked the wrath of heaven against
Caradoc, who straightaway fell dead. Beuno went back into
the church and concluded the mass, then came out and
replaced the head of Winifred on her body. The wound

---

[12] "On the feast of the saint in 1629, for example, in the midst of the
penal times, over 14,000 people and 150 priests were estimated to have
been present." *Butler's Lives of the Saints,* ed. Herbert Thurston, S. J.,
and Donald Attwater (New York, 1956), IV, 246. The legend was widely
known and had been published in English in William Caxton's *The Lyfe
of Saynt Wenefryde* (Westminster, 1485).

healed instantly, leaving only a faint red scar around her neck.

Several elements of this story appear in *The Atheist's Tragedy*. D'Amville's attempt to rape Castabella in the immediate vicinity of the church of St. Winifred parallels the central incident of the saint's legend. The rescue of Castabella by Charlemont is but a milder version of the miracle which saved Winifred. And the miraculous death of Caradoc foreshadows the manner of D'Amville's end. Also, Winifred's holy spring has an important symbolic function in the play, contrasting with the lust of Levidulcia, which she describes as the "fountain" whence flows the blood of her husband and her lover. But discussion of the important fountain and river imagery must be deferred until a later section where it can be considered in its proper relation to the full structure of action and character.[13]

From the time in Act IV when he openly doubts the ability of Rousard and Sebastian to perpetuate his line, D'Amville's faith in nature and human reason begins to be shaken, and he begins to see his whole enterprise in a clearer light. In the attempted rape of Castabella he likens himself to Tereus—a suggestion that he regards himself as a monstrous villain and foresees that his dead offspring will be served up to him. Real mental distraction comes when Charlemont appears before him as the ghost of Montferrers. The atheist is driven *by the evidence of his senses* to accept the spirit world, and he speaks of his troubled conscience, of fears of heaven and hell (IV.iii. 240–296). He interprets the name of Montferrers (Mont Fer), the brother he has murdered, as symbolizing a *mountain* about to crush him:

Mountaines o'erwhelme mee, the Ghoast of olde *Montferrers* haunts me.   (IV.iii.274–275)

---

[13] Another version of the legend of Winifred, invented by Thomas Deloney, is closely related to the events of Act V. See below, p. 85.

Of his failure in the graveyard he asks why Pluto could not

> . . . ha' suffer'd me to raise
> The mountaine o' my sinnes with one as damnable
> As all the rest; and then ha' tumbled me
> To ruine? . . .   (IV.iii.291–294)

By the end of this scene D'Amville's "braines begin to put themselves in order" (IV.iii.312), but the lesson of the contrast between his temporary distraction and the sound sleep of Castabella and Charlemont in the graveyard is not lost on him. He sees that there must be "some other happinesse within the freedome of the conscience, then my knowledge e'er attain'd too" (IV.iii.318–319). Nevertheless, when Charlemont declares himself the killer of Borachio, D'Amville determines to hazard all on one last effort to be rid of his enemy. Charlemont will stand trial for murder, and D'Amville will sit as one of his three judges.

At the beginning of Act V, D'Amville is at the peak of his worldly power. As a judge he will transcend both the blasphemer and the priest who has performed black masses, for he will be in a position allowing him to imitate the godhead. The act opens with D'Amville's final ritual. He fondles his gold, and hears in it a tinkling music "Like Angels voices" (V.i.17). He identifies himself quite clearly as antichrist, establishing his own religion with gold coins as the ministers of "Mans high wisedome the superiour power" (V.i.22–34).

Immediately, however, the ghost of Montferrers tells him that he is "a most wretched miserable foole" (V.i.38), and he is presented with the bodies of his sons. D'Amville has risen to the top of the wheel, and, since he enslaved himself to Fortune, the precipitous descent to ruin is all that is left for him. With the death of his sons and the inability of his gold to revive them

he recognizes the futility of any faith in nature or in the
"Angels" of his new religion; but he is still determined to pit
his judgment against the judgment of God "In yond' Starre
chamber" (V.i.144). By this phrase D'Amville means the high
court of man, which in England was the Star Chamber; but
in the context of the conflict between D'Amville and God,
gold and the stars, the phrase prepares the audience to behold
the judgment of God against the atheist.

The final scene of the play, D'Amville's last judgment, opens
with the punishment of the evil minor figures, Cataplasma,
Soquette, Fresco and Snuffe. Then "*Enter* D'AMVILLE *dis-
tractedly with the hearses of his two Sonnes borne after him*"
(V.ii.76–77). He has come to oppose the "providence" of his
reason to God's providence, and it is significant that his own
un-reason destroys him. Distracted by the death of his sons,
he is even further dismayed by the courage of Charlemont in
the face of death. In this he sees that he was wrong not only
about physical nature but about human nature.[14] This final
blow to his mind leads to his putting on a false courage by
drinking wine, which brings him to the folly of stepping from
the position of a judge to that of an executioner, from the godhead to the place of the fallen Satan:

> 2 JUD. My Lord; the office will impresse a marke
>   Of scandall and dishonour on your name.
> CHARL. The office fits him; hinder not his hand.
>
> (V.ii.253–255)

The axe falls and D'Amville destroys himself.[15] He is clearly

---

[14] *Cf.* Fluchère, *op. cit.*, p. 136.

[15] Ornstein suggests that D'Amville's death by striking himself in the
head with an axe may be based on a published account of the death
of Christopher Marlowe, popularly regarded as an atheist, which reported
the playwright to have stabbed himself in the head with a dagger while
attempting to kill an enemy. " 'The Atheist's Tragedy,' " *NQ*, 200 (1955),
284–285.

damned, for he dies in the act of murder, yet in death he has a moment of insight into the frailty of human reason, so easily brought to madness by grief and to folly by drink. And he sees more than the mere physical frailty of his own reason. Not chance or misfortune have killed him and his sons, but the power and the providence of God (V.ii.272–291).

The trial scene also teaches D'Amville this lesson that "mans wisdome is a foole" in more general terms (V.ii.273). Except for the divine action that has brought about his death, his plan might have succeeded; although his false rituals have failed because they have not deceived God, they nevertheless have deceived men. The dying D'Amville says to the judges :

> I came to thee for Judgement; and thou think'st
> Thy selfe a wise man. I outreach'd thy wit;
> And made thy Justice Murders instrument,
> In *Castabella's* death and *Charlemonts.*

> (V.ii.274–277)

Some critics have brushed *The Atheist's Tragedy* aside because they find the atheist's reasonings about nature puerile. This would be a good basis for rejection of the play as an atheistic tract, but it is no basis for criticism of it as a dramatic work. D'Amville thinks himself a profound reasoner, but it is obviously Tourneur's intention that *we* shall see through his pretense. Tourneur shows that the atheist position is based on an absurd contradiction : D'Amville's entire course of proof that man's reason is worthy of elevation to the godhead consists of a series of demonstrations that men are fools! The actions of Charlemont, Montferrers, Belforest and the judges have provided dramatic proof of the inadequacy of human reason.

I think much of the last scene parallels the version of the

legend of St. Winifred created by Thomas Deloney in *The Gentle Craft*.[16] The first story in the collection is of St. Hugh, who loved the fair virgin Winifred. In response to his suit for marriage, she sent him off for three months, promising to give him an answer at the end of that time. He returned to find her sitting by a well reading a holy book. She had no interest in him, for her love had fled to heaven. The disappointed Hugh then dashed off to a series of adventures in foreign lands, and when he came back to England again, he found that the Roman emperor Diocletian had sent "divers wolvish tyrants" to invade the land and persecute the Christians.[17] Upon locating Winifred among those who had been imprisoned, Hugh so commended her steadfast faith that he was imprisoned with her. They were both condemned to die for their religion. "When they were come to the place of execution, and mounted upon the Scaffold, they seemed for beauty like two bright Stars, *Castor* and *Pollux,* there they embraced each other with such chaste desires, as all those that beheld them, admired to see how stedfast and firme both these Lovers were, ready in hearts and minds to heaven itselfe."[18] They pledged themselves to constant heavenly love, and Hugh thanked Winifred for teaching him such love to replace his former "shadow of love, a sweetnesse tempered with gall-dying life, and a living death, where the heart was continually tossed upon the seas of tempestuous sorrowes, and wherein the minde had no calme quietnesse." The Christian-hating tyrant then commanded their death, and Hugh replied: "Thou tyrant . . . the very like sentence is pronounced against thy selfe; for Nature hath deemed thou shalt die likewise, and albeit the execution thereof be something deferred, yet at

---

[16] London, *c.* 1598. Quoted from the edition prepared by Merritt E. Lawlis, *The Novels of Thomas Deloney* (Bloomington, 1961).

[17] *Ibid.,* p. 105.

[18] *Ibid.,* p. 109.

86   A STUDY OF CYRIL TOURNEUR

length it will come, and that shortly, for never did Tyrant
carry gray haires to the grave." Winifred asked the executioner
to bleed her to death; "the scarlet blood sprung out in plenti-
full sort, much like a pretious fountaine lately filled with Claret
Wine," and she said, "Here doe I sacrifice my blood to him
that bought mee, who by his blood washt away all my sinnes."[19]
Hugh was executed by being forced to drink her blood mixed
with poison. Winifred was "buried by the Well where she had
so long lived."[20] Since Hugh had worked for a time as a shoemaker, he willed his bones to "the gentle craft." This is why
a shoemaker's tools were commonly called St. Hugh's bones.

Because Deloney needed St. Hugh's bones, the outcome of
this story is the reverse of *The Atheist's Tragedy,* yet the two
situations are strikingly similar. In each story young Christian
lovers are persecuted by the antichrist and face death with
exemplary courage, one of them having sought the martyrdom
because of the other. The condemnation of the tyrant in
Deloney's story implies that he, like D'Amville, will die a
victim of divine providence. The execution of Hugh, forced
to drink the poisoned blood of Winifred, may have suggested
the drunken end of D'Amville, for Deloney describes Winifred's blood as like wine, and D'Amville is given wine to drink
that looks to him like blood. Hugh rejoices in death because
the drinking of Winifred's blood is a quasi-sacramental act.
As a parody of sacrament, the drinking of wine is for D'Amville a last, fragmentary, blasted ritual, a consecration to a
death that is damnation:

[D'AM.]   . . . Why thou uncharitable Knave;
            Do'st bring mee bloud to drinke? The very glasse
            Lookes pale and trembles at it.
SERV.   T'is your hand my Lord.

[19] *Ibid.,* p. 110.
[20] *Ibid.,* p. 112.

D'AM.   Canst blame mee to be fearefull; bearing still
The presence of a murderer about me?

(V.ii.222–227)

At the end of *The Atheist's Tragedy*, after D'Amville has been punished, Charlemont is rewarded. He will be

> Lord of *Montferrers;* Lord *D'amville; Belforest.*
> And for a cloze to make up all the rest;
> The Lord of *Castabella.*

(V.ii.312–314)

The normal order of the manorial society is to be restored through the union of Castabella and Charlemont. D'Amville has desecrated funerals and weddings, the rituals through which a healthy, natural society sheds old life and begins new, by using them as instruments of an unnatural plot. The play ends with preparations for purifying those rituals through the plainly healthy and natural wedding of Castabella to Charlemont and the funeral of D'Amville and his sons.

3   CHARACTERS AND DOCTRINES IN CONFLICT

In *The Atheist's Tragedy* Tourneur examines several different ways of living without God. D'Amville and Borachio are rationalizing naturalists, Levidulcia is an instinctual sensualist, Snuffe is a man whose precisian conscience is easily overcome by the world, and the bawds and whores are simply too low to be capable of knowing God. The grotesquely comical and vicious actions of the subordinate figures provide ironic perspectives on D'Amville in dramatic parallels that parody his character, undercut his pretensions, and reveal the inherent contradictions of his view of life.

Dramatically contrasted with all the atheists are the Christians of the play. Levidulcia stands in direct opposition to Castabella, "chaste and beautiful."[21] Critics have accused Castabella of an *unnatural* chastity on the basis of her remark on the night of her wedding to Rousard that "The sweetnesse of the night consists in rest" (II.iii.33), and the speech at the end of the third act in which she says of carnality, "I am as much respectlesse to enjoy/ Such pleasure as [I'me] ignorant what it is" (III.iv.81–82). I think Castabella's critics err in overlooking the situation in which these lines are spoken: she would not say anything to arouse Rousard, and he is present in each instance. Also, in the second instance she wants to attest her innocence to D'Amville and Charlemont. If her mind is at all revolted by sexuality, it is because she finds herself "married unto hate" rather than to the man she loves (II.iii.1–15).

Another contrast—that between the two fathers concerned for their posterity, D'Amville and Montferrers—has already been discussed. Similarly, Montferrers' love for Charlemont is contrasted with the cruelty of Belforest in forcing the will of Castabella to serve his own ends.

The character of Charlemont may be studied by comparing his behavior with Rousard's and Sebastian's under similar circumstances. We see some value in his sense of honor when we compare his courtship of Castabella in I,ii, with the vulgarity of Rousard's in I,iii. But comparison with Sebastian reveals the weakness of Charlemont's common sense and reason. Sebastian, though he must die for his careless amours, is a fundamentally normal and sensible human animal. He is the only person besides Castabella who can consistently see

---

[21] William Empson discusses the contrast of Levidulcia and Castabella in *Some Versions of Pastoral* (London, 1938), pp. 53–55. *Cf.* Bradbrook, *Themes and Conventions*, pp. 48, 181.

through the hypocrisy of D'Amville and Snuffe,[22] and Tourneur shows the spiritual poverty of the early Charlemont's
impulsive sense of honor by paralleling it with Sebastian's
impulsive generosity and rightness of heart. Each of them
receives a thousand crowns from D'Amville. Sebastian uses his
to free Charlemont, because he believes he owes him his life
(III.ii.80–105). Charlemont accepts the gold of D'Amville in
order to go to the war, not heeding Montferrers. D'Amville
opens his remarks at the funeral of Montferrers with an
extended image of money-lending, implicitly associating his
loan to Charlemont with the success of his plot (III.i.3–8).
Indeed, throughout the later action of the play we see that
putting himself in debt to D'Amville, and thereby making
himself "doubly bound" to that villain, was not an entirely
honorable course for Charlemont.

The character of Charlemont is to be defined and evaluated
chiefly in relation to D'Amville, however. His progress is from
something approximating folly to wisdom, as D'Amville's
downfall is from "wisdom" to folly. The particular forms of
Charlemont's folly and wisdom can be best understood if we
first examine their contrasting forms in D'Amville.

Robert Ornstein, after studying Elizabethan refutations of
atheism, concludes that D'Amville is the "archetypal Renaissance atheist synthesized from contemporary opinion about,
and refutations of, atheism." He is a "compound of atheist,
materialist, sensualist, nature worshipper, and politician."[23]
Like the typical atheist depicted in the refutations, he fears
death, he cannot die a confirmed atheist, and he suffers an

---

[22] St. Sebastian is one of the saints invoked by the faithful for special
protection against the enemies of religion. Helen Roeder, *Saints and
their Attributes* (Chicago, 1956), p. 41.
[23] *"The Atheist's Tragedy* and Renaissance Naturalism," *SP*, LI (1954),
195.

unnatural death as punishment for his disbelief.[24] He has, again like the conventional atheist, come to his disbelief by pride of mind and naturalistic speculation.[25] The fundamental type, incorporating many of these secondary attributes, had been popularized years earlier in Nashe's *Christs Teares Over Jerusalem* (1593). Nashe describes two sorts of atheists, the hypocrite and the open one who "establisheth reason as his God."[26] By manipulation of stage conventions, Tourneur manages to give us both sorts in D'Amville. Atheists, says Nashe, are always ambitious and unscrupulous, and continue in their disbelief only so long as their designs prosper.[27] The following lines characterize D'Amville and his fate perfectly:

> Who heareth the thunder, that thinkes not of God? I would know who is more feareful to die, or dies with more terror and afrightment, then an Atheist. Discourse over the ends of all Atheists, and theyr deathes for the most parte have been drunken, violent, and secluded from repentance. The blacke swuttie visage of the night, and the shadie fancies thereof, assertaines every guilty soule there is a sinne-hating God.[28]

But our recognition that in many ways D'Amville is a "typical" atheist must not be allowed to obscure the important ways in which he is *not* typical. It is true that as a "politician" he is related to the popular stage atheist Machiavel and his counterpart in the Jacobean world, the hypocritical "new man" using religion as an instrument of policy in a ruthless attack on the traditional order of society.[29] Like the Machiavel

---

[24] *Ibid.*, pp. 201–203.

[25] Ernest A. Strathmann, *Sir Walter Ralegh: A Study in Elizabethan Skepticism* (New York, 1951), p. 90.

[26] In *Works*, ed. McKerrow, II, 118.

[27] *Ibid.*, p. 120

[28] *Ibid.*, p. 121.

[29] See the discussions of this point in Ornstein, *The Moral Vision*, pp. 26–27, 119; Ellis-Fermor, *The Jacobean Drama*, p. 165.

he has an accomplice to commit his murders for him, and he is a treacherous hypocrite who takes delight in his own cunning. On the other hand, though D'Amville is plainly an evil person, his evil is not, like the evil of the typical Machiavel, unbounded. He does not destroy his accomplice or seek to torture his victims, and his criminal intentions against society envisage the death only of his brother and his nephew.[30]

D'Amville's greatest divergence from the character of the "typical" atheist is his denial of sensuality.[31] D'Amville is all reason and no passion, one of those pathetic people who are never moved to any end by nature but always by rational plan. Tourneur has carefully constructed D'Amville as a typical atheist in most other respects to emphasize for his Elizabethan audience this very lack in his character of a usual element in the pattern.

The character of the "typical" atheist is divided among several of the characters of the play. The sensuality D'Amville lacks is represented partly in his shadow "Borachio" (drunkenness), and partly in Levidulcia, a typical Jacobean portrait of female lechery. Tourneur makes the division between the rationalist and the sensualist atheists as clear as he can. At the beginning of the play D'Amville and Borachio reject the "minutes pleasure" of sensuality as an insufficient end in life; and subsequently there is never a moment when D'Amville merely *enjoys* a sensual experience. If he drinks wine, it is to use its influence as an instrument, as he does Borachio himself. The healths he proposes at the wedding feast are to assist his plot to murder Montferrers, and the drink he takes in the

---

[30] Boyer, in *The Villain as Hero,* has a full discussion of the Machiavel type and of D'Amville's relation to it. See especially p. 168.

[31] On pp. 198–199 of *"The Atheist's Tragedy* and Renaissance Naturalism,"* Ornstein argues that D'Amville's attempt to rape Castabella proves him a sensualist. But see below.

execution scene is to bolster his courage and warm his cold blood; he anticipates no pleasure in it (V.ii.216–222).

D'Amville's attempt to rape Castabella is, likewise, purely instrumental, and the basis for it is entirely rational: he sees that if he is to have an heir he must beget one himself, and Castabella is the obvious choice for the purpose. He has no physical desire for her, and in the attempt itself reason is still his weapon:

> CASTA. My Lord! The night growes late. Your Lordship spake
>   Of something you desir'd to move in private.
> D'AM. Yes. Now I'le speake it. Th' *argument* is love.
>   The smallest ornament of thy sweete forme
>   (That *abstract* of all pleasure) can command
>   The sences into passion; and thy entire
>   Perfection is my object; yet I love
>   Thee with the *freedome* of my *reason*. I
>   Can give thee *reason* for my love.
>   (IV.iii.91–99; italics added)

Poor D'Amville cannot even make Castabella understand what he intends, and as the scene continues it becomes plain that if he triumphs, she will be the first woman ever raped by the instrument of a man's reason.

Now listen to Levidulcia's account of her passion for Sebastian, in a speech that affords a point-by-point contrast with that of D'Amville quoted just now:

>   . . . My strange affection to this Man!—
> T'is like that naturall sympathie which e'en among the *sence-less* creatures of the earth, commands a mutuall inclination and consent: For though it seemes to be the *free* effect of mine owne voluntarie love; yet I can neither restraine it, nor give *reason* for't.   (IV.v.17–21; italics added)

Levidulcia might have rebuked D'Amville for his argumentative approach to the rape of Castabella much as she rebuked Snuffe earlier, when he tried to argue Castabella into marrying Rousard :

> Tush, you mistake the way into a woman,
> The passage lyes not through her reason, but her bloud.
>
> (I.iv.67–68)

Levidulcia's faculty of reason is woefully undeveloped. Having rebuked Snuffe thus, she herself launches into an absurd argument from nature, taking a stand and using forms of logic which parody D'Amville's attempt to perform a rational rape upon Castabella. Levidulcia tries to persuade Castabella to give up the barren imaginary joy of loving the absent Charlemont, and to accept instead her "natural" role in the generation of new life by yielding to Rousard (I.iv.70–105). Levidulcia rejects reason as the way into a woman, then attempts a closely reasoned but obviously foolish argument to prove to Castabella that she should embrace the pleasures and duties of the body and forget the appeals of reason and the spirit![32] Levidulcia is all instinctual passion and D'Amville is all reason.[33] Tourneur shows the inadequacy of either half-person : D'Amville, stripped of humanity by his denial of natural sympathy, is therefore puerile in his reasonings, and the unreasoning natural sympathy of Levidulcia leads her finally to embrace a dagger. At the moment of death, each is given a flash of insight into his own imbalance.

The action shows that the forces of atheism are doomed to fail because they are divided against themselves. The passion

---

[32] Una Ellis-Fermor shows that Levidulcia's "slipshod mental process" can be seen in both her actions and her imagery. *The Frontiers of Drama* (London, 1945), p. 91.

[33] *Cf.* Bradbrook, *Themes and Conventions,* pp. 180–181.

of Levidulcia for Sebastian leads to his death, and the death of Sebastian is one of a series of events that bring ruin to the rational plot of the atheist who thinks he has no feeling of another's pain. The drama may be viewed as the external enactment of an inner conflict : the combat between reason and passion for control of the will must end in the destruction of the atheist because he lacks the divine light by which one can tell right from wrong reason, normal from excessive passion.

In addition to his denial of sensuality, there are other aspects of D'Amville's character that are not necessarily typical of the atheist. In his opposition to God and divine providence he rejects astrological fate (II.iv.157–161). In this he is closer to the divines of the period than to the naturalists.[34] Calvin and other theologians were opposed to astrology because it preached a form of materialistic determinism, limiting the freedom of man and eternally imprisoning the will of God within laws of physical causation, and so leaving Him too little room for direct action in the affairs of men.[35] Scientists, for these same reasons, were somewhat inclined to favor astrology, and it was quite possible for an atheist to write approvingly of the science.[36]

I say "science" advisedly, for in the early seventeenth century astrology was still generally regarded as such. Most men were willing to accept the idea that the moon controlled the liquid humors which were supposed to determine bodily health, and real controversy began only when astrologers claimed the ability to make specific predictions about human

---

[34] Paul H. Kocher, *Science and Religion in Elizabethan England* (San Marino, 1953), p. 202.

[35] *Ibid.*, p. 215.

[36] Lynn Thorndike, *A History of Magic and Experimental Science*, VI, 570–571.

decisions and actions.[37] Sir Christopher Heydon, to whom
Tourneur had dedicated *The Transformed Metamorphosis* in
1600, had in 1603 become the author of *A Defence of Judiciall
Astrologie, In Answer to a Treatise lately published by M.
John Chamber*.[38] Heydon's *Defence* is often cited today as
typical of respectable defenses of astrology.[39] Now, because of
his previous association with Heydon, and because his villain
atheist attacks astrology, Tourneur might himself be thought
to be writing a defense of astrology. Such an interpretation can
be dispatched in a very few words, however. First of all, no
counter-argument is offered to D'Amville's attack on astrology.
Charlemont, it is true, says in the closing lines of the play that
he will tempt his stars no longer, but this is too vague to be
anything more than conventional: his statement has no doc-
trinal content whatever (V.ii.317–318). The stars are, indeed,
God's lights in the action of the play, but they do not function
as they should if they were truly in control of the actions of
men. Instead, Tourneur treats them as a source of true light,
as shining proof that God is in His heaven. They unexpectedly
shine on the night when Borachio goes to murder Charlemont,
and D'Amville feels that their light accuses him (IV.iii.252–
258). Moreover, the play as a whole affords ample evidence
that Tourneur is eager to give God all the freedom He could
want for direct intervention in the affairs of men. A conception of divine providence is developed that is entirely alien
to astrological determinism.

Yet, since D'Amville's view of "providence" is expressed in
terms analogous to those used by astrologers, and since his

---

[37] Kocher, *op. cit.*, pp. 205–206. Cf. Don Cameron Allen, *The Star-
Crossed Renaissance: The Quarrel about Astrology and Its Influence in
England* (Durham, 1941), p. 148, on this point, and generally on most
of the questions raised in this discussion.

[38] Published at Cambridge.

[39] *E.g.*, Kocher, *op. cit.*, pp. 209–210.

understanding of human psychology is much the same as theirs, it will help us to understand D'Amville's view if we look briefly at the salient points of Heydon's treatise. We can immediately see why an atheist like D'Amville, who is only secondarily a naturalist, would associate astrology with the religious view of the universe. Heydon's whole argument assumes an omnipotent God, and the discussion is never allowed to stray very far from that assumption. In fact, Heydon represents the astrologer's as the *moderate,* the *Christian* view, opposed to philosophical extremes. He argues against both the Stoic belief that man is subject to necessity, and the Epicurean belief of many atheists that there is no necessity whatever.[40] The influence of the stars, a form of materialistic necessity, is great, but above that influence are the wholly spiritual influences of God and the angels.[41] Enlightened astrologers regard the stars only as "Gods instruments, which . . . it is in his power to alter, as best pleaseth his divine will."[42] Heydon elaborates his position in the following key paragraphs:

> Astrological signes must be confessed effectuall, and not to be frustrated but by miracle, and by his omnipotent power, to which that the Starres are subject. . . . [This] all our Astrologers doe confesse, and none but an atheist will denie. For as God is the creatour of all things, so is he the first cause of all causes, to whom all second causes are but his instruments. And therefore as the instrument worketh not of it selfe, but when it is imploied by the artificer, so the Heavens being Gods instruments, doe not exercise their force upon these inferiour things, but as God doth use their ministerie in the government of the world.[43]

---

[40] The *Defence,* p. 231.
[41] *Ibid.,* pp. 213–214.
[42] *Ibid.,* p. 30r.
[43] *Ibid.,* p. 32v.

The reformation of our purposes, whensoever they are directed to a good and right end, proceedeth from God, and not from our selves.[44]

Ptolemie . . . maketh not the influence of the starres inevitable, but ascribeth much to the *circumstances of regions, countries, lawes, education, Parents, times, place,* by which the particular decrees of the starres are often hindered. . . . For though the course, & influence of heaven in it selfe be immutable, yet the matter of these inferiour things is not so : besides as our will deliberateth, chooseth, or determineth without the helpe of any corporal instrument, it may elect, or refuse those things which are offered unto us by the senses. . . . [The stars influence the senses through the humours,] yet, sith the will freely exerciseth the actions thereof without any helpe from the body, the starres have no power over the same directly, nor other wise, then as the will is informed by the understanding, and the understanding apprehendeth by meanes of the senses, and therefore it may resist our naturall appetites, though there are few that withstand them, or that use the commaund of reason . . .[45]

Both D'Amville and Tourneur join Heydon in rejecting a universe either of chance or of absolute necessity, but they do not accept Heydon's compromise universe of conditional necessity. Instead, they both see a universe alive with purpose and action. D'Amville believes that man may use reason to manipulate the physical world by physical means, and other men by money and deceit. Tourneur questions the ability of human reason to solve by itself all the problems of human life, and asserts the supremacy of a living and active God over man and nature alike. Nevertheless, D'Amville is closer to Tourneur and to the orthodox—Anglican or Calvinist—view in his faith

---

[44] *Ibid.,* p. 87.
[45] *Ibid.,* p. 538.

in "providence" than he is to the usual forms of atheism in the philosophy of Epicurus or in materialistic determinism. Indeed, he is almost as nearly a typical Puritan as he is a typical atheist. Tourneur has made him so deliberately, and has coupled him with Snuffe to make his Puritanism obvious. Perhaps only in this way could Tourneur differentiate clearly his own idea of providence and all it connoted from that of radical Puritanism.

Robert Ornstein, though he argues that D'Amville is a merely conventional atheist, has pointed out his Puritan qualities, too : namely his materialism and "industry" and his egoistic ideas about providence.[46] In these qualities he is linked to Languebeau Snuffe, who is, of course, a caricature of all the objectionable Puritan traits.[47]

D'Amville and Snuffe are also linked through a number of plot parallels. Both are usurpers, Snuffe the tallow chandler having no more right to a chaplaincy than D'Amville has to his brother's estate (V.ii.63–70). Both are hypocrites and both are false priests : Snuffe in performing the wedding ceremony that Sebastian describes as a rape, and D'Amville in presiding over the funeral of Montferrers and Charlemont. In the graveyard scene both attempt unnatural intercourse : D'Amville would commit incest with Castabella; Snuffe, wanting to fornicate with Soquette, finds himself about to commit sodomy upon a corpse. And both are judged in the final scene of the play.

Snuffe, Cataplasma, Soquette and Fresco as a group afford an ironic perspective on the main action and characters of the play. Their gross obscenity is a monstrous caricature of D'Amville's materialistic ambitions. Their perverted wit, and

---

[46] *The Moral Vision*, p. 119.

[47] See Aaron Michael Myers, *Representation and Misrepresentation of the Puritan in Elizabethan Drama*, Univ. of Penna. diss. (Phila., 1931), p. 122.

especially Snuffe's feeble attempts at "logic," keep before us an alternative image of D'Amville's god, the all-sufficient human reason.[48]

Again and again we have seen that Tourneur demonstrates the insufficiency of human reason. The play's doctrinary atheist, who relies on reason alone to determine his plots, is destroyed because his reason leads him to false conclusions. And the weakness of the human reason is even more obviously shown in such characters as Levidulcia and Snuffe. Charlemont's reason is, like D'Amville's, an inadequate guide, and his passions, like Levidulcia's, are strong; but he transcends the destroying conflict of reason and passion by his recognition that he must accept divine guidance.

Charlemont is sometimes mistakenly described by critics as a Stoic or Senecal man.[49] If anything, *The Atheist's Tragedy* is an orthodox Christian reaction against the Stoic teaching of Epictetus and Seneca that the virtuous man's reason is a valid guide to proper action. The Stoic character, which is nothing if not whole, is destroyed here by its division between Charlemont and D'Amville. Charlemont has the acceptance of suffering and the courage in the face of death that can, it is true, be loosely described as Stoic—though they are also Christian —but he lacks the Stoic faith in reason. D'Amville, on the other hand, has the Stoic faith in reason but lacks the Stoic fortitude and virtue. Tourneur divided atheism in order to

---

[48] *Cf.* the discussion of this relationship in Bradbrook, *Themes and Conventions,* pp. 48. 184; Inga-Stina Ekeblad, "An Approach to Tourneur's Imagery," *MLR,* LIV (1959), 490.

[49] Bradbrook, *Themes and Conventions,* pp. 182–183; Henry Hitch Adams, "Cyril Tourneur on Revenge," *JEGP,* XLVIII (1949) pp. 83–84. What seems to me the correct position is taken by Michael H. Higgins, "The Influence of Calvinistic Thought in Tourneur's *Atheist's Tragedy,*" *RES,* XIX (1943), 255–262, and by Clifford Leech in "*The Atheist's Tragedy* as a Dramatic Comment on Chapman's *Bussy* Plays," *JEGP,* LII (1953), 525–530.

refute it, and it would appear that he also divided Stoicism for the same purpose.

The doctrine that triumphs in *The Atheist's Tragedy* is the orthodox Christian one that reason is to be relied upon only as it is guided by revelation and only as it regards nature as a divine order from which right reason can deduce only moral conclusions. Charlemont achieves right reason when he accepts the guidance of the revelation granted him through his father's ghost, although he has not begun the play as a possessor of right reason. It is essential to note this change that comes over him, for if we overlook it, we deceive ourselves into thinking his character is merely inconsistent.[50]

Charlemont is by nature a passionate and unthinking, even anti-intellectual young man. To him are given no speeches expressing confidence in his reason; on the contrary, in the early scenes he always either acts independently of reason or, when guided by reason unaided by revelation, infallibly errs. With Charlemont the central conflict is never that of passion with *reason* for control of the will. At his crisis, when the ghost of his father appears for the second time to forestall his impassioned murder of Sebastian, Charlemont says:

> You torture me betweene the passion of
> My bloud, and the religion of my soule.
>
> (III.ii.49–50)

But in the early part of the play, religion not yet having become an issue, his "bloud" holds complete sway, and there is an instructive contrast with D'Amville in his neglect of reason.

Charlemont is moved to the war by "inclination" and "disposition" (I.i.73, 85). He entreats his father to let him go

---

[50] As Una Ellis-Fermor does in *The Jacobean Drama,* p. 166.

by saying he feels called to the war by his "affection" and the heredity of his "bloud" (I.ii.16–17), and refuses to listen to good reasons why he should not go.

His neglect of reason is also evident in his analysis of rhetoric. To him, the purpose of a discourse is to conquer the hearer's *sense,* not his reason, and to this end a speech should be elegant and moving, its points primarily sweet, fluent and forceful (I.ii.73–92). This analysis of rhetoric itself is not being put to any rational purpose : Charlemont intends it merely as a verbal ornament to a parting kiss for Castabella. Here, as elsewhere, his imagery is "obvious and simple," contributing to the total impression that the speech is "elaborate but shallow."[51] Castabella immediately and incisively cuts away the ornament to discern the error of Charlemont's thought :

> My worthy Servant ! you mistake th'intent
> Of kissing. T'was not meant to separate
> A paire of Lovers; but to be the seale
> Of Love. . . .

(I.ii.93–96)

In these opening scenes Charlemont is never suspicious of his uncle's villainy, and places full confidence in Snuffe, accepting each for what he pretends to be. To confirm in our memories the impression that Charlemont is rather a fool, Tourneur has him reiterate his errors with regard to his departure for war and his confidence in Snuffe just before he leaves, not to return until after Castabella is married to Rousard and his father has been murdered. He says to Snuffe :

> Something within me would perswade my stay,
> But Reputation will not yeeld unto't.

---

[51] *Ibid.,* p. 161.

> Deare Sir, you are the man whose honest trust
> My confidence hath chosen for my friend.
>
> (I.ii.142–145)

When next we see Charlemont, it is at the crucial hour when his father's ghost appears to reveal the murder and to give the orthodox Christian injunction to

> Attend with patience the successe of things;
> But leave revenge unto the King of kings.
>
> (II.vi.26–27)

Charlemont, in his fatigue and his fear, at first tries to rationalize away the apparition (II.vi.29–69), but his reasoning is proved false when the ghost reappears a moment later. From this point Charlemont begins to be guided by his religion as well as by the passion of his blood.

After the ghost begins to influence him, we see Charlemont moving toward a new insight into the human reason, a movement taking him from neglect of reason through rejection of it to a Christian humility in which the reason may function in harmony with his subdued emotions, a state he has not previously known. Before his passion can be subdued by his religion, however, it is necessary for the ghost to return and repeat his command to be patient and leave revenge to God. Meanwhile Charlemont's unthinkingness is emphasized in a series of emotional outbursts. Returning from Ostend he rushes in upon Castabella, who swoons. He then says:

> I Beshrew my rash
> And inconsid'rate passion.—*Castabella!*
> That could not thinke—my *Castabella!*—that
> My sodaine presence might affright her sense.—
> I prithee (my affection) pardon mee.   *Shee rises.*
> Reduce thy understanding to thine eye.
>
> (III.i.84–89)

Castabella tells him she is married to Rousard, and he rages against her *wisdom* and her incontinence without waiting to learn that she has been forced to marry by D'Amville and her father (III.i.107–137). She points out to him the grave of Montferrers, and there he laments:

> Of all mens griefes must mine be singular?
> Without example? Heere I met my grave.
> And all mens woes are buried i' their graves
> But mine. In mine my miseries are borne.
> I pr'ithee sorrow leave a little roome,
> In my confounded and tormented mind;
> For understanding to deliberate
> The cause or author of this accident.—
> A close advantage of my absence made,
> To dispossesse me both of land and wife:
> And all the profit does arise to him,
> By whom my absence was first mov'd and urg'd.
> These circumstances (Uncle) tell me, you
> Are the suspected author of those wrongs.
> Whereof the lightest, is more heavie then
> The strongest patience can endure to beare.
>
> (III.i.151–166)

Charlemont calls upon his passionate grief to allow a little room for reason, but the action he decides on is dictated by passion, not by right reason guided by religion. The command of the ghost is overthrown, and he goes to attack D'Amville.

There the ghost arrests Charlemont's passionate fury, and D'Amville orders the arrest of his physical person. During his stay in prison, the combination of the ghost's teaching and the humbling effect of dungeon life brings him to accept the will of God in place of his own. The unaided reason, he sees, is incapable of leading man aright. It actually works with the uncontrolled emotions to increase man's confusion and suffering :

> O my afflicted soule ! How torment swels
> Thy apprehension with prophane conceipt,
> Against the sacred justice of my God?
> Our owne constructions are the authors of
> Our miserie. . . .
>
> (III.iii.13–17)

From this moment, as he goes on to say, his passions are his subjects (III.iii.42–49); he has "a *heart* above the reach" of the most violent malice (III.iii.36–37; italics added). But it is noteworthy that here, where Charlemont comes closest to the Stoic position, there is no mention of the triumphant *mind,* no sense that he is self-sufficient. On the contrary, he sees that the understanding deludes us, and he accepts the need for a greater faith in God than reason alone would dictate.

After this scene Charlemont yields himself up entirely to his religion. That is to say, he never relies on his reason alone and never submits to passion, but instead accepts divine providence as the governor of his destiny. In this he is, of course, opposed to D'Amville, who later reflects on Charlemont's imprisonment and his own "prosperity" in lines that are ironically ludicrous in the light of the events that immediately follow :

> Thus while the simple honest worshipper
> Of a phantastique providence; groanes under
> The burthen of neglected miserie;
> My reall wisedome has rais'd up a State,
> That shall eternize my posteritie.
>> *Enter Servants with the body of* Sebastian.
>
> (V.i.53–58)

With these lines we are nearly home, and it remains only to present a few more strong contrasts between human and divine providence, between those who rely on their reason and those who rely on God. In the execution scene D'Amville tries to use his dimming reason to search out the "efficient cause of a contented minde" so that he may achieve a courage like Charlemont's (V.ii.184). The Christian tells him that "The peace of conscience rises in it selfe," *i.e.*, that it has no physical cause but is of supernatural origin, being a gift of God's grace (V.ii.177). Finally, just before dying, the atheist sees the insufficiency of human reason (V.ii.273–285). The Christian does not claim any credit for his victory over the atheist, but merely confirms D'Amville's acknowledgment that the triumph belongs to divine providence :

> Onely to Heav'n I attribute the worke.
> Whose gracious motives made me still forbeare
> To be mine owne Revenger. Now I see,
> That, *Patience is the honest mans revenge.*
>
> (V.ii.300–303)

D'Amville's renunciation of an atheistic faith in human reason is corollary to his renunciation of an atheistic doctrine of nature :

> There was the strength of naturall understanding.
> But Nature is a foole. There is a power
> Above her that hath overthrowne the pride
> Of all my projects and posteritie.
>
> (V.ii.282–285)

D'Amville has hitherto regarded nature as a mechanical system governed by physical laws of cause and effect, capable of being understood and controlled by rational man in place of God.

To him natural law is physical law or amoral natural analogy. He and Borachio sometimes speak of nature as though it were a "she" having conscious purposes.[52] These, they think, are favorable to D'Amville's plans : they have made a physical analysis of the workings of nature, and reason that

> . . . it followes well;
> That Nature (since her selfe decay doth hate)
> Should favour those that strengthen their estate.
>
> (II.iv.189–191)

D'Amville usually refers to nature as "she" only when he is fearful or when his plans seem to have failed, using the personification in the former instance to bolster his courage by arguing that the universe is on his side, and in the latter to dissociate himself from defeat as much as possible (*e.g.,* II.iv. 162–191; V.i.122–146). In either instance it is plain that D'Amville is not a worshipper of a "goddess." "She" is really a personification of the order and supposed purposes his mind has rationalized out of nature, a projection of the true objects of his worship : his own ego and faculty of reason.

In his recantation, as Ornstein acutely points out, D'Amville does not go all the way over to orthodoxy. He concedes only that there is the power of God and His providence *above* nature, not that nature itself is "the harmonious, rational, moral order of the universe."[53] Ornstein contends that in the play's debates about nature, the word "nature" is entirely surrendered by the Christians to the naturalists. He cites the fact that D'Amville and Levidulcia are never said to be

---

[52] Ellis-Fermor identifies D'Amville's several meanings for "nature" as the medieval *Natura Naturans,* physical law; *Natura Naturata,* a "particular manifestation" of nature; and *Natura Dea,* "the loving Mother of us all." *The Jacobean Drama,* p. 165.

[53] *"The Atheist's Tragedy* and Renaissance Naturalism," p. 205.

"unnatural" as evidence that the Christians recognize them as "the representatives of nature in the play."[54] He concludes that Tourneur accepts the naturalist's contention that physical laws govern nature, asserting only that the moral law transcends physical law : "If nature is no longer the embodiment of the divine moral order, that moral order still exists, beyond the reach (and attack) of the empiricists."[55]

It seems to me that Ornstein goes too far. D'Amville, after all, is hardly Tourneur's spokesman, even in his recantation. At any rate, we should hardly expect D'Amville to make nice philosophical distinctions between God *in* and God *above* nature when he is dying, half mad, and somewhat drunk. Moreover, we must not lose sight of the *action* of the play, in which nature has certainly been the embodiment of the moral order in the providential illness of Rousard, the deaths of Rousard and Sebastian, and the self-murder of D'Amville. The chains of causation controlling these events are not physical and mechanical, but moral, yet they occur in and through nature, for there is no literal *deus ex machina*.

Finally, I do not think it is true that the Christians speak of nature as a merely physical machine. There are three occasions on which either Belforest or Castabella uses an argument from nature against D'Amville or otherwise disputes with him briefly about the nature of "nature." The first is on the heath just after the murder of Montferrers, when D'Amville is making a great show of grief. He asks Belforest :

> . . . Doe you thinke
> That Nature has no feeling?
> BEL. Feeling? Yes.
> But has she purpos'd any thing for nothing?

---

[54] *The Moral Vision*, p. 127.
[55] *"The Atheist's Tragedy* and Renaissance Naturalism," p. 207.

What good receives this body by your griefe?
Whether is't more unnaturall not to grieve
For him you cannot helpe with it; or hurt
Your selfe with grieving and yet grieve in vaine?
                                        (II.iv.61–68)

There is nothing in Belforest's reply that is inconsistent with
the orthodox conception of a divine purpose immanent in
nature. The second dispute occurs when Castabella appeals
to D'Amville for the release of Charlemont from prison
(III.iv.2–25). Here the case is clearer. Castabella's metaphor
of the sun raising clouds to water the earth, following as it does
a discussion of the sweet and loving favor of God's mercy,
is informed with religious significance. She seems to use the
sun itself as a symbol of God in nature. Her final argument,
that mercy can be learned from subrational creatures, is
philosophically ambiguous (Tourneur is writing a play, not a
Summa Theologiae); but again, it is not necessarily inconsistent
with orthodox belief that the universe is divinely interfused.

On the third occasion of "debate" on nature Castabella is
once more D'Amville's antagonist, and this time there can be
no doubt that her position is orthodox. She moves from a purely
theological argument to an argument from natural law, as
before, and this time she specifically notes and disputes D'Amville's claim that nature supports his view, accusing him of
having a degenerate conception of natural law :

D'AM.   Incest? Tush.
         These distances affinitie observes;
         Are articles of bondage cast upon
         Our freedomes by our owne subjections.
         Nature allowes a gen'rall libertie
         Of generation to all creatures else.
         Shall Man to whose command and use all creatures
         Were made subject be lesse free then they?

CASTA. O God! is thy unlimited and infinite
        Omnipotence lesse free because thou doest
        No ill? or if you argue meerely out
        Of Nature; doe you not degenerate
        From that; and are you not unworthie the
        Prerogative of Natures Maister-piece,
        When basely you prescribe your selfe
        Authoritie and law from their examples
        Whom you should command? I could confute you;
        But the horrour of the argument
        Confounds my understanding.—

                        (IV.iii.139–157)

I think we may safely conclude from all the foregoing that though the dying D'Amville does not entirely abandon his idea that nature is a God-less machine, conceding only that *above* nature is God, the play as a whole, through a series of natural but providential events, proves that Castabella is right to believe that nature is divinely informed with moral purpose.

None of the play's Christians ever has to brand D'Amville with the word *unnatural* because, as we have seen, the entire action of the play and the relation of the characters to that action show atheism to be against nature. However, the unnaturalness of D'Amville's doctrines, aspirations and actions *is* made plain at the purely verbal level through figures of *allegoria*, if not by the word *unnatural* itself. Consider, for example, the metaphor concluding D'Amville's key speech on his hopes of immortality and his need to plunder his brother's estate:

        And for my children; they are as neere to me,
        As branches to the tree whereon they grow;
        And may as numerously be multiplied.
        As they increase, so should my providence;

> For from my substance they receive the sap,
> Whereby they live and flowrish.
>
> (I.i.59–64)

If nature is merely, as D'Amville thinks, a mechanism governed by physical laws of cause and effect, this analogy is false, for in nature, as D'Amville is to learn, fathers and sons are not physically related as are trunks and branches. Ironically for D'Amville, this metaphor makes sense only if we believe nature is governed by *moral* laws of cause and effect : it figures forth the direct relation between the crimes of D'Amville and the impotence and death of Rousard.

4   SYMBOLIC PATTERNS

Essential to the Christian, medieval dramaturgy of *The Atheist's Tragedy,* with its ritual action and dialectical characterization, is its treatment of the material world as a poem of God. Symbolic action and symbolic characters lead us to expect symbolic verbal patterns, and these we find not only in the arguments about reason and nature in the abstract, but in the metaphors and other imagery. Tourneur makes impressive imaginative use of the traditional correspondence between the macrocosm of nature and the microcosm of man to provide a wonderfully appropriate substructure for his play.

Two of the play's symbolic motifs have been frequently noted. One is D'Amville's repeated equating of the stages in his career with those in the building and the disintegration of a house. From the laying of foundation and cornerstone to final crumbling ruin he returns to this key image that so well defines the development of the play's action.

Even more evidently symbolic is the involved *allegoria* of the stars as God's lights, to which D'Amville opposes the glitter of gold.[56] But such studies as have been made of Tourneur's symbolism are too narrow in scope ("Tourneur and the Stars"). We must not only isolate particular recurring images and study them by themselves, though that is helpful, but must consider them in connection with their full context of action and of other, related symbols. Thus the light of the stars is not only to be contrasted with the "star" light of D'Amville's gold but with lights (and dark) in whatever form they occur, metaphorically stars or not, whether in words, characters, or action.

Another central image is that of blood in the human veins and arteries or, at the level of the macrocosm, of water in springs and rivers. Through this image Tourneur presents in symbolic form the central action of the play: the blood D'Amville spills, the lusty bloods of Sebastian and Levidulcia, and the cold blood of Rousard all flow together to sweep away the foundations of the house D'Amville wants to found. In a number of speeches the rise and fall of blood pressure caused by passion is imaged in the rise and fall of the current in a river. Thus Belforest speaks of Castabella's refusal to marry Rousard:

> Her soft excuses savour'd at the first
> (Methought) but of a modest innocence
> Of bloud; whose unmoov'd streame was never drawne
> Into the current of affection . . .

(I.iv.5–8)

Again, D'Amville speaks of his fear of death:

> This argument of death congeales my bloud.
> Colde feare with apprehension of thy end,
> Hath frozen up the rivers of my veines.

(V.ii.217–219)

---

[56] See J. M. S. Tompkins, "Tourneur and the Stars," *RES,* XXII (1946), 315–319.

The movement of blood is all but synonymous with lust in many passages. Levidulcia speaks of Sebastian and her lust for him :

> A lusty bloud ! has both the presence and the spirit of a man.
> I like the freedome of his behaviour.—Ho—*Sebastian!* Gone?
> —Has set my bloud o'boyling i' my veynes. And now (like water pour'd upon the ground, that mixes it selfe with ev'ry moysture it meetes) I could claspe with any man.
>
> (II.iii.73–77)

Levidulcia and Fresco speak of Cataplasma and her suitors :

> FRES. Faith Madame, shee has suitors. But they will not suite her me thinkes. They will not come off lustily it seemes.
> LEV. They will not come on lustily, thou wouldst say.
> FRES. I meane (Madame) they are not rich enough.
> LEV. But I *(Fresco)* they are not bold enough. Thy Mistresse is of a lively attractive bloud *Fresco.* . . .
>
> (II.v.8–13)

A few lines later Levidulcia kisses Fresco :

> FRES. Your Ladiship has made me blush.
> LEV. That showes th'art full o' lustie bloud, and thou knowest not how to use it. . . .
>
> (II.v.30–32)

Charlemont returns from the war to find Castabella married to Rousard. She tells him of what Levidulcia had called the cold blood of Rousard (II.iii.50), but Charlemont nevertheless rails :

> What? marryed to a man unable too?
> O strange incontinence ! Why? was thy bloud

Increas'd to such a pleurisie of lust,
That of necessitie, there must a veyne
Be open'd; though by one that had no skill
To doe't?   (III.i.127–132)

The destructive effect of the stream of lust is symbolized in
the action of a river that washes the earth away from the roots
of a tree. At the end of the previous section of this chapter I
cited the passage early in the play in which D'Amville defined
his relation to his sons:

And for my children; they are as neere to me,
As branches to the tree whereon they grow;
And may as numerously be multiplied.
As they increase, so should my providence;
For from my substance they receive the sap,
Whereby they live and flowrish.

                                        (I.i.59–64)

After the murder of Montferrers, this image is employed again
to symbolize D'Amville and his sons. This time it foreshadows
their destruction. Cataplasma examines Soquette's needle-
work:

[CATA.] What's here? a Medlar with a Plum-tree growing hard
          by it; The leaves o' the Plum-tree falling off; the
          gumme issuing out o' the perish'd joynts; and the
          branches some of 'em dead, and some rotten; and yet
          but a young Plum-tree. In good sooth, very prettie.
SOQU.   The Plum-tree (forsooth) growes so neare the Medlar,
          that the Medlar suckes and drawes all the sap from
          it; and the naturall strength o' the ground, so that it
          cannot prosper.   (IV.i.4–11)

These trees had come to have sexual meanings frequently

exploited by the dramatists. We may infer that the plum tree, a male, perishes because it or one of its members is too lustful. Sebastian enters a few lines later and makes even clearer the sexual significance of the medlar, toward which a "Batchelers-button should have held his head up more pertly," etc. (IV.i.26–27). Sebastian is inspired to invent a fable in which the symbolic relation of the river of lust to the life of the male lover is made perfectly explicit :

> . . . But heere's a morall. A poppring Peare-tree growing upon the banke of a River; seeming continually to looke downewards into the water, as if it were enamour'd of it; and ever as the fruit ripens, lets it fall for love (as it were) into her lap. Which the wanton Streame, like a Strumpet, no sooner receives, but she carries it away, and bestowes it upon some other creature she maintaines : still seeming to play and dally under the Poppring, so long, that it has almost wash'd away the earth from the roote; and now the poore Tree stands as if it were readie to fall and perish by that whereon it spent all the substance it had.
>
> CATA. Morall for you that love those wanton running waters.
> SEBA. But is not my Lady *Levidulcia* come yet?
>
> (IV.i.33–44)

At the hour of death for Rousard and Sebastian, when streams of blood and lust have cut the ground from under D'Amville, there is a return to this imagery of plants and the roots of life. The dying groan of Rousard is to D'Amville like "the cries of Mandrakes"—the aphrodisiac plant that was supposed to make a sound like a human when it was uprooted (V.i.69). The doctor enters and begins his examination of the corpses of Rousard and Sebastian :

If any roote of life remaines within 'em capable of
Phisicke; feare 'em not, my Lord.

(V.i.89–90)

But the generating root (radix) of life, D'Amville's hope for a
posterity, is in them no more :

My Lord. These bodies are depriv'd of all
The radicall abilitie of Nature.

(V.i.101–102)

The destroying river of lust, bringing down those who stand
upon its shores, is related to one of the play's master metaphors,
Borachio's description of the overthrow of the Spanish at
Ostend ·

The pride of all their Army was drawne forth,
And equally divided into Front,
And Rere. They march'd. And comming to a stand,
Ready to passe our Channell at an ebbe,
W' advis'd it for our safest course, to draw
Our sluices up and mak't unpassable.
Our Governour oppos'd; and suffered 'em
To charge us home e'en to the Rampiers foot.
But when their front was forcing up our breach,
At push o' pike, then did his pollicie
Let goe the sluices, and trip'd up the heeles
Of the whole bodie of their troupe, that stood
Within the violent current of the streame.
Their front beleaguer'd twixt the water and
The Towne; seeing the floud was growne too deepe,
To promise them a safe retreate; expos'd
The force of all their spirits, (like the last
Expiring gaspe of a strong harted man)
Upon the hazard of one charge; but were

Oppress'd and fell. The rest that could not swimme,
Were onely drown'd; but those that thought to scape
By swimming, were by murtherers that flankerd,
The levell of the floud, both drown'd and slaine.

(II.i.60–82)

At the moment when their lust is literally to destroy Levidulcia and Sebastian, this imagery recurs. Belforest, entering
the house of Cataplasma, surprises the lovers together, and
Sebastian answers him in terms that might appropriately have
been used to warn the Spanish at Ostend :

BELFO.   Pursue the Strumpet. Villaine give mee way;
          Or I will make my passage through thy bloud.
SEBA.   My bloud will make it slipperie my Lord.
          T'were better you would take another way.
          You may hap fall else.

(IV.v.55–59)

Belforest finds the way as "unpassable" as that taken by
the Spanish at Ostend. The sexual connotation of "push o'
pike" and the assault channels and "passages," reinforcing
their close relation to lustful veins of blood, is apparent all
through the play :

LEV.   Tush, you mistake the way into a woman,
          The passage lyes not through her reason,
                                    but her bloud.

(I.iv.67–68)

Levidulcia says of Fresco's lack of passion :

          . . . Faint-hearted foole ! I
          thinke thou were begotten betweene the North-
          pole, and the congeal'd passage.

(II.v.50–52)

At the instant of his attempted rape upon Castabella, D'Amville cries:

> *Tereus*-like,
> Thus I will force my passage to—
> CHARL. The Divell. (IV.iii.190–192)

D'Amville's passage to the devil is opened only much later, when he tries to execute Charlemont:

> D'AM.   I'le butcher out the passage of his soule,
>   That dares attempt to interrupt the blow.
>   (V.ii.251–252)
> D'AM.   The lust of Death commits a Rape upon me
>   As I would ha' done on *Castabella*.
>   (V.ii.292–293)

All the deadly passages, rivers and sluices of blood, water and lust are fused in the final speech of Levidulcia, when she re-enters after Belforest and Sebastian have killed each other:

> Is this the saving of my Honour? when
> Their bloud runnes out in rivers; and my lust
> The fountaine whence it flowes? . . .
>   (IV.v.65–67)

This image is repeated almost verbatim when the judge accuses Cataplasma of maintaining a bawdy house where murder has been committed:

> . . . from the Spring of lust which you preserv'd;
> And nourish'd; ranne th' effusion of that bloud.
>   (V.ii.30–31)

This imagery of fountain and spring parallels the legend of St. Winifred. Tourneur constructs a symbolic contrast between the chaste Christian lovers, Castabella and Charlemont, linked with the holy fountain and healing waters of Winifred's well, and the atheists, drowned in seas of blood springing from their crimes.

Besides the blood of sexual crimes, there is also the unnatural *blood-letting* of D'Amville, to which all the images of destroying streams are again fully relevant. D'Amville's plans are thwarted not only by the failure of Sebastian and Rousard to beget a posterity for him, but by the blood flowing from his victim Montferrers, which finally destroys the murderer.

In the first scene D'Amville concludes that "pleasure onely flowes/ Upon the streame of riches" (I.i.33–34), and not long after we hear him finding ways to swell the current of his wealth :

> This marriage will bring wealth. If that succeede,
> I will increase it though my Brother bleed.
>
> (I.ii.252–253)

D'Amville's blood-letting and the sense of a destroying flood are brought together when he rejoices at the servants' drunkenness that is to be instrumental in his plot to murder Montferrers :

> Let them drinke healthes, & drowne their braines i' the floud;
> Ile promise them they shall be pledg'd in bloud.
>
> (II.ii.28–30)

After he and Borachio have murdered Montferrers, D'Amville calls the attention of Belforest to his victim's blood :

> Behold the lively tincture of his bloud !
> Neither the Dropsie nor the Jaundies in't.
> But the true freshnesse of a sanguine red.
>
> (II.iv.72–74)

In the graveyard, when he is frightened from his attempt to rape Castabella by what he takes for the ghost of Montferrers, D'Amville describes his crime as fornication with Murder, and himself as "like/ A Leacher emptied of his lust" (IV.iii.249–254). He goes on to say:

> I could now commit a murder, were
> It but to drinke the fresh warme bloud of him
> I murder'd; to supply the want and weakenesse
> O' mine owne; t'is growne so colde and flegmaticke.
>
> (IV.iii.269–272)

D'Amville's thirst for blood is finally quenched when he calls for wine, instrumental in his earlier murder, to help in the execution of Charlemont. Cold fear has "frozen up the rivers" of his veins:

> I must drinke wine to warme mee, and dissolve
> The obstruction, or an apoplexie will
> Possesse mee.—Why thou uncharitable Knave;
> Do'st bring mee bloud to drinke? The very glasse
> Lookes pale and trembles at it.
>
> (V.ii.220–224)

Paralleling the courses of D'Amville, Levidulcia and Sebastian until he is liberated from the passion of his blood by his religion is Charlemont, who tells Montferrers his affection to the war is as hereditary as his blood (I.ii.16–17). His speech explaining his "dream" of Montferrers' death goes far toward justifying my "argument of blood and death" by suggesting the imaginative fusion of the "push o' pike" at Ostend with rape and murder at the estates of Belforest and Montferrers:

> Tush. These idle dreames
> Are fabulous. Our boyling phantasies

Like troubled waters falsifie the shapes
Of things retain'd in them; and make 'em seeme
Confounded, when they are distinguish'd. So
My actions daily conversant with warre;
(The argument of bloud and death) had left
(Perhaps) th' imaginary presence of
Some bloudy accident upon my minde :
Which mix'd confusedly with other thoughts,
(Whereof th' remembrance of my Father, might
Be one) presented all together, seeme
Incorporate; as if his body were
The owner of that bloud, the subject of
That death; when hee's at Paris, and that bloud
Shed here. . . .   (II.vi.52–67)

Contrasting with all the unholy and violent affections of the blood is the purer spirit of Castabella, who rejects them in her definition of love :

O Love! thou chast affection of the Soule,
Without th' adultrate mixture of the bloud;
That vertue which to goodnesse addeth good :
The minion of heavens heart. . . .

                                      (II.iii.2–5)

Associated primarily with Castabella and opposed to all the evil, death-bearing streams of riches, blood and lust running from springs in the world of man are the Fountain of Winifred and the life-imparting waters of the heavens. These latter, often in the form of tears, suggest the divine grace which constantly showers down on Charlemont to preserve and then to nurture him. His father's efforts to dissuade him from the war, which are powerless against the persuasion of Charlemont's blood and the stream of D'Amville's riches, take the form of tears :

> I prithee let this current of my teares,
> Divert thy inclination from the warre.
>
> (I.ii.2–3)

Castabella's repeated use of the tears-rain metaphor is always associated with heavenly intervention in the affairs of Charlemont. First, an intervention of *prophecy to* warn him against going to war : she tells him that on the day a certain great man went to war :

> The heavie cloudes hung downe their mourning heads,
> And wept sad showers . . .
> As if that day presag'd some ill successe,
> That fatallie should kill his happinesse.
>
> (I.ii.117–120)

She fears that her eyes are like those weeping clouds :

> And as their showers presag'd so doe my teares,
> Some sad event will follow my sad feares.
>
> (I.ii.123–124)

Next a prophetic intervention of grace the moment before the return of Charlemont from his supposed death. Castabella prays God to

> . . . be not displeas'd, if on
> The altar of his Tombe, I sacrifice
> My teares. They are the jewels of my love
> Dissolved into griefe : and fall upon
> His blasted Spring; as Aprill dewe, upon
> A sweet young blossome shak'd before the time.
>
> (III.i.66–71)

A little later Charlemont is put away again by D'Amville, this time into prison. The moment before Charlemont's return—he is released by D'Amville's unintentional bounty—there is another prophetic intervention of grace as rain. This time Castabella uses rain as a metaphor for human bounty bestowed in response to God. She is begging D'Amville to release Charlemont:

> . . . Rich men should transcend the poore,
> As clouds the earth; rais'd by the comfort of
> The Sunne, to water dry and barren grounds.
>
> (III.iv.17–19)

In Borachio's artful narrative of the "death" of Charlemont at Ostend, the sea itself is represented as having wept over Charlemont: and we must remember that Charlemont is in fact graced by a supernatural visitation in a *real* storm at the front. Borachio describes how

> Hee lay in's Armour; as if that had beene
> His Coffine, and the weeping Sea, (like one;
> Whose milder temper doth lament the death
> Of him whom in his rage he slew) runnes up
> The Shoare; embraces him; . . .
>
> (II.i.91–95)

John Peter points out that the weeping of the sea in this passage is similar to the hypocritical weeping of D'Amville over the body of Montferrers.[57] Pretending piety, D'Amville seeks the grace of tears. But whereas Castabella's tears always prayed grace for another, D'Amville, in his egoism, puts the prayer into his *brother's* mouth and seeks the relief of grace only for himself. His brother was, he says,

---

[57] *Complaint and Satire,* p. 274.

> . . . So deerely pittifull,
> That e're the poore could aske his charity
> With dry eyes, hee gave 'em reliefe wi' teares
> —With teares—yes faith with teares.
>
> (II.iv.83–86)

Then D'Amville weeps :

> . . . All these
> Wordes were but a great winde, and now
> This showre of teares has layd it, I am calme
> Againe . . .   (II.iv.92–95)

For the Renaissance poet, the rivers of life lead almost inevitably to the sea of death. Commonly in the Elizabethan drama the dying compare themselves to vessels embarking on a voyage into an unknown sea, and it is no surprise that Levidulcia and Charlemont should both use the figure in anticipating death. What is interesting is the way Tourneur correlates their uses of the figure with the metaphor of the action at Ostend and the reference to the Pillars of Hercules in the speech D'Amville delivers at the funeral of Montferrers and Charlemont.

In Borachio's narrative of Ostend, the sea is a veritable *mare mortuum,* for the drowned Charlemont is described as having been deposited on the shore by the "full-stomack'd Sea" that slew him (II.i.85–119). In more senses than Borachio intends, Charlemont goes the journey through the sea of death and returns to the shore of life—a symbolic pattern he often repeats in action and metaphor, as we have seen. Borachio, of course, means only to say that Charlemont is dead. For the atheist, the voyage into the sea of death is final; there can be no return to the shore of life and there is no new land beyond the sea. D'Amville's assertion of the finality of death is made through the same basic metaphor. He has just "buried" Montferrers and Charlemont, and is hypocritically praising their virtue, saying it can never be surpassed:

> . . . So that on
> These two Herculean pillars, where their armes
> Are plac'd; there may be writ, *Non ultra*. . . .
>
> (III.i.50–52)

The ancient notion that no land lay beyond the Straits of Gibraltar had long since become a symbol for the limitations not only on human travel but on all human aspiration, spiritual as well as physical. D'Amville, under the pretext of praising the virtue of his victims, is above all trying to seal their tombs.

In the speech of Levidulcia immediately before her suicide is the full series of symbolic terms leading from the fountain of lust through rivers of blood to a sea of death. Levidulcia, the sensualist atheist, assumes that life ends with physical death, though she fears that her *shame* will not end with death. With Sebastian dead, and Belforest dying, she says:

> Their bloud runnes out in rivers; and my lust
> The fountaine whence it flowes . . .
>
> (IV.v.66–67)
>
> Now I can weepe. But what can teares doe good;
> When I weepe onely water, they weepe bloud?
> But could I make an Ocean with my teares;
> That on the floud this broken vessell of
> My body, laden heavie with light lust
> Might suffer shipwrack, and so drowne my shame:
> Then weeping were to purpose; but alas!
> The Sea wants water enough to wash away
> The foulenesse of my name. . . .
>
> (IV.v.73–81)

In contrast to Borachio, D'Amville and Levidulcia, Charlemont uses the metaphor of the sea voyage to assert his Christian faith in a life beyond death. He answers *Plus ultra* to the atheists' *Non ultra,* and substitutes for their broken vessels a warlike navy bound on a voyage of conquest :

> CHARL.   *D'amville!* to shew thee with what light respect
> I value Death and thy insulting pride;
> Thus like a warlike Navie on the Sea,
> Bound for the conquest of some wealthie land,
> Pass'd through the stormie troubles of this life,
> And now arriv'd upon the armed coast;
> In expectation of the victorie,
> Whose honour lies beyond this exigent;
> Through mortall danger with an active spirit,
> Thus I aspire to undergoe my death.
>
> (V.ii.135–144)

Charlemont sees that it is not death but *life* that is the stormy sea, as Belforest has done in rebuking D'Amville for his laments over the body of Montferrers :

> Lament him not. Whether our deaths be good
> Or bad; it is not death but life that tryes;
> Hee liv'd well, (therefore) questionlesse, well dyes.
>
> (II.iv.57–59)

What Tourneur has achieved through all these passages is a remarkably complex symbolic land- and seascape revealing the true face of nature. The atheists, however, reject the orthodox cosmology and therefore the ability to see the analogous systems of order in the cosmos and the individual. The purely discursive reason of D'Amville and Borachio rejects the interpretation of reality possible only through intuitive imaginative modes of thought, and as a result they repeatedly are exposed to the irony of their own words.

This tendency toward unintentional irony is never clearer than in the series of "house" images D'Amville uses to trace the rise and fall of his plot. To us, his speeches seem always to imply his overthrow or point to the absence of real foundation for his "house," but D'Amville is oblivious to these implications. Thus when Charlemont goes to war, D'Amville says to Borachio:

> Well! *Charlemont* is gone. And here thou seest,
> His absence the foundation of my plot.
>
> (I.ii.224–225)

Which is as much as to say the plot has no foundation at all. Later D'Amville rejoices to note that Borachio's tale of Ostend has its desired effect on Montferrers:

> So. The foundation's laid. Now by degrees,
> The worke will rise and soone be perfected.
> O this uncertaine state of mortall man!
>
> (II.i.137–139)

The first two lines are spoken aside, and the last is part of D'Amville's act for the benefit of the others, to convince them that he has all the conventional pious beliefs. As Inga-Stina Ekeblad has remarked, he thinks the foundation really *is* certain, and is inwardly scoffing at the sentiment in the third line. From the hearer's point of view, however, the irony is in his unconscious forecast of his own ruin.[58]

The servants obligingly make themselves instruments of D'Amville's plot by getting drunk. In thanking *Fortune* for his success, he again implies his ultimate downfall, cast low by Fortune's wheel:

---

[58] "An Approach to Tourneur's Imagery," pp. 494–495.

Fortune I honour thee. My plot still rises,
According to the modell of mine owne desires.—

(II.ii.34–35)

While D'Amville and Belforest accompany Montferrers across
the fields, Borachio prepares to commit murder:

      Enter BORACHIO *warily and hastily over the Stage,*
       with a stone in eyther hand.

BOR.   Such stones men use to raise a house upon;
      But with these stones I goe to ruine one.

(II.iv.1–4)

He means to ruin the house of Montferrers, but his words come
to apply ironically to the house of D'Amville, too, for these
same stones are to be the ruin-causing cornerstone for D'Amville's mansion:

D'AM. Upon this ground Ile build my Manour-house;
      And this shall be the chiefest corner stone.
BOR.   T'has crown'd the most judicious murder, that
      The braine of man was e'er deliver'd of.

(II.iv.118–121)

This speech marks the completion of D'Amville's plot, his
accession to power. The figure of the house does not recur
until the counter-action of divine providence is well begun.
Then it marks two crises: the failure of D'Amville's final effort
to generate a posterity when he cannot seduce Castabella, and
the end of all his remaining hopes in the death of his sons.
He tries to seduce Castabella with an argument which, if he
interpreted the symbols he uses in anything but the most purely
local and discursive fashion, must seem an argument *against*
his position:

> All the purposes of Man
> Aime but at one of these two ends; pleasure
> Or profit : And in this one sweet conjunction
> Of our loves, they both will meete. Would it
> Not grieve thee, that a Stranger to thy bloud,
> Should lay the first foundation of his house
> Upon the ruines of thy family?
>
> (IV.iii.125–131)

D'Amville, after all, is the very stranger to her blood who is attempting to found a house on the ruins of her family and the family of Charlemont, the family she soon will be a part of.

The dying groans of Rousard mark the fall of the house of D'Amville :

> D'AM. His gasping sighes are like the falling noise
> Of some great building when the ground-worke breakes.
> On these two pillars stood the stately frame,
> And architecture of my loftie house.
> An Earthquake shakes 'em. The foundation shrinkes.
> Deare Nature ! in whose honour I have rais'd
> A worke of glory to posteritie;
> O burie not the pride of that great action,
> Under the fall and ruine of it selfe.
>
> (V.i.92–100)

Again D'Amville fails to take into account the symbolic values of his own words. The two pillars he intends are Rousard and Sebastian, but we remember that the foundation of the house was an absence and its cornerstone a murder, that the word *pillars* has come from D'Amville's own mouth to describe the monuments erected over the graves of Charlemont and Mont-ferrers.

This "house" imagery also draws attention to the play's various *structures* and their relation to the conflict between the

houses of Montferrers and D'Amville. The encroachment of
the house of the un-godly on that of the godly is reflected in
the invasion by the licentious inhabitants of Cataplasma's
bawdy house into the grounds of the nearby house of St.
Winifred. Enclosing the entire action is "this great chamber
of the world," which D'Amville regards as a God-less structure (IV.iii.246). In the passage containing these words,
D'Amville acknowledges forces opposed to him at work within
nature, but he does not yet acknowledge them to be of God.
The question whether the universe is God's continues through
D'Amville's appeal to the "Starre chamber," a term referring
as well to a superior civil court as to the "loftie houses" of
God's stars (cf. V.i.142–144, and V.i.25). The conflicts over
the mastership of the house of the universe and of the houses
of D'Amville, Montferrers and Belforest are all resolved on
the scaffold, the final structure. From that baleful eminence the
face of God is unmistakable. There the spirit of Charlemont
triumphs and D'Amville finds defeat and death.

Tourneur's symbolism of pillars and stars is perfectly adapted
to his theater, with its two pillars supporting a star-fretted
canopy over the stage. The "Starre chamber" is a great unifying symbol, relating the conflict between the houses to the
central question of authority and truth, symbolized in the
contrast between true and false lights. God's stars are, of
course, the chief of the true lights, and the chief symbol in the
dialectic on authority. The central elements in this conflict of
true and false lights we have already noticed in other con-
nections: D'Amville asserts that gold coins, not stars, are the
ministers of fate, and thereby he claims the authority of God
for the human reason deploying the coins (V.i.18–34).

Reason and wealth are not the only false lights, however.
Castabella and Levidulcia are associated with contrasting
"lights." The chaste, shining beauty of Castabella is described
by Snuffe:

> Shee's like your Dyamond; a temptation in every mans eye,
> yet not yeelding to any light impression her selfe.
>
> (I.ii.175–176)

Levidulcia, on the other hand, is *Levi* + *dulcia*—"light" (inconstant) and "sweet" or "yielding." She believes of ladies that

> . . . Hot diet and soft ease makes 'em (like wax alwaies kept
> warme) more easie to take impression.
>
> (II.v.23–25)

Castabella, unlike Levidulcia, is not light and yielding to all men. She resists the advances of Rousard :

> [CASTA.]   . . . What favour would you have?
> ROUS.   Any toy : any light thing.
> CASTA.   Fie. Will you be so uncivill to aske a light thing
> at a Gentlewomans hand?
>
> (I.iii.18–21)

She finally gives him a favor :

> CASTA.   Then with all my hart, Ile give you a Jewell to
> hang in your eare.—Harke yee—I can never love
> you.   *Exit.*
> ROUS.   Call you this a Jewell to hang in mine eare? T'is
> no light favour, for Ile be sworne it comes somewhat
> heavily to mee.
>
> (I.iii.51–54)

This contrast of Castabella with Levidulcia is twofold : Castabella's light is true and her substance is as firm as a jewel; Levidulcia's light love is false and she is soft, like warm wax.

Her light is the weak light of earthly love, commonly symbolized by Cupid's candle, as in one of Francis Quarles'
Emblems, Divine and Moral:[59]

> Do, silly Cupid, snuff and trim
> Thy false, thy feeble light,
> And make her self-consuming flames more bright;
> Methinks she burns to dim.

(ll. 1–4)

Here we meet the rascal who is the very soul of false light,
Languebeau Snuffe, the "pleasant-tongued" hypocrite Puritan
whose action in the play begins with false witness and pro-
gresses through all forms of corruption, both spiritual and
sensual. Tourneur has a great deal of fun with "Snuffe,"
exploiting nearly all the word's several meanings.

According to the *N.E.D.*, the snuff of a candle is the partly
burned portion of the wick that must be snipped off if the
candle is not to burn dimly. The snuff is therefore associated
with a faint light, and by extension may be used to refer not
to the burned wick but to a candle that has burned so low it is
on the point of expiring. To snuff a candle is to pinch off the
burned portion of the wick, to suppress a flame temporarily,
or to put a light out completely. Snuff is also the word for the
part of a drink left in an emptied glass. The snuff, in all these
cases, is something of no value. To take snuff at something is to
take offense, so a person in a snuff is in a passion.

"Snuffe's" significance as one who is a false light and who
puts out the light of others is explicated for us:

[1. Judg.] Where tooke you your degrees of Schollership?
Snuffe.   I am no Scholler my Lord. To speake the sincere
            truth, I am *Snuffe* the Tallow-Chandler.

---

[59] *Ed. cit.*, Book II, pp. 56–57.

2. JUDG.   How comes your habite to be alter'd thus?

SNUFFE.   My Lord *Belforest* taking a delight in the cleanenesse
             of my conversation; withdrew mee from that un-
             cleane life, and put me in a garment fit for his
             societie and my present profession.

1. JUDG.   His Lordship did but paint a rotten post;
             Or cover foulenesse fairely. Monsieur *Snuffe!*
             Backe to your candle-making. You may give
             The world more light with that, then either with
             Instruction or th' example of your life.

SNUFFE.   Thus the *Snuffe* is put out.   *Exit Snuffe.*
                                                   (V.ii.63–75)

As Snuffe the candle-maker, Languebeau is the absolute
hypocrite, incapable of speaking sincerely, *i.e.* "without wax."
We know he lies, for example, when, after he has been bribed
by D'Amville, he claims to speak sincerely in trying to persuade
Castabella that Charlemont is unworthy of her love :

> Since *Charlemont's* absence, I have waighed his love with the
> spirit of consideration; and in sinceritie I finde it to be
> frivolous and vaine. With-draw your respect; his affection
> deserveth it not.
>
>   (I.iv.40–42)

Sebastian, of course, sees through Snuffe's pretenses : "What
does the Stinkard here? put *Snuffe* out. He's offensive"
(IV.i.63–64).

Snuffe's sensuality snuffs the feeble light of his spirit, and
he seeks out Soquette to be the "socket" to his candle. She
says to him, "You purpose i' the darke to make me light," but
the feeble light of his candle seems not to have the potency
required (IV.iii.60). When the watch enters Cataplasma's
licentious house to arrest bawds and lechers together, Snuffe
suggests his own impotence : "May not *Snuffe* be suffer'd to
goe out of himselfe?" (IV.v.92).

"Snuffe" as the dregs of drink is involved with D'Amville's use of liquor to snuff the light of the servants' torches so that he may murder Montferrers in the dark. This reference comes in the midst of a cascade of symbolic "lights" in the early scenes of Act II, from the beginning of the wedding feast until after the murder of Montferrers (i–iv). In the first three of these scenes Tourneur introduces all the play's lights in rapid succession in order to prepare the audience for the drama of the lights in night's dark fields.

The whole of Act II takes place at night, and the stage would have been lighted by torches from its beginning. The motif of the lights begins in earnest after Borachio has burst upon the scene with his story of the death of Charlemont at Ostend. Snuffe urges Montferrers to change his will, and D'Amville says:

> I have my wish.—Lights for my Brother.
> MONT. Ile withdraw a while;
> And crave the honest counsell of this man.
> (II.i.153–155)

"This man" unfortunately is Snuffe, and so Montferrers leaves to be counselled by the dim light of the candle-making hypocrite. The scene shifts to the room where the servants are drinking:

> 1. SER.   Boy! fill some drinke Boy.
> FRESCO.   Enough good Sir; not a drop more by this light.
> 2.   Not by this light? Why then put out the candles and
>   wee'l drinke i' the darke and t'wut old Boy.
> (II.ii.2–5)

Fresco will drink no more, but the two servants continue until their minds and bodies are equally weakened by the liquor. D'Amville enters with Borachio and hears them quarrel drunkenly over their emptied flasks:

1.	You ha' left a damnable snuffe here.
2.	Doe you take that in snuffe Sir?
1.	You are a damnable rogue then. *—together by th' eares.*
D'AM.	Fortune I honour thee. My plot still rises, According to the modell of mine owne desires.— Lights for my Brother.—What ha' you drunke your selves mad you knaves. (II.ii.31–37)

"Lights for my Brother!" The "snuffe" of the servants shall be a device to snuff those lights. D'Amville takes each of them aside and tells him to attack the other:

> Dost 'heare? that fellow is a proud knave. Hee has abus'd thee. As thou goest over the fields by and by, in lighting my brother home, Ile tell thee what' sha't doe. Knocke him over the pate with thy torch, Ile beare the out in't.
>
> (II.ii.40–43)

Then they depart:

> *Enter* MONTFERRERS *and* BELFOREST, *attended with lights.*
>
> MONT. Brother now good night.
> D'AM. The skie is darke, wee'l bring you o'er the fields.
> (II.ii.58–60)

The scene shifts again, this time to the wedding chamber of Castabella and Rousard. Castabella speaks a few lines alone. Then to her

> *Enter* LEVIDULCIA, ROUSARD, CATAPLASMA, SOQUETTE, *and* FRESCO *with a lanthorne.*
>
> LEV. Mistresse *Cataplasma,* good night. I pray when your Man has brought you home, let him returne and light me to my house. (II.iii.16–20)

Where Levidulcia will want him to make her "light." Levidulcia turns to Rousard and Castabella :

[LEV.]	O here's your Bride.
ROUS.	And melancholique too, me thinkes.
LEV.	How can shee choose? your sicknesse will Distaste th' expected sweetnesse o' the night. That makes her heavie.
ROU.	That should make her light.

(II.iii.25–30)

The newlyweds leave Levidulcia alone, and she speaks of her
inflamed lust. Sebastian enters and offers to "quench the fire"
(II.iii.58). Fresco comes with a lantern to light Levidulcia
home, and they depart together.

We join the little group escorting Montferrers across the
fields by the light of torches borne by the two drunken servants :

*Enter two Servants drunke fighting with their
torches,* D'AMVILLE, MONTFERRERS, BELFOREST,
and LANGUEBEAU SNUFFE.

BEL.	Passion o' me you drunken knaves, you'l put The lights out.
D'AM.	No my Lord; th' are but in jeast.
1.	Mine's out.
D'AM.	Then light it at his head, that's light enough.— Foregod, th' are out. You drunken Rascals backe And light 'em.
BEL.	T'is exceeding darke. *Exeunt Servants.*

(II.iv.5–14)

In the darkness D'Amville hurls Montferrers down into the
gravel pit, where he is murdered by Borachio. The servants

return with new lights, and D'Amville gloats over the inability of God's stars to pierce the clouds of the night, under cover of *bewailing* the darkness that brought on his brother's "accident" (II.iv.43–55).

Belforest goes off with the body of Montferrers, and D'Amville is joined by Borachio. Together they rejoice at the success of their plot for darkening lights and so blinding the eye of observation. They review in detail each step leading to the fatal climax: the healths proposed by D'Amville which lightened the heads of the servants and then put them into a snuff, the instigation of the servants to fight with their torches, and the "accidental fall" in the ensuing dark (II.iv.142–161). The murderers conclude that the cloudiness of the night is evidence that "propitious Nature" has "favour'd our successe" (II.iv.186, 188). The scene, and with it this portion of the motif of lights, ends with an apostrophe to the power of darkness:

> D'AM.   . . . Now farewell blacke night;
> Thou beauteous Mistresse of a murderer:
> To honour thee, that hast accomplish'd all;
> Ile weare thy colours at his funerall.
>
> (II.iv.203–206)

D'Amville plans for Borachio's attempt to murder Charlemont to be similarly "favour'd by the darknesse of the night" (IV.ii.27), but he has presumed too far on nature. Borachio fails, and the stars give enough light for D'Amville to see and be terrified by the ghostly form of Charlemont and by the skulls in the charnel house. The imagery of bawd and mistress with which D'Amville then reproaches the sky for letting light shine into his black soul echoes the language he had so happily praised her with before (IV.iii.244–258).

From this hour commences the distraction that finally destroys D'Amville. Act V opens with an emblematic scene:

Musicke. A Clozet discover'd. A Servant sleeping with lights and money before him. (V.i.1–2)

D'Amville enters and fondles his gold, which he is told is revenue from Montferrers' estate. The false light of D'Amville's reason and of the artificial stage light darken his vision, and he imagines that the gold coins are brighter than stars, more melodious than angel voices. Heaven's eyes are lesser than these; these are the ministers of fate; and man's reason is the superior power in the universe (V.i.16–34).[60]

Through this symbolic structure of light and darkness Tourneur reinforces the three-cornered structure of the conflict between rational atheism, sensual atheism, and the power of God. Each has its symbolic lights. The light of mere reason and its instruments is opposed to the light of Cupid's candle, and both these sets of lights are opposed to the light of God's stars and of Castabella's true beauty. The great orbs of heaven may be darkened for a time, but they can never be extinguished. The weak, earthly lights of men are, like the servants' torches, unreliable. They are too easily extinguished by various aspects of Snuffe—the man, drink, or passion— and, because they shine but from a finite point, they cast shadows that disguise and distort the face of reality.

The symbolic patterns are linked to the series of rituals giving form to the plot of the play. The imagery of the lights casts the shadow of the murder of Montferrers behind D'Amville's ritual of self-deification. The symbolic pattern of houses and other structures is associated with nearly every ritual. Since it is used in direct relation to the play's central action, the atheist's attempt to found a dynasty, it recurs at every crisis to mark his rise and fall. It is, however, most notably related to the rituals of wedding and funeral. The wedding is

---

[60] Note that the symbolic true and false lights are much the same as those in *The Transformed Metamorphosis.*

the union of the houses of D'Amville and Belforest. The tombs and the monumental pillars D'Amville erects for Montferrers and Charlemont are the foundation and cornerstone of his manor house.

Powerfully suffusing every part of the play are the two great metaphors of the flood at Ostend and the fountain of Winifred. War, opening the sluices at Ostend, releases the torrents of rape and murder which undermine society. Winifred's is the fountain of life and grace, bringing regeneration to those who accept it. This imagery of fountain and river, as we have seen, is related to the pledges in wine at the wedding feast. Through the feast itself, this imagery is further related to the supper at which D'Amville and Charlemont pledge eternal friendship. The sharing of bread and wine is associated with rituals of brotherhood, and D'Amville violates the bond of brotherhood, committing the crime that has the primal eldest curse upon it, when he murders Montferrers. The wine drunk at the wedding feast may be regarded symbolically as the source of the river of death which destroys Montferrers. But it destroys D'Amville as well; his last drink is the blood-like wine at the scaffold.

The blood of Montferrers poisons the fountain of the new blood-line D'Amville would establish, so that the wedding of Rousard, instead of being a fountain of new life, directly causes his impotence and subsequent death. In this way the symbolic pattern of the fountain, river and sea of death parallels the ritual movement from wedding to funeral.

5   CONCLUSIONS ON *The Atheist's Tragedy*

Critics dealing with Tourneur in short span have usually devoted most of their space and praise to *The Revenger's Tragedy*, brushing off *The Atheist's Tragedy* with a few largely derogatory remarks. One important critical objection

to *The Atheist's Tragedy* is that its characterizations lack the
human depth and sympathetic insights we associate with the
greatest tragedies.[61] The characters in *The Revenger's Tragedy*
are mostly flat, too, but at least Vindici is passionate, and not
a feeble rationalist like D'Amville, who is too puny and
materialistic to fit the Marlovian or the modern idea that an
atheist may be a heroic, spiritual figure.[62]

The Atheist's Tragedy has also suffered by comparison with
The Revenger's Tragedy because in its action it is not a good,
sound, naturalistic play, as at times *The Revenger's Tragedy*
seems to be. Coincidence, writes Clarence Boyer, might be
accepted in the simultaneous deaths of Rousard and Sebastian,
but Tourneur goes too far in depending on fortuitous circumstances to save Charlemont from Borachio's pistol, Castabella
from D'Amville's attempt to rape her, and Charlemont from
D'Amville's axe. All of these coincidences cause "the frail
structure of the drama to collapse."[63]

Such a judgment is possible only when a critic insists on
applying to all plays the standards of naturalistic dramaturgy.
By the play's "structure" Boyer evidently means its status as
a realistic construct. It is not the work itself he judges, but its
credibility as a historical reproduction of reality. *The Atheist's
Tragedy* is not history but a work of dramatic art, in which
experience is given form to reveal the order of reality lying
beyond history. It is precisely the structure of the drama that
does not collapse, when that structure is understood as an
imaginative arrangement of action, character and verbal pattern designed to illuminate the tragic conflict of the atheist
with God, nature and society. Events and words are molded
to stand in symbolic relation to one another and to the action

---

[61] *E.g.*, Henry W. Wells, *Elizabethan and Jacobean Playwrights* (New
York, 1939), p. 32.
[62] *Cf.* Ornstein, *The Moral Vision*, p. 119.
[63] In *The Villain as Hero in Elizabethan Tragedy*, p. 170. See also
Ornstein, *The Moral Vision*, pp. 120–121.

of the play, each element interacting with the others to reveal the significance of the whole.

Considered in this way, I think *The Atheist's Tragedy* is one of the most interesting achievements of the Jacobean drama. If it is ultimately a failure on the naturalistic stage, it is at least a great experiment, a full realization of the artistic possibilities of the medieval conception of tragedy and action. From the morality tradition, especially, the play inherits its coherence of structure. Nothing is irrelevant; Tourneur grasps the contradiction inherent in the atheist's search for immortality among the dying creatures of this world, and he shapes his drama so that the actions of the atheist always reveal in their fullest the implications of denying the fatherhood of God.

Though his dramaturgy may have been medieval, one side of the story Tourneur tells is recognizably contemporary. As *The Honest Man's Revenge,* the play has "assimilated many plot elements—and the theatrically most striking ones—from the Revenge tradition."[64] If we compare plot summaries, we are struck by the degree of Tourneur's borrowing from *Hamlet.*[65] In both plays, the hero's father is murdered by a villainous brother, and the murdered man's ghost appears to sentinels at night in order to counsel his son. D'Amville is a mad revenger in his effort to get justice for the death of his sons. Other common features of the two plays and of the genre are the swordfights, the suicide and the meditation in the graveyard.

The Atheist's Tragedy is even more closely related to the genre of the tragedy of ambition that was given impetus in the plays of Marlowe. After *Tamburlaine,* the heroism of the

---

[64] Ekeblad, "On the Authorship of *The Revenger's Tragedy,*" *ES,* XLI (1960), 234.

[65] For a full discussion of these parallels see Ashley H. Thorndike, "The Relations of *Hamlet* to Contemporary Revenge Plays," *PMLA,* XVII (1902), 194–200; and Elmer E. Stoll, *John Webster* (Boston, 1905), pp. 111–112.

ambitious and godless hero of this tradition rapidly declined as the playwrights presented the more nakedly evil ascent to power of Machiavellian atheists or analogous native types. In Marlowe there is a precipitous descent from Tamburlaine to Barabas, *The Jew of Malta*. Shakespeare takes up where Marlowe left off, beginning with the hideously evil Aaron of *Titus Andronicus* and the anti-heroic Richard III. From these he re-developed the type of the ambitious atheist villain in more complex forms, notably in Iago, Edmund and Macbeth.

The dramatist in this tradition to whom Tourneur stands closest is George Chapman, whose *Bussy D'Ambois* and *The Revenge of Bussy D'Ambois* taken together combine, as does *The Atheist's Tragedy*, the story of an overreacher with a story of revenge. Tourneur borrows Chapman's French setting and some names: D'Amville from D'Ambois, Montferrers from Montsurry, and Charlemont from Clermont. Tourneur apparently imitated *The Revenge of Bussy D'Ambois* in order to criticize the Stoic rationalism and self-sufficiency of Clermont, the avenger of the play.[66] The ghost of Bussy, unlike that of Montferrers, demands revenge against his murderer. His brother Clermont accepts the duty of revenge, having reservations only about undertaking evil action to secure it. He finally forces an honorable duel upon his cowardly enemy, and kills him. Then he commits suicide, calling on his patron in the hour of death. To Clermont the *mind* of man is the soul of the soul. When he is asked wherein men differ from beasts, Clermont refers to faith as well as reason, thus distinguishing himself from D'Amville by paying something more than lip service to faith. But his reliance on reason and learning is

---

[66] This relation of *The Atheist's Tragedy* to *The Revenge of Bussy D'Ambois* was first discussed in some detail by Higgins in "The Influence of Calvinistic Thought in Tourneur's *Atheist's Tragedy*." A fuller examination of the problem is by Clifford Leech, "*The Atheist's Tragedy* as a Dramatic Comment on Chapman's *Bussy* Plays." See also Section 3 of this chapter.

more Stoic than Christian, as is the basis for his scruples against violent action. Tourneur divides *Clermont D'Ambois* into *Charlemont* and *D'Amville,* assigning the non-Christian elements of Stoicism to the atheist. Charlemont rejects Clermont's Stoic goal of self-sufficiency, and finds the right guide for human action in revealed truth, leaving reason to be D'Amville's instrument. In Tourneur's view, suicide is damnation, not evidence of spiritual self-mastery; and all revenge—not only vicious revenge—is evil.

The Christianity dramatized by Tourneur is at once popular and eclectic, and does not seem to be associated with the doctrines of any particular sect. It is popular and Catholic in its acceptance of ghosts. It follows the popular tradition in demonstrating that virtue earns material rewards and that sinners are punished by God.[67] Though Tourneur's emphasis on divine retribution and his loathing of sin are sometimes cited as evidence that he had been strongly influenced by Calvinism,[68] I think that his Calvinism scarcely differs from that of the Anglican Church. He parodies the Puritan Calvinist in Snuffe, and attacks Puritan "industry," materialism and egoistic ideas about "providence" in D'Amville. And he goes against even moderate Calvinism in his acceptance of ghosts.

The brilliant image of the defense of Ostend dominates *The Atheist's Tragedy* at many levels. Tourneur's overriding purpose is to defend the traditional Christian positions on nature, providence and the need for divine grace against attack from all the philosophies that were undermining religious

---

[67] Willard Farnham shows that these ideas of reward and retribution were to be found in Lydgate and other writers of *de casibus* tragedy before the time of Calvin. *Medieval Heritage,* p. 162ff.

[68] Higgins, "The Influence of Calvinistic Thought in Tourneur's *Atheist's Tragedy.*" But John Peter shows that the loathing of sin expressed by Tourneur is not necessarily derived from Calvin more than from the tradition of medieval complaint literature. *Complaint and Satire,* p. 268.

orthodoxy in Jacobean England : the atheism growing out of the new science, the radicalism of Puritan and Machiavel, and the Stoic rationalism revived by the humanists, which threatened the religious basis for moral philosophy.[69] For Tourneur the tragedy of the atheist is in denying that man's one hope is still that *God* reigns. Nature is God's, for moral rather than physical causation is its ultimate law. Divine grace makes truth available to man through revelation.

---

[69] See Ornstein, *The Moral Vision,* Chapter I.

IV

The Anonymous Revenger's Tragedy

1 AUTHORSHIP

MOST OF US FIRST READ *The Revenger's Tragedy* IN THE Mermaid volume along with *The Atheist's Tragedy* as the work of Cyril Tourneur, and as a result of this early association we later find it hard to believe those who would convince us that the play was written by Thomas Middleton. Outside the works of Shakespeare, few authorship problems have attracted as much attention, and the literature of the subject has become extensive as scholars have attempted a variety of approaches to the problem.

Because of the unreliable source from which the fragmentary external evidence of authorship is taken, scholars have sifted internal stylistic evidence, but the results have been inconclusive : here, at any rate, it seems impossible to distinguish imitation from common authorship with any certainty. The failure of stylistic evidence leads us to try analyzing some aspect of a play's language less likely to be subject to imitation. Such a test was developed by Cyrus Hoy for his study of the

144

Beaumont and Fletcher canon.[1] Hoy examined the frequency
of occurrence of certain pronouns, verb forms and colloquial
contractions in the unassisted writings of Fletcher, Beaumont,
Massinger and the other collaborators. He found that, armed
with knowledge of an author's preference for *doth* or *does*, *'em*
or *them,* or his tendency to write *h'as* for *he has,* and so forth,
it is possible to detect that author's work in a collaboration
and to distinguish it from the work of his collaborators. Since
Hoy's division of the Beaumont and Fletcher canon corres-
ponds to that of most earlier researchers, his method is probably valid, and can be applied, with due caution, to other
works of uncertain authorship.

I have modified Hoy's method slightly by introducing
separate analyses for preferred spellings and for preferred
linguistic forms. Thus modified, the method yields results
leaving little doubt that Thomas Middleton and not Cyril
Tourneur is the author. I have also made a closer analysis of
the external evidence for attribution of the play than appears
to have been made hitherto. I want first of all to consider this
evidence and then to try to throw some fresh critical light on
the literary evidence. In this way a context will be established
for interpreting the linguistic and spelling data.

Although the external evidence for the authorship of *The
Revenger's Tragedy (RT)* is inconclusive, it lends more sup-
port to the claim of Middleton than is generally recognized.
The *RT* was entered with a Middleton play in the Stationers'
Register by George Eld on 7 October 1607 :

> Twoo plaies th[e] one called *the revengers tragedie*
> th[e] other. *A trick to catche the old one.*[2]

---

[1] See especially "The Shares of Fletcher and his Collaborators in the
Beaumont and Fletcher Canon (I)," *SB,* VIII (1956), 129–146.
[2] Ed. Arber, III, 360.

In the entire period from 5 July 1605 to 26 June 1610 there is not another entry in the Register linking two works so closely as to list them in a single clause. Works now ascertained to be of separate authorship were usually given entirely separate entries in the Register, or else appeared as distinct items when recorded in a single entry. Thus, on 6 August 1607, only two months before entering *RT* and *A Trick to Catch the Old One,* George Eld had listed *The Puritan* and *Northward Ho* in separate, though adjacent entries.[3]

Only with great hesitation can we conclude from these facts that the form of the joint entry is itself evidence of common authorship of Middleton's *Trick* and of the *RT,* since there is no real evidence that the keepers of the Stationers' Register would have related differences in the form of publishers' entries to the authorship of the works entered. Moreover, since the form of this entry is unique in its period, it cannot be compared with similar instances in order to judge its significance. One thing must be clear, however. The joint entry proves that Eld had both books in hand at one time, and the normal inference would be that he received them simultaneously. Indeed, the simplest explanation would be that they arrived together from a common source. Since the title pages assert that they were enacted at different theaters, it would be natural to infer that the common source was a single author, or a single author by way of an intermediary. It must be conceded that this is only an inference, and it is perhaps best to conclude by simply emphasizing that the joint entry does, inescapably, suggest an association between the *RT* and *A Trick* that can be explained neither by their having originated at the same theater nor by their being written in the same genre.

In a 1609 court case, Middleton swore that some years

---

[3] *Ibid.,* p. 358.

before he had written a tragedy entitled *The Viper and Her Brood,* and it has been suggested that this may be a stage or alternative title for the *RT.*[4] As R. A. Foakes points out, the argument from *The Viper* is self-defeating, for if it is another title for the *RT,* which was in print in 1609, why did not Middleton simply refer to it *as* the *RT,* and so prove his point? Foakes' question is not easily answered, but *The Viper* has importance because it shows Middleton writing a tragedy having a title appropriate to the *RT* at the time when those opposed to his authorship of the play insist he was interested only in writing comedies of London life.

The final piece of external evidence is an entry in Edward Archer's list of Elizabethan and Jacobean plays together with their authors, published in 1656. This list does actually associate the title, *The Revengers Tragedy,* with the name "Tournour," but it is dated forty-nine years after the publication of the play, and about twenty years after the death of both Middleton and Tourneur.[5] Archer's list, the similar list of Rogers and Ley[6] and, subsequently, that of Francis Kirkman,[7] are all known to contain many errors of attribution. The testimony of Archer, repeated by Kirkman, that Tourneur wrote the *RT,* is today acknowledged to have weight only because most of the errors of attribution in the lists are in the direction of assigning important doubtful works to prominent authors, not to minor figures like Tourneur. Considered with

---

[4] Harold N. Hillebrand, "Thomas Middleton's *The Viper's Brood,*" *MLN,* XLII (1927), 35–38. R. A. Foakes advanced the argument against identification of *The Viper* with the *RT* in "On the Authorship of 'The Revenger's Tragedy,' " *MLR,* XLVIII (1953), 129–138.

[5] In the list of plays appended to *The Old Law;* see Appendix II of *A List of English Plays Written Before 1643 and Printed Before 1700,* ed. Walter Wilson Greg (London, 1900), p. cii.

[6] Appended to *The Careless Shepherdess* (1656); See Greg, *loc. cit.*

[7] Kirkman's list appeared with *Tom Tyler and His Wife* (1661), and was later enlarged and reissued with *Nicomede* (1671). Kirkman's conflated list is in Greg, *loc. cit.*

this in mind, Archer's attribution of the *RT* to Tourneur is not to be lightly brushed aside.

It may be an error, however, to consider the entire list of Archer as forming a single class of attributions, and it is certainly an error to ignore what we can deduce from the lists themselves about the methods of their compilers. Let us estimate the value of the attribution of the *RT* made in these lists by examining the fate of the attributions of the other eight plays printed by George Eld within a year of his publication of the *RT* (1607–08). Of the plays Eld printed in this period, all except the *RT* and *A Trick to Catch the Old One* had authors' names or initials on their pages when first printed, and in all these instances the lists of Rogers and Ley, Archer, and Kirkman—where they list one of these plays at all—follow the attribution they find the printer making, or list the play with *no* author's name. Most of these attributions are in accord with modern opinion, but in one instance the playlists are certainly wrong. The title page of *The Puritan, or The Widow of Watling Street* testifies that the play was "Written by W.S." Rogers and Ley did not list the play, but Archer and, following him, Kirkman, duly expand the *W.S.* to Will Shakespeare, an assignment of the play that no modern scholar accepts. Neither the correct attributions of the plays bearing their proper authors' names nor this error with respect to *The Puritan* suggest that Archer had any information on the authorship of these plays beyond what he found on printed copies of them.

Still more illuminating is the record of the playlists in the attribution of *A Trick to Catch the Old One* and the *RT,* works already associated in the Stationers' Register and associated again by the fact that both were first printed anonymously. There was, however, a second issue of *A Trick* in the same year as the first issue—1608—bearing the words "composde by T.M." on its title page. Rogers and Ley list both *A*

Trick and the *RT* as anonymous. Archer attributes *A Trick* to Shakespeare and the *RT* to "Tournour." Kirkman assigns *A Trick* to Middleton and the *RT* to Cyril Tourneur. What most probably happened is evident. Archer had a copy of *A Trick* from the early, anonymous issue, and he guessed or was misinformed that it was by Shakespeare. For some reason he assigned the *RT* to Tourneur. Kirkman, having a copy of *A Trick* from the second issue with Middleton's initials on it, or a copy of the edition of 1616 with Middleton's whole last name on the title page, was able to correct Archer's misassignment of that play, but since *all* copies of the *RT* are anonymous, he could not use similar evidence to check Archer on its attribution. He may merely have repeated Archer's testimony. Now, in this account there is much uncertainty, but one thing is clear. For these nine plays, there is no indication that Archer had any reliable evidence of authorship other than that to be found on printed copies of the plays themselves. When such evidence was not available in the case of *A Trick*, his judgment erred.

It seems hardly unfair to suggest that Archer's error in the case of *A Trick* may have an analogue in the case of the *RT*. It would appear that Archer *guessed* in the case of the *RT*, perhaps allowing himself to be swayed by the similarity of the title of *The Revenger's Tragedy* to that of *The Atheist's Tragedy*, and that Kirkman merely repeated his guess, having no contrary information. In any event, the record shows that Archer erred in two of three doubtful plays of the nine printed by Eld in 1607–08, leaving only the question whether he did not also err concerning the third doubtful play, the *RT*.

Still it cannot be denied that Archer and Kirkman *may* have had good reasons to attribute the *RT* to Tourneur, and as a consequence we are not in a position to disregard their testimony completely. But we will want to remember that their attributions of the *RT* to Tourneur are the only known basis for all the references to the play as his work that have followed, including the several modern editions of the play from which we today have learned to associate the play and the name.

If our doubts about the validity of the external evidence for Tourneur's authorship of the *RT* are not so great as to allow us to ignore that evidence, they are, on the other hand, great enough to permit us to hear testimony based on internal evidence.

All of the important parallels in moral outlook or dramatic technique between the *RT* and the works of Middleton or the works of Tourneur either can be interpreted as imitation or convention, or find their basic similarity in aspects of the works so abstracted from the qualities of the plays themselves as to have little value for the determination of authorship. From the beginning of the controversy, Middleton's proponents have been inclined to concede that the bitter moral didacticism of the *RT* fitted better with the attitudes of Tourneur expressed in *The Transformed Metamorphosis* and *The Atheist's Tragedy (AT)* than with the attitudes of Middleton, of whom E.H.C. Oliphant could say that he "never shows any concern whatever with moral problems."[8] This extreme view is no longer popular, but its legacy is a cognate belief, held on both sides of the controversy, that the sinful characters in Middleton's plays act in ignorance of orthodox morality, unlike the sinners of the *RT*, who enjoy sin partly because it *is* forbidden.[9] Lines epitomizing this sense of sin in the *RT* are the following:

[8] "Tourneur and 'The Revenger's Tragedy,'" *TLS*, Dec. 18, 1930, p. 1087.

[9] See, *e.g.*, Samuel Schoenbaum, "'The Revenger's Tragedy' and Middleton's Moral Outlook," *NQ*, CXCVI (1951), 9, and Inga-Stina Ekeblad, "An Approach to Tourneur's Imagery," p. 494n.

Enter the Bastard *meeting the* Dutchesse

Spu.   Had not that kisse a taste of sinne 'twere sweete.
Dutch.   Why there's no pleasure sweet but it is sinfull.
Spu.   True, such a bitter sweetnesse fate hath given;
               Best side to us, is the worst side to heaven.

(III.v.218–222)

But do we not find similar imagery expressing an identical attitude in Middleton's *Women Beware Women*?

Sin tastes at the first draught like wormwood-water,
But drunk again, 'tis nectar ever after.

(II.ii.481–482)[10]

Middleton's tragic characters generally are well aware they are violating a moral order.[11] That order is for Middleton, as it is for Tourneur, the morality taught by the Anglican Church, and so it is impossible to distinguish their work by reference to basic differences in religious views.

The main reason why many critics refuse to grant the *RT* to Middleton is that the traditional view of the play as a neurotic document showing its author obsessed with evil cannot be reconciled with Middleton's apparently objective realism elsewhere. This is a problem of interpretation that cannot be dealt with in brief space here. Succeeding sections of this chapter will show that whoever was the author of the *RT*, that play is no evidence of *his* neurosis. There is evidence aplenty of *Vindici's* neurosis, but it is a misreading of the play to detach Vindici from his dramatic context and attribute his twisted emotions to the author.

If some critics are too quick to attribute the *RT* to Tour-

---

[10] In *The Works of Thomas Middleton*, ed. A. H. Bullen (London, 1885), VI, 292.
[11] *Cf.* William L. Power's 1955 Vanderbilt University dissertation; *The Ethical Pattern in the Plays of Thomas Middleton, DA*, XV, No. 9 (1955), 1615.

neur because of its moral tone, others are too quick to associate the play's ironic retributions with Middleton.[12] The belief that clever evil men may outwit themselves and be hoist with their own petard is, as the source of the figure reminds us, fundamental to Elizabethan and Jacobean tragedy and thus hardly original with Middleton. Moreover, Tourneur's *AT* is as ironic as one could wish, and so once again we are dealing with a characteristic that cannot be used to distinguish his work from Middleton's.

The *RT*, like Tourneur's *AT*, is often symbolical and allegorical, and the prevailing view is that Middleton's tragedies are not—that their power is in their realistic insight into character.[13] But Middleton's plays are no more and no less realistic than the *RT*: the important and extensively developed symbolic relation between stolen treasure and stolen sensual pleasure in *Women Beware Women* functions as a structurally important expanded metaphor, and other Middleton plays, like *The Phoenix,* with its disguised duke-to-be moving among his people in order to reform them, or like *A Game at Chess,* are allegorical from their very titles on.

Parallels between the *RT* and the signed works of Tourneur or Middleton can be endlessly spun out, but they can almost always be traced to common ancestors external to the works of either man. The plays the *RT* is most closely akin to in symbol and action are—aside from the tragedies of revenge—the comical or tragical satires of John Marston and Ben Jonson. The plot, much of the manner, and the central malcontent-revenger of the *RT* are probably all derived from Marston's

[12] See Samuel Schoenbaum, *Middleton's Tragedies: A Critical Study* (New York, 1955), pp. 160–161; Richard Hindry Barker, *Thomas Middleton* (New York, 1958), pp. 65, 70, *et passim.*
[13] John D. Jump, "Middleton's Tragedies," in *The Age of Shakespeare,* Vol. II of Penguin's *A Guide to English Literature,* ed. Boris Ford (London, 1956), p. 355.

Malcontent (1604). The idea that the world of the *RT* is an
evilly *transformed* world, and the use of torchlight as a symbol of evil within that world, seem to link the play to Tourneur's *Transformed Metamorphosis* (1600), in which an evil
transformation overcomes the world, replacing the true light
of stars with hellish torchlight. But these symbolic values, and
others associated with them that might be cited, are basic to
the satires of Jonson and Marston, and still more to the
English conception of Italy (see Section 2 of this chapter).

Two efforts by Inga-Stina Ekeblad to prove Tourneur the
author of the *RT* lack force because they seek similarities in
admitted differences of tone or dramatic method. In one article
she argues that the imagery is functional, though in different
ways, in both the *RT* and the *AT,* and concludes that therefore the plays are by a single author.[14] In a second article she
shows that the *AT,* like the *RT,* is compounded of elements
from the revenge tradition, the satires and the moralities. But
in the *AT* a fourth element is added—"the study of the
Christian-Stoic individual"—and as a result the *fusion* of
diverse elements achieved in the *RT* is replaced by a mere
mixture of the elements. "The satire is detached from the main
plot," and "none of its realism and directness of language gives
life to the frequently symbolic situations."[15] These remarks are
part of a paper which contains a sound analysis of the various
elements in each of these two plays. The value of the analysis
as evidence for Tourneur's authorship of the *RT* is slight,
however, since only a potential similarity is argued in the face
of recognized profound differences between the *RT* and the
AT.

Yet it is also true that there are substantial differences
between the *RT* and the surviving works of Middleton written

---

[14] In her "An Approach to Tourneur's Imagery."
[15] "On the Authorship of *The Revenger's Tragedy,*" pp. 234–235.

in the period 1602–1609, which are all comedies. Genre distinctions are all-important, and we must look for Middleton's work comparable to the *RT* among his surviving tragedies, written years later, and in such an unclassifiable work as *A Game at Chess*. In this last play, and also in *Women Beware Women,* are the moral concern, the possibly prurient interest in seduction, the representation of a Latin country as demonically corrupt, and the fusion of morality, satire and revenge so characteristic of the *RT*.

On thematic and structural grounds, then, a case may be made for either Tourneur or Middleton as the author of the *RT*. When we turn to stylistic evidence we find much the same thing to be true, although here at first glance the data seem to point almost overwhelmingly to Middleton. Scholars have found dozens of verbal parallels between the *RT* and both early and late plays of Middleton. Some twenty-five of these parallels are close and un-conventional.[16] To counter this there are very few echoes of the *RT* in the *AT* or vice versa, and those few are all conventional or are to be found in Middleton as well.[17] The method of citing parallel passages has been generally discredited, however, because it permits no distinction between imitation and common authorship. It may be noted, though, that if imitation is the explanation here, we first have Tourneur imitating satirical comedies in writing a satirical tragedy, followed by an imitation by Middleton, working in several genres, of Tourneur's tragedy—a rather

---

[16] See E. H. C. Oliphant, "The Authorship of *The Revenger's Tragedy,*" *SP*, XXIII (1926), 157–168; Wilbur D. Dunkel, "The Authorship of *The Revenger's Tragedy,*" *PMLA*, XLVI (1931), 781–785; Schoenbaum, *Middleton's Tragedies*, pp. 177–181; and Barker, *Thomas Middleton*, pp. 166–169.

[17] H. Dugdale Sykes cites what parallels there are in "Cyril Tourneur: 'The Revenger's Tragedy': 'The Second Maiden's Tragedy,' " *NQ*, V (1919), 225–229.

complex pattern of imitation and counter-imitation.

Studies of versification generally show that the RT correlates better with the works of Middleton than with the AT.[18] However, much of the "verse" of the AT was printed as prose in the only seventeenth-century edition of the play, and the results of some metrical tests are therefore vitiated because the versification examined was that established by a modern editor. Nevertheless, the verse of the RT, seeming to move with passionate, irregular force, contrasts with a slower, more regular reflectiveness in the AT. This same difference may be observed in the imagery of the two plays: Marco K. Mincoff writes that in the RT the speed of the action and dialogue demands the compression of simile into metaphor.[19] Mincoff concludes that the imagery of the AT and the RT are radically and fundamentally different: Tourneur is "slow of inspiration, a philosophizer and a plagiarist, vaguely visual in his imagery and fond of Nature and inclined also to diffuseness," but the author of the RT is "quick and energetic, brutally direct . . . , overflowing with imagination of an intellectual type, . . . opposed to all romanticism in his imagery . . . , powerful and original."[20] All these characteristics of the "unknown author" of the RT, Mincoff goes on to find in Middleton's *Women Beware Women*.

Similarities and differences of this sort are entirely relevant to questions of authorship, yet at the same time extremely treacherous to interpret. Unknown to Mincoff, Una Ellis-Fermor had earlier published an independent study of the

---

[18] See E. E. Stoll, *John Webster* (Boston, 1905), p. 212; Oliphant, "The Authorship of *The Revenger's Tragedy*," p. 159; Fred L. Jones, "Cyril Tourneur," *TLS*, 18 June 1931, p. 487; and Barker, "The Authorship of the *Second Maiden's Tragedy* and *The Revenger's Tragedy*," *SAB*, XX (1945), 127.

[19] In "The Authorship of 'The Revenger's Tragedy,'" *Studia Historico-Philologica Serdicensia*, II (1940), 7.

[20] *Ibid.*, pp. 56–57.

imagery of the *AT* and the *RT,* and reached the conclusion that the same man must have written both plays![21] Mincoff's is the more detailed and convincing study, and since Miss Ellis-Fermor neglects to compare the *RT* with any of Middleton's plays, one must be more impressed by Mincoff's conclusions; but the very fact that two scholars could apply the same method and obtain diametrically opposed results must cast grave doubts on the usefulness of the test involved.

Mincoff himself notes the limitations on the study of imagery as a test of authorship in his introductory discussion of method. As he points out, differences in imagery may occur within the work of a single author as that author develops, or as he works in different literary forms. A crucial further limitation on the method which he notes but does not always observe in the discussion of results, is that to yield information on authorship, an image must be attributable directly to the author and not to the character uttering it.[22] We must ask, of course, whether we can *ever* believe with confidence that the imagery of a play may be thus directly related to the author. Rosemond Tuve warns us that "some of the factors which influenced a dramatist *writing* images and which we neglect at our peril in *reading* them are : general purpose (*e.g.*, satire; *cf.* philosophical reflection), immediate purpose, subject matter, character speaking, source, type of scene, audience, type of company, stage conditions, pace or tempo of scene." Miss Tuve concludes that we cannot use imagery in any simple way to determine authorship.[23]

By paying proper attention to these many factors, Tourneur's supporters have found it easy to explain the stylistic differences between the *AT* and the *RT*. Harold Jenkins argues

[21] "The Imagery of 'The Revengers Tragedie' and 'The Atheists Tragedie,' " *MLR,* XXX (1935), 289–301.

[22] *Op. cit.,* p. 5.

[23] *Elizabethan and Metaphysical Imagery* (Chicago, 1947), p. 238n.

that the shift from the passionate speed and compression of the
RT to the slower pace of the *AT* is to be explained as resulting
from Tourneur's development of mind in "the supplanting of
a fiery instinct by a reasoning purpose."[24] Or alternatively we
may look back at the descriptions of Tourneur and the "unknown author" quoted from Mincoff's essay and see that they
are, respectively, excellent characterizations of the atheist,
D'Amville, and the revenger, Vindici![25]

We may conclude this review of the literary evidence by
observing that the limitations on the use of imagery to determine the authorship of a work apply to the use of *any* elements
of a play that may be adapted by an author in his imitation of
an action through plot structure, character and style. Since
the *AT* and the *RT* have greatly different unifying actions, it
naturally follows that they will have greatly different styles.
For example, the rapid movement of the verse in the *RT* and
the corresponding speed and compression of its imagery reflect
the theme of the play, which concerns in part the speed with
which men may hurry to damnation.

For these reasons we must remain unconvinced one way or
the other by the literary evidence. It may be generally agreed
that the *RT* is within the range of capability of both Tourneur
and Middleton. As Samuel Schoenbaum writes, "the situation,
as it stands, is that neither Middleton's nor Tourneur's advocates have been able to bring forward the kind of proof to
which one party or the other must submit." In Schoenbaum's
revision of the *Annals of English Drama, 975–1700*, the authorship entry for the *RT* will be: "Anonymous (Tourneur, C. ?
Middleton, T. ?)."[26]

---

[24] In "Cyril Tourneur," *RES*, XVII (1941), 25.
[25] Una Ellis-Fermor discusses the close relation of imagery to character
in both the *RT* and the *AT: The Jacobean Drama*, p. 161: *The Frontiers
of Drama*, pp. 90–91.
[26] From "Internal Evidence and the Attribution of Elizabethan Plays,"
NYPLB, LXV (1961), 122.

We may now proceed to a consideration of the kind of internal evidence that derives from such elements of a play's text as most authors probably regard as sub-literary, elements over which most authors probably exercise less conscious control than they do, say, over imagery. This evidence is obtained by bibliographical and linguistic analyses of the texts in question.

George R. Price has published the results of a bibliographical analysis of the 1607 quarto of the *RT*. He found some evidence that two compositors set up the play, but their typesetting was so faithful to the copy that Price had difficulty distinguishing their work with any certainty from variations in the reproduction of any linguistic or spelling forms.[27] From the fact that many stage directions are lacking and from the form of those that are present, Price deduces that the printer's copy was probably an authorial or scribal manuscript not intended either for immediate use in the theater or for printing.[28]

Price's study of the punctuation and spelling in the *RT* indicates that the play is Middleton's. As in the holograph Middleton manuscript of *A Game at Chess,* there is frequent use of the comma, sometimes even to end speeches, and infrequent use of the colon and period. In this respect the *RT* contrasts with the works of Tourneur, which have consistently heavy punctuation.[29] Price notes several unusual spellings in the *RT* that are characteristic of Middleton's holograph and printed work, and that contrast with spellings in Tourneur's four acknowledged works.[30]

Several scholars have noted that the author of the *RT* shares with Middleton a liking for a number of peculiar words or phrases. These linguistic parallels include the use of *unbribed*

---

[27] "The Authorship and the Bibliography of *The Revenger's Tragedy,*" *The Library,* 5th series, XV (1960), 272–273.

[28] *Ibid.,* pp. 263–265.

[29] *Ibid.,* pp. 266–267.

[30] *Ibid.,* p. 268.

and *hereafter* as adjectives, of the rare word *luxur,* of the inter-
jection *push* (versus the *AT*'s *tush*), and of *comfort, slave,
honour* and *covetous* in special senses.[31]

But any attribution of the play ought to have a more substantial basis than this. Suppose we concede that the *RT* is
closer to Middleton than to Tourneur in the spelling or use of
a few scattered words. How many hundreds of words may
have escaped our notice that are used and spelled identically
in the *RT* and the *AT*, in a way contrasting with Middleton's
usage? What happens, that is, when we make a close analysis
of a large group of forms?

In the preparation of this study, I have determined both the
frequency of occurrence and the spelling for all colloquial
contractions of prepositions, articles, personal pronouns and
verbs, and their combinations with one another. In addition
to these colloquial contractions, the author's choice of *has*
or *hath, does* or *doth,* has been determined in every play
examined. These forms have been examined not only in the
RT and the *AT* but also in plays by George Chapman,
Barnabe Barnes, John Marston and the combination of
Thomas Dekker and John Webster (all printed by George Eld
in 1607–08), in Ben Jonson's *The Alchemist,* printed by
Thomas Snodham in 1612 (Snodham printed the *AT* at the
end of 1611), and in other works of both Tourneur and Middleton dating from various periods of their development. The data
obtained from the plays of Jonson, Marston and Dekker-
Webster were checked against others of their works published

---

[31] Most of these are reviewed in Schoenbaum, *Middleton's Tragedies,*
pp. 175–176. Charles Barber writes of "A Rare Use of the Word *Honour*
as a Criterion of Middleton's Authorship" in *ES,* XXXVIII (1957), 161–
168. Francis Berry has suggested that the use of *thou* in the *RT* to address
the skull and other symbols may be a characteristic which could help
determine authorship. Unfortunately, this use of *thou* was standard for
both Tourneur and Middleton. See Berry's *Poets' Grammar* (London,
1958), p. 102.

by still other printers at about the same time.[32] The data obtained are reported in Tables I–V (pp. 174–189).

The chief data are summarized in Tables I and II. Table I reports the *spelling* of the forms studied. For the purposes of this table, for example, *w'are* and *we're* are regarded as different forms of contraction for *we are*. The table excludes only those forms that are spelled the same by both Tourneur and Middleton, or for which no really significant spelling correlation can be shown because the spelling in question occurs too rarely in the *AT* or the *RT* to establish a preference.

In Table II the spellings of the forms are disregarded, and only the frequency of occurrence of a contraction is considered. For the purposes of Table II *w'are* and *we're* are regarded as a single form, each instance of either having equal significance as a contraction for *we are*. Every contraction of the class studied is included in the table if it occurs more than once in the *RT* or in any of the Tourneur or Middleton plays examined.

---

[32] The texts used are as follows: for the *RT*, Xerox prints of the Folger Library copy of the qto. of 1608; for the *AT*, Xerox prints of the Yale University Library's microfilm of the Elizabethan Club copy of the qto. of 1611. Both these texts were checked against Nicoll's old-spelling edition. Photostat facsimiles of the Henry E. Huntington Library copies of the qtos. of 1607–08 were used for Middleton's *Your five Gallants, A Tricke to Catch the Old-one, A Mad World, My Masters* and *The Phoenix. A Game at Chesse* was consulted in the edition of the Middleton holograph Trinity manuscript prepared by R. C. Bald (Cambridge, 1929). The copy of the qto. of 1608 in the Horace Howard Furness Memorial Library at the University of Pennsylvania was used for Chapman's *Conspiracy and Tragedy of Charles Duke of Byron*. Barnes' *Devil's Charter* was studied in the *Student's Facsimile Edition*, 1913, pt. 8. Jonson's *Alchemist* was studied in *The English Replicas* facsimile of the qto. of 1612 (London, 1927). Jonson's other plays were checked in *Ben Jonson*, ed. C. H. Herford and Percy Simpson (Oxford, 1925–52). Dekker and Webster's *Northward Ho* and *Westward Ho* were studied in Vol. II of *The Dramatic Works of Thomas Dekker*, ed. Fredson Bowers (Cambridge, 1955). Marston's *What You Will* and *Parasitaster, or The Fawne* were studied in Vol. II of *The Plays of John Marston*, ed. H. Harvey Wood (Edinburgh, 1938). Tourneur's poems were studied in Nicoll's edition of the *Works*.

The first question to ask of the data is whether the forms reported in the tables are really those of the respective authors, or whether they come from the compositors who set the type. It would be helpful if we could make a detailed comparison of the forms in the *AT* with those in a number of other plays printed in the same shop at about the same time. Snodham, however, printed only one other play within a year of the *AT*, and that was Jonson's *Alchemist*. Comparison of the spellings and use of colloquial contractions in *The Alchemist* with the *AT* on the one hand (Table III), and with Jonson's late comedies on the other, indicates that the compositors followed copy in *The Alchemist*, and as a result we can use the data from this play a little later on when we want representative figures for Jonson's practice. But, since Jonson's interest in getting printers to reproduce his text accurately was unusual, the fact that Snodham followed copy for him proves little with regard to the printing of Tourneur's play.

The only proof we have that Snodham's compositors also followed copy in printing the *AT* is that its spellings are identical to those dominant in Tourneur's other signed works, *The Transformed Metamorphosis*, printed by Valentine Sims in 1600, the *Funeral Poem Upon the Death of . . . Sir Francis Vere*, printed for Eleazar Edgar in 1609, and the *Grief on the Death of Prince Henry*, printed by Nicholas Okes in 1613. Composite figures for these three works show the following spellings dominant: *t'is*, *t'was*, *'em*, *does*, *is't*, *hee'l*, *o'th*, and *th'are*. Other typical Tourneurisms are frequent use of *th'*, fairly frequent use of the then rare *'s* possessive—found in the *AT* but never in the *RT* or the works of Middleton—elisions like *heav'n* and *gen'rous*, and occasional infinitive contractions like *t'offend*. These results corroborate George Price's conclusion, based on the spelling of *hable* and other words, that the *AT* was printed from a manuscript in Tourneur's own hand, and they indicate that the compositors who set type for the play were not tampering with the forms of the manuscript.

The data in Tables I and IV prove that George Eld did not alter the forms in the texts brought to him for printing in 1607–08. My specific conclusions with regard to the *RT* would be better founded if I could identify the individual compositors who set the type for the play and study their work there and in other texts to see whether they followed copy; but that has proved impossible. Price, as I have noted, was unable to discover for either of the two *RT* compositors any peculiar spellings or linguistic traits. Nor did Fredson Bowers identify any of Eld's compositors in preparing his edition of *Northward Ho*.[33] This in itself is good evidence of the compositors' faithfulness to the copy. Since we cannot make a rigorous study of identified compositors, we must be satisfied with the next best thing : surely by studying *all* the plays of known authorship printed by Eld in 1607–08 we can establish a reasonable basis for the presumption that somewhere among them we shall cover the work of the compositor(s) of the *RT*. In this connection it is important to note that Eld's shop added no apprentices between the beginning of 1607 and 15 December, 1608.[34]

Contractions of the sort under study are rare in Barnes' *Devil's Charter* and George Chapman's *Conspiracy and Tragedy of Charles, Duke of Byron*, indicating that Eld's compositors were not in the habit of introducing such forms willy-nilly into texts they printed. There is variation in the frequency and the spelling of these forms from playwright to playwright, and remarkable consistency of both the frequency and the spelling of the forms between the average figures for the two Middleton plays printed by Eld in 1607–08—*A Trick to Catch the Old One* and *Your Five Gallants*—and the average figures for two other Middleton

---

[33] Edition of Dekker, II, 408.
[34] See D. F. McKenzie, "A List of Printers' Apprentices, 1605–1640," *SB*, XIII (1960), 120.

plays printed in the same period but by other printers—*The Phoenix*, printed by Edward Allde, and *A Mad World, My Masters*, printed by Henry Ballard. And the spellings in both pairs of plays conform to Middleton's practice in the holograph *A Game at Chess*, with its use of *e'm, a, ath, ith, dos* or *do's, ist, Ile, I've, youle* and *heele* or *hee'le*, and so on. That is, there is consistency in these matters where one would expect to find it if the forms printed had come from the manuscripts presented to the printer. We find that Middleton's preference, consistent in the texts studied, for contractions of *in the* omitting the apostrophe after the *th*, is not preferred in Dekker and Webster's *Northward Ho*, and that *in the* is never contracted at all by Barnes, Marston or Chapman. Middleton occasionally uses *h'as* or *ha's* not only for *he has* but for *has* alone; Dekker, Webster and Marston never do. *Has* itself is rare in *Byron's Tragedy*, unknown in *The Devil's Charter*. Middleton has, likewise, a consistent preference for *y'are, yare,* or a variant of *youre,* and of *dos* or *do's,* which contrast with the dominant *does* and *ya're* in *Northward Ho*. These and the other data indicate no determining printer's preference at work.

In those cases in which Marston's or Dekker-Webster's preferred spelling of a form coincides with Middleton's in these plays printed by Eld in 1607–08, it can be shown that these same forms are preferred in other plays by the same authors printed at about the same time but by different printers : *ha, ist, Ile,* and contractions of other pronouns with *will* or *shall* having a final *e,* as in *heele,* are preferred in Marston's *Parasitaster, or The Fawn,* printed by Thomas Purfoot in 1606, and in Dekker and Webster's *Westward Ho,* printed in 1607 by William Jaggard.

Table IV shows, without regard to spellings, the frequency of occurrence of the forms under study in *Westward Ho, Northward Ho, What You Will* and *Parasitaster*. Agreement of frequencies between works of common authorship is good, implying that these forms have not been altered in the printing process. In neither of his plays does Marston use any contractions of *them,* of *on, of* or any other prepositions with *the* (as in *o'th'*), or of pronouns with any verb except *will* or *shall* (*Ile* and *youle* but not *I'm, you've,* or *they'd,* etc.). These are all rather common forms in the Middleton plays. There are differences between *Parasitaster* and *What You Will,* too, but they are not of the sort that can be traced to the printer. *Has, ha',* and *hath* all occur more frequently in *Parasitaster* than in *What You Will,* but the use of *ha'* and *hath* is much more frequent in *either* Marston play than in any Middleton play studied.

In general, a sharp distinction may be made between the Marston plays and the Middleton plays, but not between Eld and the other printers. The Marston play printed by Eld agrees better with the Marston play printed by Purfoot than it does with either Middleton play printed by Eld in regard to the frequency of about 90 per cent of the forms for which any distinction can be made (counting the *has/hath* and *does/ doth* ratios as the significant values to be derived from counts of the four forms).

Agreement of frequencies between the two Dekker-Webster plays is not likely to be as close as between the two Marston plays, since Dekker and Webster may have written different proportions of their two collaborations. Nevertheless, the agreement between *Northward Ho* and *Westward Ho* is considerable. The frequencies of 78 per cent of the forms for which any distinction can be made agree more closely between the Dekker-Webster play printed by Eld and their play printed by Jaggard than between the Eld play by Dekker-Webster and either Eld play by Middleton (again taking as the significant values the ratios of *has* to *hath* and *does* to *doth*).

There is still more evidence that for the most part Eld's workmen simply reproduced what they found in the manuscripts presented to them for printing. As George Price pointed out in his study of the play's bibliography, the *RT* uses a number of Middleton's characteristic spellings, including *forcst* (*forced*), *damb, relligion, chast* and *hast, closse,* and *tennants.* To these may be added the distinctive Middleton preference for *ei* spellings in such words as *peice.* These are the spellings preferred in the Middleton holograph portion of the Trinity manuscript of *A Game at Chess.* The inference that these Middleton spellings in the *RT* are valid evidence that he wrote the play is supported by the fact that none except *chast* is consistently preferred in the other plays printed by Eld in 1607–08 :

Game at Chess and RT	CHAPMAN'S Byron	MARSTON'S What You Will	BARNES' Devil's Charter	DEKKER-WEBSTER'S Northward Ho
peice	peece	peece	peece	peece
dambd	—	damn'd	damn'd	dambd
forcst	forc't	—	forc'd	devorst
relligion	religion	—	religion	—
closse	—	—	—	close
tennants	—	—	—	tenants
chast	chast	tast	hast	chast

The evidence presented so far has eliminated the possibility that the printshop workers materially altered the forms occurring in the *RT,* the *AT,* or any other plays we have studied. We are now ready to discuss in detail the data in Tables I and II that enable us to make a comparison of the forms in the *RT* with those in Middleton's plays and in Tourneur's *AT.*

Table I, containing data for the spelling of colloquial contractions, *has,* and *does,* shows that *in every one* of the eighteen spelling conflicts between Tourneur and Middleton the pattern of spellings occurring in the *RT* is closer to Middleton's than to Tourneur's. Although some of the spelling differences between Middleton and Tourneur concern only the use of the apostrophe, others reveal basic differences in the two authors' methods for forming colloquial contractions. In this important category fall the contrasts between Middleton's (and the *RT*'s) *tas, 'tas,* or *t'as* and Tourneur's *t'has,* Middleton's *the're* or *they're, we're* or *wee're* and Tourneur's *th'are* and *w'are,* and Middleton's *thourt* or *thou'rt* and Tourneur's *th'art.* In each of these contractions of a personal pronoun with a following verb, Middleton preserves the pronoun (*we're*) and Tourneur the verb (*w'are*).

These results are of the greatest importance. There can be no doubt that spelling is sub-stylistic and therefore not subject to change as a writer moves from poetry to prose or from tragedy to comedy. Since the spellings in the *AT* have been shown elsewhere in his signed works to be those of Tourneur, and since there is no evidence that George Eld altered the forms in the plays he printed in 1607, these spelling results are the strongest possible evidence that Tourneur was *not* the author (or scribe) and that Middleton *was* the author (or scribe) of the *RT*.

Table II summarizes the frequency of use of the colloquial contractions and of *has, hath, does* and *doth.* There are thirty-four frequencies reported, counting not the actual occurrence of *has, hath, does* and *doth* but the percentage *hath* and *doth* represent of the total *has + hath* and *does + doth,* respectively. For twenty-five of these thirty-four frequencies the value for the *RT* is closer to Middleton than to Tourneur; for eight it is equally close to them both; and for one it is closer to Tourneur than to Middleton. This correlation of the *RT* with Middleton is so good that even if other evidence had not narrowed our choice down to Tourneur or Middleton as author of the play, and we were groping among all these authors to assign the *RT* solely on the basis of the linguistic data, we should still have no trouble attributing the play to Middleton. We can apply a mathematical test to the data to determine the degree of confidence with which we can reject the hypothesis that this correlation with Middleton is a mere coincidence, which would be the case if Middleton were not the author of the *RT*. If the play were by none of the five writers (Middleton, Tourneur, Jonson, Marston or Dekker-Webster), so that chance determined the correlation, we should expect an equal number of the forms to correlate with each writer. The departure from this expectation in the direction of correlation with the average values for Middleton is so great that, by applying the *chi*-square test of significance, we may assign a confidence level of greater than 99.95 per cent to our rejection of the hypothesis that the correlation is a matter of chance. That is to say, we should not expect to find so exact a correlation between Middleton's work and a play he did *not* write more often than one time in two thousand. If we apply this same test to the correlation of the *RT* with *each* of the four Middleton plays written within a few years of the *RT*, we find that we can reject the hypothesis that chance governs the correlation with 97 per cent certainty for *Mad World* and about 98 per cent certainty for *A Trick*, for *The Phoenix* and for *Your Five Gallants*.

Thus far we have seen a distinct numerical correlation between the *RT* and the works of Middleton. When we analyze the linguistic practices behind the numbers, this correlation seems to be confirmed. The one form for which the frequency of use in the *RT* correlates with Tourneur better than with Middleton is *o'th'*. But this correlation is achieved only by including all occurrences in Tourneur of *o'the* as well as of *o'th'* and equating them with Middleton's and the *RT*'s *ath*, *a'th*, and *ath'*. The forms are probably not the same, however. Tourneur mostly uses *o'th'* and *th'* before words beginning with vowels, with *ha,* or with *wo.* When the word following begins with a consonant, the *AT* usually uses *the* and *o'the.* If Tourneur is the author of the *RT,* somewhere in the transmission of his text someone has levelled *o'th'* and *o'the* to *ath, a'th,* and *ath'.* In addition, this person has eliminated most of the occurrences of *th'* before words beginning with vowels, for the *RT,* like Middleton, is at least as likely to use *ath* or *th'* before words beginning with a consonant as before those beginning with a vowel. If we were to consider these changes unlikely, and decide to regard *o'the* and *i'the* as occurrences of *o'* and *i'* but not as contractions with *th',* we could present the data in the first part of Table II thus:

		Middleton	the RT	the AT
	o'th'	6	18	5
	i'th'	16	14	7
[other prep.]	th'	10	7	1
other	o'	14	17	47
other	i'	0	0	21

Such a rearrangement of the data, while it does not enhance the correlation of the *RT* with Middleton, eliminates the one point of correspondence between the *RT* and the *AT.*

The *RT*'s and Middleton's *a* is not really equivalent to Tourneur's *o',* which is used much more exclusively to mean *of.* Also, the *AT* uses *o'* nineteen times before personal pronouns; the *RT* and the typical Middleton play seldom so use *a.* Typical of Middleton's use of *a* are the following, the total list from *Mad World: cloth a gold, a comming, cloth a tissue, a one side, now a daies, long a making ready, Innes a courtman, wrought a purpose, a my credit, a my troth* (2), and *riding a horse back.* Compare these with the *RT*'s uses of *a* : *cloath a silver, Bucket a water, a comming* (2), *a both sides, a quoyning, a dying, a hunting, a foot* (2), *a bed* (2), *a horse-back, a peices, a cold, a your trick, a conscience.*

There is a notable correlation between the *RT* and Middleton's average practice, and a difference between the *RT* and the *AT*, in the use of contractions of personal pronouns with following verbs in such forms as *I'll, I'm* and *we're*. Here, since the situation in a play may influence the use of *we'll* as against, say, *they'll,* I have reported not only the totals for the occurrence of the forms but the percentage these totals represent of all the times they and their expanded forms occur: % I'll = I'll × 100 / (I'll + I will + I shall). With respect to both total use and percentage of use it can be seen that Middleton and the author of the *RT* use these forms much more freely than Tourneur does.

Space will not permit similar detailed treatment of every form, but several others must be at least briefly discussed. The widest disparity between Middleton and the *RT* on the one hand and Tourneur on the other is observed in the use of *th', ha',* and *on't*. Tourneur, as we have seen, quite frequently omits the terminal *e* of *the* to elide a syllable in verse when *the* is followed by a word beginning with a vowel. Similarly, Tourneur often shortens *have* to *ha'*. Middleton and the author of the *RT* rarely use these contractions. Middleton's favorite contractions do not promote metric regularity or euphony but rather the flavor of idiomatic speech. The contraction *on't*, usually having the idiomatic meaning *of it,* occurs an average of nineteen times in the Middleton plays studied, eighteen times in the *RT,* and only once in the *AT*.

Middleton and the *RT* are not only more idiomatic than Tourneur, they are more modern. *Doth* was in the process of giving way to *does* in the early seventeenth century. In Middleton *doth* is quite rare, usually occurring only in quoted songs or proverbs. *Doth* occurs only twice in the *RT,* once to rhyme with *truth*. In the *RT,* as in Middleton generally, *doth* is used only 7 per cent of the time, *does* 93 per cent. In the *AT, doth* is used 38 per cent of the time. Analysis of Tourneur's use of *doth* and *does* in the *AT* shows that he had a rational basis for selecting one form or the other. All but two occurrences of *doth* are in verse, and the two in prose are spoken by the Puritan, Snuffe. *Does* occurs only six times in the verse : twice in non-auxiliary constructions in which its use seems to have become somewhat standard at an earlier date than in other constructions, twice for the sake of euphony when *d* is the initial letter of the next word, once in the lines of the usually prose-speaking Levidulcia, and only once under other circumstances. This rationale does not fit the *RT. Does* is used indiscriminately in prose or verse and is not used as a characterizing word in any way. Of the writers studied, this more modern lack of discrimination is typical only of Thomas Middleton.

One important objection to the reasoning behind this analysis must be considered. It may be argued that these differences in usage between the *AT* and the *RT* are the result of deliberate choice of diction level : that somehow Tourneur felt that a satirical atheist's tragedy set in a manorial society, even though it contains long passages of prose spoken by low figures, contrasts with a satirical tragedy of Italianate revenge in calling for less idiomatic English and a verse style using contractions chiefly to assist in getting iambic pentameter rhythm and line length. This contention can be used to account for the higher percentage of *hath* and *doth* in the *AT,* and for the use in the *AT's* verse of such contractions as *m'unhappy* (*my unhappy*), *t'have* (*to have*), and *t'begins* (*it begins*)—all of which, according to this theory, would be inappropriate to the decorum of the *RT.* This theory can also be used to account for the decrease in the total number of the contractions studied from 548 in the *RT* to 408 in the *AT*—a decrease chiefly in the idiomatic forms like *on't*, in *'twas* and *'tis* and *'em*, and in contractions of personal pronouns with verbs.

This counter-argument in favor of Tourneur considers the use of colloquial contractions, *hath*, and *doth* as *stylistic*— as an element of a play adaptable to the central unifying action in the same way as imagery would be. It cannot be denied that the frequency of these forms varies within the work of most Jacobean dramatists as they shift from genre to genre : Jonson in *Sejanus* uses *hath* and *doth* almost exclusively, and makes many fewer contractions than in *The Alchemist*, and Marston's tragedies differ similarly from his comedies.

A general defense of Tourneur's claim to the *RT* could be stated like this : Just as the swiftness of the action in the *RT* demands rapid plot events, compressed and concise imagery, and rapid verse movement, so it also demands compression of words into contractions and the conciseness of idiomatic talk. It allows no time for careful, regularizing verse elisions of the sort common in the *AT*. The unifying action of the *AT*, on the other hand, is the search for human fulfillment in a material or spiritual eternity, an action in which the mere *minute* of fulfillment is rejected by Christian and atheist alike. Such an action, having eternity as its goal, permits a slower verse, freer use of simile rather than compressed metaphor, and a correspondingly lesser use of contractions.

No doubt this argument from style actually does explain some of the differences between the *AT* and the *RT*, regardless of who wrote the anonymous play, and if the *positive* correlation with Middleton were not so remarkable we might be tempted to throw up our hands in despair of resolving the issue. We need not despair, however. There is a fatal number of facts this argument cannot explain. Let us reconsider the data in Tables II and IV in such a way as to be sure that we are distinguishing dramatic dictional levels (which may vary with the genre, speaker, occasion and so on) and differences resulting from variation in the range of the forms familiar to a writer.

Instead of studying the absolute frequencies of occurrence, we shall shift our attention to relative frequencies of occurrence within related groups of forms. The argument from decorum may explain the great drop from the *RT* to the *AT* in the total number of contractions of *I* with verbs; but how can it explain the disproportionately great drop in *I'm,* a drop reducing *I'm* to the level of use of *I've* and *I'd?* How can it explain the absence of *sha't* and *sha'not,* used both in prose and verse in the *AT,* from the *RT,* where other contractions involving verbs are so plentiful? How can it explain the fact that in the *RT i'* occurs only in combination with *th'* as *i'th',* whereas the *AT* uses it also in conjunction with other words? *O'th'* and *i'th'* are common in the *RT* and in the *AT:* why is *th'* so rare in the *RT?* And why are prepositions other than *of, on* or *in* frequently contracted with *th'* only in the *RT?* Prepositions are often contracted with *th'* and with *it* (e.g., *for't*) in both plays: why are they contracted in significant numbers with *his* only in the *AT?* In each of these cases and others which the argument from decorum cannot explain, the *RT* is closer to Middleton than to Tourneur.

If we use this sort of analysis to determine with which of the several writers studied the *RT* correlates best, we again find a highly significant correlation with Middleton. By the *chi*-square test we find that we may reject the hypothesis that this correlation is caused by chance with a confidence of greater than 99.5 per cent.

We have seen that both the preferred spellings and the frequency of occurrence of the large group of forms studied in the *RT* correlate very strongly with the practice of Thomas Middleton and of no other author, and certainly not with that of Cyril Tourneur. The evidence points to a choice among

three conclusions : that Thomas Middleton wrote *The Revenger's Tragedy*, that he revised it, or that he made a copy of it
that was in the line of transmission of the text to the printer in
which he systematically altered the author's forms and imposed
his own. I think most scholars are ready to agree that the great
weight of the internal evidence of style and imagery indicate
that if we must choose among these three hypotheses, we must
say that Middleton *wrote* the play, and did not merely revise
or copy it.

2   THE WORLD OF THE PLAY

Although the evidence strongly supports Middleton's claim
to *The Revenger's Tragedy,* the tests I have used leave a slight
chance that Tourneur is the author. So long as we study this
problem from a text at least one remove from the author's
papers, we can never do more than establish a *probability* of
authorship by means of linguistic and spelling tests, and that
probability is only as good as the inferences about scribes and
compositors on which it is based. Moreover, other statistical
analyses than those I have made will yield different degrees of
certainty for assignment of the play to Middleton, some of
them no doubt less than that I have shown.

I think it necessary, therefore, to include here a study of *The
Revenger's Tragedy*. The reader may, after all, prefer literary-
critical reasons for deciding whether the play belongs in the
Tourneur canon, and he will then expect a verification of the
assertions about the play's structure, symbolism, literary ante-
cedents and outlook on life that I made in the early part of
my discussion of its authorship. In this connection it is
especially necessary to show that the play on the one hand does
have the "realistic" psychological interest we have come to
associate with Middleton, and on the other hand is not the

TABLE I

SPELLINGS OF COLLOQUIAL CONTRACTIONS, *has* and *does*

EXPANDED FORM	SPELLINGS OBSERVED	PLAYS PRINTED BY ELD IN 1607–08 N-W Ho[a]	WYW[b]	AVERAGE FOR TWO MIDDLETON PLAYS[c]	AVERAGE FOR TWO MIDDLETON PLAYS[d] BY OTHER PRINTERS	RT[e]	AT[f]
of, on	o'	0	—	0	0	0	34
	a	20	—	10	20	17	3
on, of the	*spellings with:*						
	o', *e.g.* o'th'	0	0	0	1	0	5
	a, *e.g.* ath	1	0	6	7	18	0
in the	i'the	0	0	0	0	0	15
	i'th'	0	0	0	0	0	5
	i'th	0	0	1	11	3	2
	it'h	0	0	0	5	0	0
	ith	10	0	11	2	11	0
	'ith	1	0	0	3	0	0
	ith'	17	0	3	0	0	0

a *Northward Ho*, by Thomas Dekker and John Webster, printed in 1607.
b *What You Will*, by John Marston, printed in 1607.
c *Your Five Gallants*, printed in 1607, and *A Trick to Catch the Old One*, printed in 1608.
d *The Phoenix*, printed by Edward Allde in 1607, and *A Mad World, My Masters*, printed by Henry Ballard in 1608.
e *The Revenger's Tragedy*, printed by George Eld at the end of 1607.
f *The Atheist's Tragedy*, printed by Thomas Snodham in 1611.

for it	for't	9	0	1	4	3	7
	fort	0	3	2	0	6	0
does	does, doe's	12	1	3	2	4	16
	dos, do's	1	3	7	16	22	0
have	ha'	0	0	0	0	0	35
	ha	15	21	6	9	3	0
it has	tas, 'tas, t'as	0	0	3	1	5	0
	t'has	0	0	0	0	0	3
do it	doe't	0	1	0g	0	0	8
	do't, doo't	0	4	7g	2	4	0
is it	is't	0	0	0	1	0	8
	ist	11	17	6	8	13	0
them	'em	15	0	11	13	21	18
	e'm	0	0	15	29	11	0
	em	3	0	20	10	5	0
I will or I shall	I'le	0	—	0	2	0	17
	Ile	90	—	39	48	51	30
	ile	16	—	27	21	23	0

g These figures are for *Your Five Gallants* only.

TABLE I (Continued)

Spellings of Colloquial Contractions, *has* AND *does*

Expanded Form	Spellings Observed	Plays Printed by Eld in 1607–08		Average for Two Middleton Plays[c]	Average for Two Middleton Plays[d] by Other Printers	RT[e]	AT[f]
		N-W Ho[a]	WYW[b]				
I am	*spellings with terminal* e, *as:*						
	I'me or Ime	25	0	16	27	23	0
	vs. I'm	0	0	0	0	0	3
I had *or* I would	I'de	0	0	1	3	1	2
	Ide, ide	3	0	7	3	8	0
you, he she, we, *and* they will *or* shall	*spellings with terminal* e, *as:*						
	youle	44	17	30	20	25	0
	vs. youl	4	1	3	1	0	15
has *and/or* he has	has	24	11	36	28	38	45
	h'as, ha's	0	0	4	17	7	3
thou art, *etc.* hast, *and* wouldst, *etc.*	thou'rt, *etc.*	0	0	7	7	10	0
	th'art, *etc.*	0	0	1	1	1	17

ye *and/or* you are	y'are, yare	0	0	4	12	9	12
	ya're	5	0	0	0	0	0
	your, you're, youre	0	0	10	7	2	0
we *or* they are	th'are, w'are	—	0	1	2	0	7
	we're, theyre, *etc.*	—	0	8	16	19	0
it was, were, will, would	t'was, *etc.*	0	0	0^{g}	6	3	13
	'twas, *etc.*	3	7	8^{g}	0	7	0
	twas, *etc.*	9	15	15^{g}	12	43	0
it is	t'is	0	—	0^{g}	2	1	50
	'tis	11	—	20^{g}	1	17	0
	tis	35	—	40^{g}	59	74	1

g These figures are for *Your Five Gallants* only.

TABLE II

FREQUENCY OF OCCURRENCE OF COLLOQUIAL CONTRACTIONS, has, hath, does AND doth

The spellings are modernized and the frequencies corrected to a quarto play length of seventy pages.

EXPANDED FORM	CONTRACTION	MIDDLETON 5 PLAYS AVERAGED[a]	Revenger's Tragedy	Atheist's Tragedy
of the, on the	o'th'	6	18	18
in the	i'th'	16	14	20
to, for, etc., + the	[other prep.] th' e.g., toth', forth'	10	7	1
other of, on	o' + a	14	17	34
other in	i'	0	0	8
with	wi'	0	0	2
other the	th'	2	2	35
on it	on't	19	18	1
in, to, etc., it	[other prep.] 't	22	21	17
on, in, etc., his	[prep.] 's	1[b]	2	6
have	ha'	7	3	31
has, he has	has, h'as	46	45	43
hath, % hath		3, 6%	7, 13%	13, 23%
she, it has	sh'as, 'tas	5	9	4

a *Game at Chess, Your Five Gallants, A Trick, A Mad World* and *The Phoenix.*
b Calculated from a 20% random sample of each of the five plays.

it is	'tis	59	92	46
it was, were, will, would	't[was, etc.]	26	53	12
it and verbs other than has, had, is, was, etc.	't[lies, etc.]	0	0	2
does	——	13	26	14
doth, % doth	——	1, 7%	2, 7%	9, 38%
do it	do't	3	4	7
is it	is't	7	13	7
have, see, etc., it	[other verb]'t	10	8	10
to with infinitive	t'[offend, etc.]	0	0	2
shalt, shall not	sha't, sha'not	0	0	7
let us	let's	7[b]	14	5
them	'em	47	37	16
me, my, ye, you, we	m', y', w'	0	0	5
he, she is	he's, she's	25[b]	22	17
thou art, wast, hast, hadst, wilt	thou[rt, lt, st, dst]	7	11	15

[b] Calculated from a 20% random sample of each of the five plays.

TABLE II (Continued)

FREQUENCY OF OCCURRENCE OF COLLOQUIAL CONTRACTIONS, has, hath, does AND doth

The percentages given below are those of the contracted form as a fraction of the total contractions plus un-contracted forms; e.g., % I'm $= 100$ x I'm/ (I'm + I am).

EXPANDED FORM	CONTRACTION	MIDDLETON 5 PLAYS AVERAGED	Revenger's Tragedy	Atheist's Tragedy
I will, shall	I'll	65, 78%[c]	74, 77%[d]	42, 49%[d]
I had, would, should	I'd	7, 29%	9, 31%	2, 11%
I am	I'm	22, 48%	23, 54%	3, 8%
I have	I've	5, 9%	7, 28%	2, 9%
Personal pronouns other than it, thou and I with will, shall, are, had, would, should and have	*e.g.* you'll	66, 54%	69, 43%	36, 31%

[c] Percentages in this column calculated from a 20% sample of each play.
[d] Percentages in these columns calculated from a 50% sample of the play.

TABLE III

FREQUENCY OF OCCURRENCE AND ORIGINAL SPELLINGS

of COLLOQUIAL CONTRACTIONS AND *does, doth, has* AND *hath*

EXPANDED FORM	SPELLINGS OBSERVED	PLAYS PRINTED BY THOMAS SNODHAM IN 1611–1612	
		Alchemist (88 pages)	*Atheist's Tragedy* (78 pages)
of the, on the	o'the, o'th'	46, 0	15, 5
in the	i'the, i'th', i'th	39, 0, 0	15, 5, 2
other prep., with the	upo'the	1	1
other of, on, in	a + o', i'	21, 9	37, 9
other prep.	*e.g.*, wi'	0	2
other the	th'	22	39
on it	on't	15	1
in, to, *etc.*, it	[*other prep.*]'t	16	19
on, in, *etc.*, his	[*prep.*]'s	—	6
have	ha'	89	35
he has, has	ha's & h'as, has	2, 55	3, 45
hath	hath	19	14
she, it has	sh'has & t'has, sh'as	1, 0	3, 1

TABLE III (Continued)

FREQUENCY OF OCCURRENCE AND ORIGINAL SPELLINGS
of Colloquial Contractions and *does, doth, has* and *hath*

EXPANDED FORM	SPELLINGS OBSERVED	PLAYS PRINTED BY THOMAS SNODHAM IN 1611–1612	
		Alchemist (88 pages)	*Atheist's Tragedy* (78 pages)
it is	'tis, tis, t'is	41, 1, 0	0, 1, 50
it was, were, will, would	't[was, *etc.*], t[was], t'[was]	15, 1, 1	0, 0, 13
it *and other verbs*	t'[lies, *etc.*]	0	2
does	dos & do's, does & doe's	26, 2	0, 16
doth	doth	13	10
do it	doo't & do't, doe't	11, 0	0, 8
is it	is't	12	8
other verb it	[see, *etc.*]t	14	11
to *with infinitive*	t'[offend, *etc.*]	14	2
shalt, shall not	sha't & sha'not	0	8
is not, will not	i'not & wi'not	3	0
give *and* gave	gi' & ga'	12	0
let us	let's	—	5
them	'hem, 'em	53, 0	0, 18
his	'is	3	0
you, ye, me, my, we	yo', y' & m' & w'	3, 0	0, 5

thou art, hast, wast hadst, wilt, wouldst	th'[art, etc.], thou'[rt, etc.]	3, 1	17, 0
he is, she is	h'is & sh'is, he's & she's	13, —	0, 19
I will, shall	I'll, Ile & I'le	79, 18	0, 47
I had, would	I'lld & I'ld & I'had, I'de	5, 0	0, 2
I am	I'am, I'm	4, 0	0, 3
I have	I'have, I've	3, 0	0, 2
Personal pronoun other than I, thou, *and* it *with:* will *or* shall	[you, *etc.*]ll, [you, *etc.*]'l	62, 3	0, 15
had, would, should	[you, *etc.*]'ld, [you, *etc.*]'had, [th, sh, h]'ad		
are	[yo, they]'are, [y, w, th]'are	2, 2, 0	0, 0, 3
have	[yo, you]'have, y'[have, ave]	9, 2	0, 19
were	yo'were	3, 0	0, 3
		3	0

TABLE IV

FREQUENCY OF OCCURRENCE OF COLLOQUIAL CONTRACTIONS, has, hath, does AND doth

The spellings are modernized and the frequencies corrected to a play length of seventy pages. For the expanded forms see Table II.

FORM	JOHN MARSTON ELD, 1607 What You Will	PURFOOT, 1606 Parasitaster	DEKKER-WEBSTER ELD, 1607 Northward Ho	JAGGARD, 1607 Westward Ho	CHAPMAN ELD, 1608 Byron's Trag., pt. 1	BARNES ELD, 1607 Devil's Charter
o'th'	0	0	1	3	0	1
i'th'	0	0	32	14	0	0
[other prep.] th'	0	0	—	—	0	0
other o', a	—	—	23	—	0	0
other i'	0	0	0	—	0	0
other th'	2	2	0	0	25	12
on't	5	5	5	3	1	0
[other prep.] 't	7	6	21	18	1	3
ha'	25	49	17	18	0	0
has	14	44	28	31	3	0
hath	26	41	33	41	55	34
% hath	65%	48%	54%	57%	95%	100%

sh'as, 'tas, sh'ad, 'tad, h'ad	0	0	0	1	0	0
does	5	20	15	16	4	0
doth	11	10	7	7	19	18
% doth	69%	33%	32%	30%	82%	100%
do't	—	—	—	—	2	0
is't	20	14	13	6	1	2
[other verb]'t	21	10	7	5	0	0
'tis	69	63	53	30	22	19
't[was, etc.]	27	9	14	9	8	0
't[lies, etc.]	0	0	0	0	0	0
t'[offend, etc.]	4	1	0	0	8	2
sha't, sha'not	—	—	—	—	—	—
thou'[rt, st, lt, dst]	1	4	2	4	0	1
I'll	108	31	121	100	27	5
I'd	0	0	3	10	0	0
I'm	0	0	29	20	0	0

TABLE IV (Continued)

FREQUENCY OF OCCURRENCE OF COLLOQUIAL CONTRACTIONS, has, hath, does AND doth

FORM	JOHN MARSTON ELD, 1607 *What You Will*	PURFOOT, 1606 *Parasitaster*	DEKKER-WEBSTER ELD, 1607 *Northward Ho*	JAGGARD, 1607 *Westward Ho*	CHAPMAN ELD, 1608 *Byron's Trag.,* pt. 1	BARNES ELD, 1607 *Devil's Charter*
I've	0	0	0	0	0	0
you'll, we'll, they'll, he'll, she'll	22	14	54	45	5	2
you'd, we'd, they'd, he'd, she'd	0	0	2	4	0	0
you're, we're, they're	0	1	6	5	5	1
you've, we've, they've	0	0	0	0	0	0
'em	0	0	21	65	0	0
m', y'	0	0	0	0	0	0

TABLE V

FREQUENCY OF OCCURRENCE OF COLLOQUIAL CONTRACTIONS, has, hath, does AND doth

The spellings are modernized, but the frequencies are those observed, not corrected for a play length of seventy pages. For the expanded forms, see Table II.

FORM	Revenger's Tragedy (70 pp.)	A Trick to Catch the Old One (59 pp.)	A Mad World My Masters (64 pp.)	Your Five Gallants (69 pp.)	The Phoenix (74 pp.)	A Game at Chess (69 pp.)
o'th'	18	3	9	8	6	3
i'th'	14	16	34	12	10	4
[other prep.]th'	7	8	28	8	5	0
other o', a	17	14	15	5	25	5
other th'	2	1	1	3	1	4
on't	18	12	27	24	13	18
[other prep.]'t	21	13	37	26	14	19
[prep.]'s	2	—	—	—	—	—
ha'	3	6	4	8	15	2
has, h'as	45	42	53	41	45	38
hath	7	3	2	4	3	4
sh'as 'tas	9	2	8	4	4	4
'tad	1	1	0	2	1	2

TABLE V (Continued)

FREQUENCY OF OCCURRENCE OF COLLOQUIAL CONTRACTIONS, has, hath, does AND doth

FORM	Revenger's Tragedy (70 pp.)	A Trick to Catch the Old One (59 pp.)	A Mad World My Masters (64 pp.)	Your Five Gallants (69 pp.)	The Phoenix (74 pp.)	A Game at Chess (69 pp.)
'tis	92	56	56	60	66	42
't[was, etc.]	53	25	20	23	22	32
does	26	7	16	12	18	8
doth	2	1	1	1	1	0
do't	4	—	2	7	2	1
is't	13	5	13	7	5	4
[other verb]'t	8	8	14	13	9	5
let's	14	—	—	—	—	—
'em	37	35	65	56	38	35
he's, she's	22	—	—	—	—	—
thou'[rt, etc.]	11	10	10	5	4	3
I'll	74	67	70	64	70	39
I'd	9	7	6	7	6	8
I'm	23	6	26	25	28	24
I've	7	0	9	6	8	2

Personal pronouns
other than I, thou,
and it, *with:*

will, shall	25	36	22	29	19	10
had, would, should	9	1	3	0	1	12
are	30	15	45	50	29	17
have	5	7	5	5	4	6

neurotic document that could only have been written by the supposedly narrow, obsessed moralist, Cyril Tourneur—certainly never by the broadly humorous Thomas Middleton of *A Trick to Catch the Old One* or *Your Five Gallants.*

Thus the central purpose of these pages will be to demonstrate the dramatic and psychological validity of Vindici's character in relation to the total action, and to elucidate the play's complex, unified structure. In this way I can show that the author was governed by moral and psychological insight and aesthetic principles, not by neurosis. Only such a demonstration will enable us to see how so objective a satirist as Middleton could have written the play.

But the discussion of the play will not be a polemic on the question of authorship. There are enough questions of *interpretation* to occupy a legion of polemicists, and I shall rest my case for the authorship of *The Revenger's Tragedy* with the arguments in the last chapter. Here I shall demonstrate the interpretation of the play that is the basis for some of those arguments, treating the play as the anonymous work it is, referring to no author by name.

The action the play imitates through the forms of plot, characters, and diction is the effort to make moral and physical transformations. The play depicts a world of inverted values, a dark world in which torchlight makes an "artificiall noone" for scenes of evil (I.iv.33), and there is always a sense that the day is "out ath-socket,/ That it is Noone at Mid-night" (II.ii.257–258). People disguise themselves and dissemble their true intentions, and their expectations are transformed by ironic reversals in action and word.[35] Transforming puns, metaphors and personifications are everywhere.[36]

---

[35] *Cf.* James L. Rosenberg, *Cyril Tourneur: The Anatomy of Evil,* an unpublished Univ. of Denver diss., 1954, pp. 129–131.

[36] See Peter Lisca, *"The Revenger's Tragedy: A Study in Irony," PQ,* XXXVIII (1959), 242–251.

We must not be tempted to associate this theme of transformation exclusively with Tourneur's *Transformed Metamorphosis* and thus to use it as an argument for his authorship of the play. The corrupt world, especially the world spawned by the hectic imaginings of Englishmen fascinated by Italy, was commonly represented as "transformed" in Jacobean literature. Besides the transformed world of Tourneur's poem, there is the world of Jonson's comedies:

> Call Divels, Angels; and Sinne, pietie :
> Let all things be preposterously transchangd.[37]

There are also the "Mad World" of Middleton's *A Mad World, My Masters*, and the Italy of his *Changeling*. Perhaps closest to what we find in *The Revenger's Tragedy* is the Italianate hell of John Marston:

> . . . *Lorenzo Celso* the loose *Venice* Duke,
> Is going to bed, tis now a forward morne
> Fore he take rest. O strange transformed sight,
> When princes make night day, the day there night.[38]

In the transformed world of *The Revenger's Tragedy* nothing is as it should be : "Time hath severall falls./ Greefes lift up joyes, feastes put downe funeralls" (V.i.178–179). Revels for funerals! and the revels, in which courtiers should masque as virtues,[39] are instead the vehicles for murder and rape.

"Judgment in this age is nere [*i.e.*, near] kin to favour" and speaks "all in gold" (I.iv.61,67). Ethical principles of justice

---

[37] *Every Man in His Humour,* V. iii. 306–307; ed. Herford and Simpson, III, 284–285.
[38] *What You Will,* I. i; ed. Wood, II, 243.
[39] See L. G. Salingar, " 'The Revenger's Tragedy' and the Morality Tradition," *Scrutiny,* VI (1938), 414.

are lost to sight, and replacing them is a demonic, ironic justice, oblivious of good and evil, but working to destroy evil-doers. Honesty is but "heavens beggar," chastity a "foolish —Country girle" (II.i.205,94). "Fayths are bought and sold,/ Oths in these daies are but the skin of gold" (III.i.7–8). The people in the ducal family are so depraved that they are ready to "call foule Incest but a Veniall sinne" (I.ii.191). They find true delight only in stealth (I.iii.118); "There's no pleasure sweet but it is sinfull" (III.v.220). "Forty Angells can make fourescore divills" (II.i.101), and the court is so given up to evil that those who would purge it must disguise themselves as Vices, reversing the normal process of the morality play, in which Vices disguise themselves as Virtues. The members of the ducal family are overcome only by treachery and force, and at the last the opening wish of the bastard, Spurio, comes true, and all the court is "turnde into a coarse" (I.ii.40).

The society controlled by this devilish ducal court is described by Vindici as corrupted by gold and sensuality. The taking of Lussurioso's gold in a demonically inverted ritual of sacrament is a symbol of Vindici's moral poisoning, and Vindici regards the commercial society as capable of similar evil transformations of everything it touches. "A right good woman in these dayes" is easily "changde/ Into white money" (II.ii.31–32), lordships are sold to maintain whoredoms, ironically called "Lady-ships" (III.v.77), and fruitfields are "turnd into bastards" (I.iii.58). "It was the greatest blessing ever happened to women;/ When Farmers sonnes agreed, and met agen,/ To wash their hands, and come up Gentlemen;/ The common-wealth has flourisht ever since" (II.i.240–243). A mother who lives off her daughter's whoredom may call her eyes her "Tennants," count her "yearely maintenance upon her cheekes," and take "Coach upon her lip" (II.i.108–110).

Family relations are out of joint. Lussurioso is twice duped

into attacking his father, and Hippolito and Vindici brandish
daggers against their mother; thus sons are "turnd monsters"
(IV.iv.7). The Duke and Duchess have no children in common,
and the paternity even of Lussurioso, the Duke's heir, is held
doubtful (I.ii.218–220). Spurio suggests that "some stirring
dish/ Was my first father" (I.ii.201–202). Brothers murder
brothers and undertake to act as panders to their sisters. The
name of bawd "Is so in league with age that now adaies/ It
do's Eclipse three quarters of a Mother" (I.iii.175–176), and
Gratiana is "bewitcht" or "transported" by a "fury" into being
a bawd to Castiza (IV.iv.42,103), who implores God "Hence-
forth to make the Mother a disease" (II.i.264). Castiza sums
up much of this in the commonplace:

> The worlds so changd, one shape into another,
> It is a wise childe now that knowes her mother.
>
> (II.i.187–188)

For the action of the play the central symbol of the evil
transformations this hellish world has wrought is the transformation of the head of the poisoned Gloriana to a skull,
"deaths vizard" (I.i.54). By means of this skull, a mask or
"shell" of death (I.i.18), the disguisings, paintings and dissimulations of the play are immediately related to the traditional
theme of *memento mori* and its moralizing on the vanity of
sin in a world where even Ambitioso is taught that "there is
nothing sure in mortalitie, but mortalitie" (III.vi.118–119).
Vindici contrasts the bare truth of the skull to the falseness
of the heavily painted or gorgeously masked faces of the
courtiers and ladies who dance and feast by the deceptive light
of torches[40] (I.i.17–52; III.v.58–101). Human flesh is but

---

[40] *Cf.* Salingar, "Tourneur and the Tragedy of Revenge," in *The Age
of Shakespeare,* Vol. 2 of Penguin's *A Guide to English Literature,* ed.
Boris Ford (London, 1956), p. 344.

another mask, struck off by death, and penetrable, like other masks, by the eye of God (I.iii.72–75).

Repeated allusions to human brows, faces and heads keep the image of Gloriana's skull ever before our minds, as it is constantly before the mind of Vindici. The head of the Duchess' youngest son, Junior, actually appears on stage, and faces are disguised, painted or figuratively burned with hot irons (II.i.259). The standard Elizabethan idea that on the brow of a person is charactered his honor or dishonor is used everywhere in *The Revenger's Tragedy*. The most common of these brow-ornaments are of course the cuckold's horns, but also the Duke is concerned for the "for-head of our state" (I.ii.7), Ambitioso speaks of the "iron for-head" of the law (I.ii.37), Vindici tells Castiza her forehead will "dazle the world with Jewels" if she submits to Lussurioso (II.i.212–213), and had Gratiana succeeded as a bawd "that Office would have cling'd unto" her forehead (IV.iv.72). All these allusions to brow heraldry unite with the symbol of the skull in the revenge of Vindici on the Duke. The incestuous kisses of Spurio and the Duchess, one of which the lecherous Duke is forced to watch as he dies, eat into his forehead "like strong poyson" (II.ii.187–188), even as the corrosive poison from the skull of Gloriana hideously transforms his face.

The "grave" transformation of Gloriana, besides acting as a symbol of all the evil transformations in the world, is related in several ways to the tragic transformation of Vindici that the play dramatizes. "Still sighing ore deaths vizard," Vindici is immediately shown to be obsessed (I.i.54). Gloriana's death is the motivating force driving him to seek revenge, and we can trace the degeneration of his character through subtle changes in his attitude toward Gloriana and her skull: transformation begets transformation.

Gloriana's skull undergoes a fearful transformation into a

painted and masked semblance of a living woman when Vindici obtains his revenge. The power of paint and a mask to disguise death with the semblance of life indicates that masks and disguises are agents transforming more than the mere superficial appearances of things. Vindici disguises himself as Piato, thinking he can return to his "true" character at will, but as Piato he experiences a disillusionment that must permanently alter his outlook and his actions.

Vindici's lines referring to his entrance into the identity of Piato always suggest that the process is a transformation : "Ile quickly turne into another" (I.i.153); "What brother? am I farre inough from my selfe?" (I.iii.3). He even invokes "Impudence," the "Goddesse of the pallace," to alter his countenance and character :

> Strike thou my fore-head into dauntlesse Marble;
> Mine eyes to steady Saphires : turne my visage,
> And if I must needes glow, let me blush inward . . .
>
> (I.iii.7–12)

And when his disguise leads him to pretend to be Lussurioso's pander to Castiza, Vindici, having allowed himself to be "entered" by the "Indian divill" of gold, cries "Now let me burst, I've eaten Noble poyson./ We are made strange fellowes, brother, innocent villaines" (I.iii.191–192). A little later Hippolito rages against Lussurioso, "O villaine!/ To make such an unnaturall slave of me" (II.ii.12–13).

Masks and dissimulations abound as evil characters try to transform evil into a semblance of good, to rub "hell ore with hunny" (II.ii.26), and as the virtuous try to test the evil by pretending to be evil themselves.[41] Thus Castiza as well as

---

[41] Cf. Lacy Lockert, "The Greatest of Elizabethan Melodramas," in *The Parrott Presentation Volume,* ed. Hardin Craig (Princeton, 1935), pp. 103–126.

Vindici tempts Gratiana, pretending in IV, iv, to be ready to serve the pleasure of Lussurioso.

> A maske is treasons licence, that build upon;
> Tis murders best face when a vizard's on.
>
> (V.i.196–197)

Vindici builds upon this by appearing as Piato in the murder of the Duke, as a railing malcontent under his own name at the "murder" of Piato, and in the masque that is to end with the murder of Lussurioso.[42] Junior and his cohorts had worn "better faces then their owne,/ Being full of frawde and flattery" when they raped Antonio's wife during a masque (I.iv.35–36). Ambitioso and Supervacuo dissemble their true feelings under false tears and false rhetoric when they receive the report of what they presume to be the death of Lussurioso (III.vi.45–52). The ludicrous irony of their failure to secure Lussurioso's death through dissembling at this juncture does not deter them from wearing masks as "murders best face" in the revels of Act V in order to make another attempt on his life. Their earlier wiles have cost them the life of Junior, their younger brother; this time they are the agents of their own well-merited destruction.

The crucial transformations in the play are effected by poisoning, figurative or literal. One of those the Duke refers to when he says "Many a beauty have I turnd to poyson" is Gloriana (II.ii.357), and in repayment her skull poisons him. Vindici eats the "noble poyson" of Lussurioso's gold, and, as we have noted, the society as a whole is poisoned by gold. The transforming power of poisonous gold is related to the other symbols of transformation through the name "Piato" which Vindici chooses when he masks himself. This word

---

[42] Cf. Salingar, " 'The Revenger's Tragedy' and the Morality Tradition," pp. 409–410.

meant several things in Italian. One of them has been noted : ". . . flat, squat, cowred downe, hidden."[43] More subtly related to the meaning of the play is "plated."[44] As "oths in these daies are but the skin of gold" (III.i.8), the disguise of Vindici, after he is sacramentally poisoned by gold, is metaphorically a "plating" of gold over his features.

The sins of the ducal court are clearly those popularly regarded as "Italianate"; the people of the court are vainglorious, vengeful, treacherous, factious, dissembling, lustful and adulterous.[45] The central episode of the plot was probably derived from accounts of the murder of Duke Alessandro de Medici by Lorenzino, his nephew and bosom companion in vice. Alessandro asked Lorenzino to procure his sister Laudomia for his pleasure, and Lorenzino pretended to arrange a rendezvous. When Alessandro arrived, Lorenzino is supposed to have said, "My Lorde, I wil nowe goe seeke her, which can not enter into this chamber without blushing, howbeit I truste before to morrowe morning she wyll be very glad of you."[46] He then retired to re-enter not with Laudomia but with the villain Scoronconcolo, and after a fierce struggle they dispatched the duke. Lorenzino wished to finish his revenge by killing "five or sixe of them which were nerest to the Duke, and best beloved of him," but was persuaded to flee by his henchman.[47]

---

[43] R. A. Foakes, "On the Authorship of 'The Revenger's Tragedy,'" p. 135.

[44] John Florio, *A Worlde of Wordes* (London, 1598), p. 276, under the alternate spelling, "Piatto." Other meanings of the name, "platter" and "pleader," are considered below in Sections 3 and 4, respectively.

[45] These characteristics are ticked off in successive paragraphs of Fynes Moryson's account of Italians in *Shakespeare's Europe,* ed. Charles Hughes (London, 1903), pp. 402–413.

[46] William Painter, *The Palace of Pleasure* (London, 1566–7), ed. Joseph Jacobs (London, 1890), II, 77; the fifty-fourth novel.

[47] *Ibid.*, p. 78. An account of the whole affair is in G. F. Young's *The Medici* (New York, 1913), I, 506–508. Samuel Schoenbaum, in " 'The Revenger's Tragedy' : A Neglected Source," *NQ,* 195 (1950), 338,

Italy was a place where the English upper class could learn to exploit the poor,[48] a place from which it was thought many gentlemen and nobles of the court of Elizabeth had brought affectations and vices to poison England :

> *Italy,* the Paradice of the earth and the Epicures heaven, how doth it forme our yong master? . . . From thence he brings the art of atheisme, the art of epicurising, the art of whoring, the art of poysoning, the art of Sodomitrie. . . . it maketh a man an excellent Courtier, a curious carpet knight : which is, by interpretation, a fine close leacher, a glorious hipocrite. It is nowe a privie note amongst the better sort of men, when they would set a singular marke or brand on a notorious villaine, to say, he hath beene in *Italy.*[49]

In Nashe, as in *The Revenger's Tragedy,* the epitome of evil in royal courts is the Italianate :

> Tis rare to finde a true frend in Kings Pallaces : Either thou must be so miserable that thou fall into the hands of scornful pitie, or thou canst not escape the sting of envy. In one thought assemble the famous men of all ages, and tel me which of them all sate in the sun-shine of his soveraignes grace, or wext great of low beginnings, but he was spiteblasted, heaved at, & ill spoken of : and that of those that bare them most countenaunce. But were envy nought but wordes, it might

---

notes that the historical source is Lorenzino's murder of Alessandro. N. W. Bawcutt, in " 'The Revenger's Tragedy' and the Medici Family," *NQ,* 202 (1957), 192–193, points out that the story can be found in English in Painter, whom I've quoted, or in the twelfth novel of the Queen of Navarre's *Heptaméron,* included in the selection from that work published in England in 1597. Pierre Legouis, in "Réflexions Sur la Recherche des Sources à Propos de la 'Tragedie du Vengeur,' " *Etudes Anglaises,* XII (1959), 47-55, also discusses these sources.

[48] Lewis Einstein, *The Italian Renaissance in England* (New York, 1902), p. 142.

[49] Thomas Nashe, *The Unfortunate Traveller, Or, the Life of Jacke Wilton* (London, 1594), in *Works,* ed. McKerrow, II, 301.

seeme to bee onely womens sinne : but it hath a lewde mate
hanging on his sleeve, called Murther, a sterne fellowe, that
(like a Spanyard in fight) aymeth all at the heart : hee hath
more shapes than *Proteus,* and will shifte himselfe, uppon any
occasion of revengement, into a mans dish, his drinke, his
apparell, his ringes, his stirrops, his nosegay.

O Italie, the Acadamie of man-slaughter, the sporting place
of murther, the Apothecary-shop of poyson for all Nations :
how many kind of weapons hast thou invented for malice?[50]

Under hypocrisy Nashe comprehends :

all Machiavilisme, puritanisme, and outward gloasing with a
mans enemie, and protesting friendship to him that I hate and
meane to harme, all under-hand cloaking of bad actions with
Common-wealth pretences; and, finally, all Italionate convey-
ances, as to kill a man, and then mourne for him, *quasi vero*
it was not by my consent, to be a slave to him that hath injur'd
me, and kisse his feete for opportunitie of revenge, . . . to
use men for my purpose and then cast them off, to seeke his
destruction that knowes my secrets; and such as I have
imployed in any murther or stratagem, to set them privilie
together by the eares, to stab each other mutually, for feare
of bewraying me; or, if that faile, to hire them to humor one
another in such courses as may bring them both to the
gallowes. These, and a thousand more such sleights, hath
hypocrisie learned by travailing strange Countries.[51]

These passages precisely describe the Italy given to us in *The
Revenger's Tragedy,* and we can see throughout them the
shadows of Lussurioso and Vindici. England and the English
court have eaten the "noble poyson" of the Italianate, and now
England is "the Players stage of gorgeous attyre, the Ape of all

---

[50] *Pierce Penilesse His Supplication to the Divell* (London, 1592), ed.
McKerrow, I, 186.
[51] *Ibid.,* p. 220.

Nations superfluities, the continuall Masquer in outlandish habilements."[52]

The author of *The Revenger's Tragedy* is not primarily dramatizing Italian decadence or the corrupting influence of Italy on England, however. He is rather, as Robert Ornstein suggests, using Italy as a convenient model for representing *English* evils, whether those evils be native or imported.[53] The social and economic abuses castigated by Vindici in his tirades against usury, and against farmers' sons who have decided to become gentlemen, are English and clearly so, aimed at the typical targets of most satirists of the period. In later sections of this chapter I shall consider the various elements of the play's satire as they become relevant to the tragic action. It is important not to try to discuss the satire apart from the tragedy, for this would tend to separate the satire from the play as a whole and make it seem to be bitter ranting by the author when it is really an integral part of the characterization and the development of dramatic theme. After discussing the action of the play in the next section, I shall examine its structure as a moral allegory and then finally come to the question of the author's relation to the bitterness of Vindici's satire and to the evil of the world of the play.

3   THE PLAY'S STRUCTURE AND THE DAMNATION OF VINDICI

The play's structure can be best perceived if we define its unifying action of *transformation* as going out in one form and returning in another. This formulation is broad enough to describe the arrangement of events in the plot structure, to define the dramatic and verbal ironies and poetic justices, and to shed some light on the tragedy of Vindici-Piato.

---

[52] Nashe, *Christs Teares over Jerusalem* (London, 1593), ed. McKerrow, II, 142.

[53] *The Moral Vision,* pp. 24–26, 116.

The action develops scene by scene to the climax at the virtual center of the play in the murder of the old Duke (III.v); in the second half a series of scenes parallel in reverse the scenes of the first half and so afford ironic contrasts with them. Thus in I,iii, Vindici hires himself to Lussurioso as Piato in order to penetrate the court and get his revenge. This action leads him to subvert and then to curse his mother. Paralleling this, in IV,i–ii, Vindici hires himself to Lussurioso, ostensibly so that Lussurioso can get *his* revenge on Piato, and Lussurioso is led to attack and unwittingly to curse his dead father.

In II,i Vindici overcomes Gratiana, and she attempts to subvert Castiza. Reversing this, in IV,iv Gratiana is reconverted to good and Castiza pretends to try to subvert *her*.

In I,ii the Duke, conducting the trial of Junior for a crime of which he, too, is guilty, lets him *escape* for the time and seems concerned only for his own "honor," not for justice. At the end of the play the wheel comes full circle, and Antonio, the new duke, *condemns* Vindici and Hippolito for a crime of which he, too, may be morally guilty, and appears to be concerned primarily for his own welfare. Human justice is lacking at the end of the play as at the beginning.

The incidents of the play also imitate the action of "going forth in one form and returning in another" in dramatic irony and poetic justice. Reversals of action occur at every point in the development of the plot. The multiple reversals of the denouement, bloodily transforming the expectations of Lussurioso and his stepbrothers, culminate in the irony of Vindici's fate. Even though he knows that only "an Asse" would reveal himself as a murderer, and that he has been secure in the ducal palace only because he has masked his identity and dissembled his true intentions, his pride in his wit is so great that he cannot resist bragging about the clever way the old Duke was murdered. Antonio is the one man in the court whom Vindici trusts to be of a mind with himself, since the wrongs they have suffered at the hands of the ducal family are so alike; yet it is Antonio who destroys him.

The irony in all these incidents is "that in the imminent shadow of death man should strive to damn himself."[54] Vindici sees this, and in the closing lines of his opening soliloquy and in his long speeches in the climactic III,v, he preaches sermons on the vanity of sin, opposing the reality of the skull to the sensuality of the court. Nevertheless—and this is the tragic irony of Vindici's character—his obsessions drive him likewise to embrace damnation.

At the end of the seventeenth century, evidently through the error of Gerard Langbaine, *The Revenger's Tragedy* acquired an alternate title, *The Loyal Brother*.[55] This title was no doubt preserved by subsequent editors because it focuses so many ironies of the play and reveals important elements in the structure of the plot. First consider Vindici and Hippolito as loyal brothers. Loyal they are to each other, yet they lead one another into a course of action that can end only in death. And in what does their loyalty to Castiza consist? They would preserve her honor at any cost, but behave as though they hoped to corrupt her! Ambitioso, Supervacuo and Junior are stepbrothers of Lussurioso, who is a half-brother of Spurio. There is little loyalty between Lussurioso and Spurio or between either of them and any of their stepbrothers. The relation of Ambitioso and Supervacuo to their youngest brother is, however, remarkably similar to that of Vindici and Hippolito to Castiza. The "loyalties" and the events they motivate are arranged so that there are many ironic contrasts-

---

[54] Lisca, *op. cit.*, p. 246.

[55] Nicoll, p. 18n of intro. to *The Works of Cyril Tourneur*. Eighteenth-century compilers probably met the alternate title not in Langbaine's 1688 dictionary—in which, as Nicoll notes, *The Revenger's Tragedy* is omitted and *The Loyal Brother* listed under Tourneur—but in *The Lives and Characters of The English Dramatick Poets*, "First begun by Mr. Langbain . . . ," ed. Charles Gildon (London, [1699?]), where, on p. 142, appears the entry "*The Loyal Brother; or The Revenger's Tragedy*, 4to."

in-parallel between the quest of Vindici and Hippolito for revenge and of Supervacuo and Ambitioso for power.

Thus the desire of Vindici and Hippolito to guard their sister is paralleled in the desire of Ambitioso and Supervacuo to save Junior. In each case the brothers enter into false pleading that ironically endangers their intentions. Ambitioso's hypocritical "we are sory/ That we are so unnaturally employde/ In such an unkinde Office, fitter farre/ For enemies then brothers," spoken when he and Supervacuo hope to have Lussurioso executed, would be sincere if he knew the result would be the death of Junior, and could as well be spoken by Vindici in reference to his attempt to procure Castiza (III.iii.4–7).

Later this parallel is carried further in juxtaposed scenes of Act IV (iii–iv). First we see Ambitioso and Supervacuo considering when to use their rapiers to end the dishonor caused by their mother's incestuous lust for Spurio. Then "*Enter* Vindice *and* Hippolito, *bringing out there Mother one by one shoulder, and the other by the other, with daggers in their hands*," preparing to purge her of the dishonorable office of bawd to her own daughter. At the end of the play the "para'lel" gives way to virtual fusion, and the author makes us see that the drive of Vindici and Hippolito to transform an evil court into a good one by violence ends in the same way as the drive of Supervacuo and Ambitioso to overthrow the state and obtain power for themselves.[56] Supervacuo and Ambitioso mask

---

[56] It is obvious that Supervacuo should die along with Ambitioso and Spurio at V, iii, 66–82—not simply disappear without a trace. Commentators have suggested that the text is garbled here, as it may be at the end of V, i, in the assignment of speeches to Supervacuo and Ambitioso. All through their conspiracy against Lussurioso in Acts II–IV, Ambitioso has seemed to be the older of the two (see especially the opening lines of III, i). C. S. Napier, in a letter on *The Revenger's Tragedy* in *TLS*, 3/13/37, p. 188, argues that in V, iii, the author has forgotten which brother is older, and that Supervacuo, not Spurio, should have the line, "Then I proclaime my selfe, now I am Duke" (V. iii. 78). Clifford Leech makes the same suggestion in "A Speech-Heading in

themselves in the revels to murder Lussurioso, and Vindici and his party do the same. In fact, Vindici and Hippolito will be physically indistinguishable from Supervacuo and Ambitioso :

> The Masking suites are fashioning, now comes in
> That which must glad us all—wee to take patterne
> Of all those suites, the colour, trimming, fashion,
> E'en to an undistinguisht hayre almost.

(V.ii.16–19)

Nearly every character in the play makes an attempt to transform something or someone. Those who are not busy trying to subvert justice, overturn the state or seduce others are trying to reform sinners or purge the evil court and make it good through blood revenge. Vindici is, of course, chief among those pursuing this last course of action. *Vindici* signifies "a revenger of wrongs. a redresser of things, and abuses. a defender, one that restoreth and setteth at libertie or out of danger, a punisher of things done amisse."[57] But it would be a mistake to assume that the title of *The Revengers Tragœdie* refers only to the revenge of Vindici.[58] Nearly all the evil figures of the ducal court are motivated at some time in the play by a desire for revenge : the Duchess against the Duke for not sparing Junior, Spurio against the Duke for his bastardy, Supervacuo and Ambitioso against Lussurioso for the death of Junior, Lussurioso against Piato for leading him to attack his

---

The Revengers Tragaedie," *RES*, XVII (1941), 335–336. At least as probably correct is the change—also resulting in the death of Supervacuo—suggested by Eugene M. Waith in "The Ascription of Speeches in *The Revenger's Tragedy*," *MLN*, LVII (1942), 119–121. He would add V, iii, 78 to the end of Ambitioso's speech, and give the next line to Supervacuo.

[57] *Florio, A Worlde of Wordes*, p. 449.

[58] Henry Hitch Adams discusses the multiple revenges of the play in "Cyril Tourneur on Revenge."

father's bed, and Ambitioso and Supervacuo against Spurio for his incest with their mother. These peripheral revenge actions parody the aims of Vindici, keeping ever in view the possibility that "Revenge" may serve no good purpose.

To transform evil into good, Vindici enters upon a course of action in which he transforms good into evil: as he purges the court, he creates a terrible darkness in his own soul. At the beginning of the play he has our sympathy, for surely his desire for revenge is well motivated. His betrothed—tantamount to a wife in Elizabethan England[59]—has been treacherously murdered and his father allowed to die in neglect and discontent. The second scene of the play demonstrates the corruption of court justice in a parallel case, suggesting that if Vindici would see his injuries requited he must use his own devices.

An understanding of the expected attitudes of the audience toward the Revenger in such a play may serve to illuminate Vindici's character and its transformation. There seems to have been no universally accepted doctrine of revenge. The orthodox Christian position was that God would avenge: "Vindicta Mihi." This divine vengeance might be direct and miraculous, or it might come through magistrates, or it might occur through the mental agonies of the wicked. There was no place for private revenge.[60] English law likewise forbade private revenge, holding it to be no more than premeditated murder.[61]

Vindici's victims are the rulers of the state, and his acts are therefore not only murder but regicide. Though such victims

---

[59] Bowers, *Elizabethan Revenge Tragedy*, p. 132.

[60] Lily Bess Campbell, *Shakespeare's Tragic Heroes: Slaves of Passion* (Cambridge, 1930), p. 24; also her "Theories of Revenge in Renaissance England." John Reynolds, in *The Triumphs of Gods Revenge Against the Crying and Execrable Sinne of (Wilful and Premeditated) Murther,* 5th ed. (London, 1670), includes both miraculous punishments and judicial trials among his stories. Innocents who murder for revenge have embraced malice (the devil), and must die.

[61] Bowers, *op. cit.,* p. 10.

might be tyrants, the doctrine of the Tudor and Stuart monarchs and of the Reformed Church was that subjects must obey tyrants and that kings could be punished only by God.[62]

Alongside these official Tudor and Reformed traditions opposing private revenge was an older tradition, not officially accepted, but alive among the people, which did sanction revenge. The doctrine of revenge inherited from the ancients sanctioned private revenge for blood kin, but urged that moderation must govern the revenge, which should be motivated by a desire for justice and not by passion.[63] Early medieval theorists had supported tyrannicide and Sidney, in Book II of the *Arcadia*, calls it heroic.[64] Though the courts forbade *murder* as revenge for *murder*, victims of *mayhem* were permitted to retaliate in kind.[65] In this the doctrine of "Vindica Mihi" was balanced by the Old Testament doctrine of vengeance in the law of "an eye for an eye." Both were living moralities in early seventeenth-century England, and even some protestants accepted the idea of revenge.[66]

The net result was that the English people expected a man to see that the murder of his kin was avenged. If civil justice did not take effect, or if the wrong suffered had been perpetrated inhumanly, so that the reprisals of civil justice were insufficient to repay truly, private revenge was accepted.[67]

---

[62] Sister Mary Bonaventure Mroz, *Divine Vengeance* (Washington, 1941), pp. 88–89, 140.

[63] *Ibid.*, p. 115.

[64] *Ibid.*, pp. 85–88, 92–93.

[65] Willard Thorp, *The Triumph of Realism in Elizabethan Drama, 1558–1612*, Princeton Studies in English, No. 3 (Princeton, 1928), p. 128.

[66] Mroz, *op. cit.*, pp. 72–73. Thus Thomas Beard and Thomas Taylor, two "reverend Doctors in Divinity," in speaking of "God's Judgements of Murtherers," quote God speaking to Noah: "Whosoever sheddeth mans bloud, by man also shall his bloud be shed." In several stories in the book, tyrants and villains are killed by private individuals who go unpunished. *The Theatre of Gods Judgements*, 4th ed. (London, 1648), pp. 185, 206, etc.

[67] Mroz, *op. cit.*, pp. 71 and 79. This summation is generally supported by modern authorities. *Cf.* Bowers, *op. cit.*, pp. 37, 39–40, 10, and 35.

Furthermore, the instinct to avenge kin-murder was regarded as a manifestation of natural law, the final court of appeal; the avenger suffered no pangs of conscience so long as his revenge did not exceed the bounds of right nature.[68]

The revenge of passion, however, was always thought of as evil. Barnabe Barnes, in *Foure Bookes of Offices,* identifies passion-revenge with cruelty:

> Against gentlenesse being the second part of temperance, the devouring fire, vengeance, or crueltie, standeth opposite: Adjunct thereto, mercilesse, or (as it were) steeled immanitie.[69]

Such revenge proceeds from man's animal nature, for the passions have physiological causes. Choler makes the blood boil, furious vapors in spirits blind the eyes, and the person is transported beside himself. This revenge of passion is often personified as "envious Ate," a Fury, or "*Revenge* who makes her abode in hell."[70]

The Italian doctrine of revenge is stated in Elizabethan adaptations such as Sir William Segar's *The Booke of Honor and Armes:* "for revenge of . . . cowardlie and bestiall offences, it is allowable to use any advantage or subtiltie, according to the Italian proverbe, *Ad una sopercheria, si conviene un'altra sopercheria, & ad un tradimento un altro tradimento,* which is, that one advantage requireth another, and one treason may be with another acquited."[71] In the Italian popular tradition, private revenge was admissible when the law did not act. Once private revenge was undertaken, there were standards to be met. The revenge had to destroy the spirit as well as the body

---

[68] Mroz, *op. cit.,* p. 80. See also Ernst De Chickera, "Palaces of Pleasure: The Theme of Revenge in Elizabethan Translations of Novelle," *RES,* XI (1960), 1–7.

[49] (London, 1606), p. 16. Quoted from Mroz, *op. cit.,* p. 108.

[70] Mroz, *op. cit.,* pp. 106–108.

[71] (London, 1590), p. 20.

of the victim, in order for the pride of the revenger to be assuaged.[72]

The more treacherous and cruel "Italianate" revenges were condemned by the English, who feared their importation.[73] The Italians were reputed to exact a terrible penalty for even the slightest injury, to carry on long vendettas in which isolated enemies were overwhelmed by bands of ruffians, to destroy accomplices when they had outlived their usefulness, and to torture their dying victims in both body and soul so as to secure their damnation:[74] "Such are those which tyrannize over captives, persons prostrated; nay, such will not spare the dead, but like wilde beastes feede upon them with the fangues of malicious and venemous rancour."[75]

Since Vindici's betrothed has been murdered and no civil justice is possible, we may conclude that Elizabethan audiences would sympathize with his desire for vengeance. His name would suggest to them, though, that as the very personification of *Italianate Revenge,* he would eventually prove a passionate Fury, malicious "above thought" (III.v.112).

Most of the characters in the play are but two-dimensional figures, constructing the façade of the popular English conception of an evil court. Vindici, however, is a complex and ambiguous figure, difficult to analyze. Some critics, baffled by his complexity, have regarded him as a dramatic failure— as a character not complex but merely contradictory and therefore unconvincing. Because they can see no coherently expressed moral attitudes, these critics condemn the play as meaningless.[76] Then, having found no dramatic basis for Vin-

---

[72] Jacob Burckhardt, *The Civilization of the Renaissance in Italy,* trans. S. G. C. Middlemore, (New York, 1904), p. 227.

[73] Bowers, *op. cit.,* p. 55.

[74] *Ibid.,* pp. 51–52.

[75] Barnes, *loc. cit.,* quoted from Mroz, *op. cit.,* p. 108.

[76] Chief among those inclining toward the view that the play has no ethical purpose, that it fails to "assimilate different attitudes," is Madeleine Doran, *Endeavors of Art* (Madison, 1954), pp. 94, 358.

dici's character, they attribute his bitterness to his creator. To prove these criticisms groundless and so to free the dramatist of the burden of Vindici's sick emotions, we must demonstrate the dramatic validity of his character, following step by step the evil transformation he suffers.

Vindici's soliloquy opening the play subtly combines exposition and characterization. In the first few lines he shows us his enemies and tells of their lust, the appetite which will enable him to penetrate their citadel and destroy them. Then he turns to the skull of Gloriana, contrasts her former beauty with her present "ragged" state, and tells of her murder by the old Duke. The speech ends with his assertion of the motive to revenge that is to mold his action.

Though the opening lines of the soliloquy employ the modes and terms of chorus and satire, I think it a mistake to regard Vindici as receding "into his plot-part" only when he turns to the skull,[17] for he is at no time a detached commentator. Every word reveals his motivation and the triple obsession with death, usury and lust controlling his behavior. He turns from the *lusts* of the ducal family to the *skull* of Gloriana, and from his determination for *revenge* to the vanity of *costly* flesh. These obsessions are closely linked with one another in all of Vindici's words and actions.[18] Whoredom is "usury" throughout the play, and in the opening speech itself are such epitomizing lines as "Age as in gold, in lust is covetous," and "*Vengence* thou murders/ Quit-rent,[19] and whereby/ Thou shoust thy selfe Tennant to Tragedy" (I.i.41–43).

---

[17] Inga-Stina Ekeblad, "An Approach to Tourneur's Imagery," p. 495.

[18] *Cf.* the parallel discussions of these obsessions in Fluchère, *op. cit.,* pp. 63, 81; Ornstein, *The Moral Vision,* p. 110; Parrott and Ball, *op. cit.,* p. 217, and especially John Peter, "*The Revenger's Tragedy* Reconsidered," *EIC,* VI (1956), 132–133.

[19] Quit-rent: "Established rents of freeholders and ancient copyholders of a manor, which could not be departed from or varied. . . . The tenant was quit and free of all other services." Paul S. Clarkson and Clyde T.

The final union of lust with death comes, of course, when the lustful Duke kisses the skull of Gloriana and suffers the sadistic "minute" of Vindici's vengeance instead of the expected "bewitching minute" of sexual rapture (III.v.78,126). The image of the lustful usurer's son, introduced in I,i,29–32, culminates in a fusion of lustful usury with death after the old Duke is dead, when Vindici is pretending that he is a "parlous melancholy," having "wit enough/ To murder any man" (IV.ii.105–106). Then he momentarily cuts Lussurioso to the nerve with a terrifying image :

A usuring Father to be boyling in hell,
and his sonne and Heire with a Whore dancing over him.
                                                        (IV.ii.90–91)

Vindici's obsessions are the natural consequences of the wrongs he has suffered. His betrothed has been murdered by an old lecher, and his father has died in poverty caused by the Duke's disfavor (I.i.136–143; III.v.180–182). A nobleman's son suffering in honest poverty, he vents his spleen against the corrupt, opportunistic, "usuring" commercial class he sees destroying the remnants of the feudal society and its values.[80] Although Vindici's chief motive for murdering the Duke is to revenge the murder of Gloriana which has occurred nine years before the action of the play begins (III.v.126), it seems that he has reached his present state of mind only after the more recent death of his father :

For since my worthy fathers funerall,

Warren, *The Law of Property in Shakespeare and the Elizabethan Drama* (Baltimore, 1942), p. 96.
[80] John D. Peter notes that in part the usurer and "The impoverished gentleman's son" go together as cause and effect; *Complaint and Satire in Early English Literature,* p. 128.

My life's unnaturally to me, e'en compeld
As if I liv'd now when I should be dead.

(I.i.133–135)

The macabre association of sexuality and death, nine years in
the making as the skull came clean, now is fused with the
newer emotions rising from the death of his father.

Critics write of Vindici's cynicism and of his attitude toward
women as though these were undramatic, not changing in
response to events in the play,[81] and therefore to be attributed
to the author. This is surely an error. Vindici's attitudes alter
radically after he succeeds in persuading his mother to prosti-
tute her own daughter. When the play opens, Vindici is
already cynical, in a general sense, but his misanthropy seems
well founded. As we can see for ourselves, the ducal family are
lecherous murderers and there is no justice in the state. Antonio
seems just as cynical as Vindici (I.iv.59–61). Where Vindici
has reason to believe in virtue—in the memory of Gloriana, in
his mother and sister—he is ready enough to do so until he
is (as he thinks) proved wrong. Then, indeed, he yields to
despair.

The belief in feminine chastity is obsessive with Vindici : he
must retain faith in the virtue of Gloriana or be utterly lost.
In order to believe in Gloriana, he must also believe in the
chastity of his sister. For him the lust of Lussurioso for Castiza
leads to a nightmarish transformation of his role in relation to
Gloriana at the time of her murder. As Fluchère notes, Vindici
is driven by his obsession to tempt Castiza so that he can prove
the existence of the value his vengeance is to affirm.[82] When

---

[81] E.g., Ornstein, "The Ethical Design of The Revenger's Tragedy,"
ELH, XXI (1954), p. 86; Sidney Thomas, The Antic Hamlet and
Richard III (New York, 1943), p. 49; Lockert, op. cit., pp. 123–124;
Alvin Kernan, The Cankered Muse: Satire of the English Renaissance
(New Haven, 1959), p. 229.
[82] Fluchère, op. cit., p. 65.

Gratiana turns bawd, his faith in Castiza's virtue is shaken. The effect of this disillusionment upon his attitude toward the dead Gloriana is dramatized in his treatment of her as the Duke's concubine during the murder scene. Thus it is at least as much the unnaturalness of his treatment of Gloriana as the unnaturalness of his revenge against the Duke that is the measure of his departure from himself.

The shifting attitudes of Vindici toward women in general and toward Gloriana, Castiza and Gratiana in particular can best be seen first of all in his short speeches having immediate and obvious relevance to the action. Although in the early scenes he does not exonerate women from sexual guilt, he usually blames men for lust up until Gratiana turns bawd in II,i. Women are primarily "easie in beleefe," and Vindici dares, significantly, to stake his soul on the virtue of Castiza and Gratiana (I.i.105–108). The second scene, after showing the corruption of justice, ends with the Duchess seducing Spurio. By way of contrast, in the fourth scene we see the fate of the virtuous wife of Antonio in this perverted world. Vindici is on stage in neither scene, and the most striking effect of the contrast is to dramatize for the benefit of the audience the alternative views of woman with which he is struggling.

Vindici thinks he can resist corruption by the world, that he can "put on" the character of pander "for once" and return to himself safely, and perhaps he is not quite serious when he calls Lussurioso's payment of money to him a sign of his possession by the devil. He does not know the form temptation will take for him. He cynically says "Our maides are wiser; and are lesse ashamd" than the virtuous maids of long ago (I.iii.17), and disguised as Piato he claims to "have beene witnesse/ To the surrenders of a thousand virgins" (I.iii.54–55), but even in the guise of Piato, when Lussurioso suggests that he try to make a bawd of Gratiana, he bursts out :

> O fie, fie, that's the wrong end my Lord. Tis meere impossible
> that a mother by any gifts should become a bawde to her
> owne Daughter! (I.iii.170–172)

Lussurioso's reply strikes directly to the heart of Vindici's
obsession:

> Nay then I see thou'rt but a puny in the subtill Mistery of
> a woman:—why tis held now no dainty dish: The name
> Is so in league with age that now adaies
> It do's Eclipse three quarters of a Mother.
> (I.iii.173–176)

Lussurioso means that the reward of bawdry nowadays over-
whelms the loyalties of motherhood, but his lines, through the
metaphor of "dish" for bawd, apply directly to Vindici. As
Piato he is "a platter, a dish, a charger, a plate, a messe or
dish of meat . . . a course served in at any feast,"[83] and the
common idea that lust is an appetite is projected everywhere
in the play. Sexuality thrives amid banquets and revels, and
the characters speak of lust in terms of eating. Lussurioso
would "tast of that yong Lady" (II.ii.174), and Antonio
describes how Junior had "long lust to eat/ Into" his chaste
lady, and so in a revel "fed the ravenous vulture of his lust"
(I.iv.38–39, 50). Lussurioso's lines, then, at once suggest that
"Piato" can eclipse the mother and seize upon Vindici's obsession by suggesting he is but a "puny" in the "subtill Mistery
of a woman."

Though some scholars speak of the "purely arbitrary and
dissociated nature of Vindice's different personalities," it is
certainly not true that "the two halves of Vindice's character

---

[83] Florio, op. cit., p. 276, under Piatto; cf. his Queen Anna's New
World of Words (London, 1611), p. 378, for the recognition that Piato
and Piatto are alternate spellings of the same word.

are kept sharply distinct : it would be possible to draw a line
separating them off."[84] Vindici disguised as Piato is still clearly
Vindici. Piato has all Vindici's attitudes : at every step of the
conversation with Lussurioso he harps upon the sin of lust and
insists that damnation is its consequence.[85] Not even in his
willingness to undertake evil does Piato move beyond Vindici,
for it was as Vindici that he decided to enter upon the role of
pander. The new name and the disguise are intended to fool
Lussurioso, but *we* should not be fooled by them into seeing
a contradiction of character where none in fact exists.

Lussurioso makes Vindici swear to serve him truly, and
almost immediately Vindici says "I've eaten Noble poyson,"
and that he has become an "innocent villain" (I.iii.191–192).
Vindici is not actually corrupted by Lussurioso's gold. He
regards his acceptance of the gold as a kind of ritual whereby
he is obliged to swear that he will serve Lussurioso. He believes
that it is this oath, in turn, which compels him to tempt Castiza
and Gratiana, although he is in fact compelled by his sexual
obsession. He rationalizes this compulsion in the speech that
ends the third scene, concluding with an important couplet
reasserting his willingness to stake his soul upon their virtue :

> . . . I durst almost for good,
> Venture my lands in heaven upon their good.
>
> (I.iii.206–207)

---

[84] Muriel C. Bradbrook, *Themes and Conventions of Elizabethan
Tragedy,* pp. 166, 72. See also pp. 69, 130, 165. Elmer Edgar Stoll also
found Vindici "a mechanical combination of the incompatible, and in
themselves sufficiently unpleasant, individuals — malcontent, revenger, and
tool-villain, — he is too chaotic to be either a character or a moral entity."
John Webster, p. 129. Stoll's analyses of *The Revenger's Tragedy* and
The Atheist's Tragedy are marred by rather serious errors in reading. He
thinks the Duke has *murdered* Vindici's father, and that the father of
Castabella is D'Amville. *Ibid.,* pp. 105, 106, 112.

[85] *Cf.* John Peter's discussion of this matter in *"The Revenger's
Tragedy* Reconsidered," pp. 134ff.

When Castiza strikes him he rejoices, but still feels himself compelled to try Gratiana:

> Thou art approv'd for ever in my thoughts.
> It is not in the power of words to taynt thee,
> And yet for the salvation of my oth,
> As my resolve in that poynt; I will lay
> Hard siege unto my Mother, tho I know,
> A *Syrens* tongue could not bewitch her so.
>
> (II.i.56–61)

Even in his attempts to seduce Gratiana and Castiza, Vindici-Piato is frank in admitting that what he advocates is evil. He shares with the other sinners in the play an intense awareness of his own sin, and in view of his many expressions of this awareness it seems strange that a critic should apologize for suggesting that Vindici was aware of the evil of his own actions.[86] The only justification Vindici offers for whoredom and bawdry is summed up in the line, "Tis no shame to be bad, because tis common" (II.i.130). He then offers Lussurioso's gold to Gratiana, explicitly remarking the moral implication of her "entrance" by the "Indian divill": "can these perswade you/ To forget heaven—and—" (II.i.133–134). She is transformed into a bawd by the comfortable shine of the gold, and is no longer "troubled with the mother" (II.i.139–140).

Immediately Vindici recoils from himself in horror, fully aware of the evil he has performed:

> O suffring heaven with thy invisible finger,
> Ene at this Instant turne the pretious side
> Of both mine eye-balls inward, not to see my selfe.
>
> (II.i.142–144)

---

[86] John Peter, in a note on pp. 485–486 replying to T. W. Craik's note on "The Revenger's Tragedy," in *EIC,* VI (1956), pp. 482–485.

Castiza re-enters, and Vindici and Gratiana take turns trying
to break her resolve. Gratiana's arguments are consistently self-
interested, and they contrast in tone with Vindici's lines, which
throughout suggest implicitly or explicitly the evil of the course
he proposes, as in the following :

> 'Tis honestie you urge; what's honestie?
> 'Tis but heavens beggar . . .
>
> (II.i.204–205)

When Castiza denounces them both, Vindici rejoices, thinking
the trial of her virtue at an end. Then comes the final blow to
his faith, causing him to have a lingering doubt of the virtue
of Castiza. Gratiana says :

> Peevish, coy, foolish—but returne this answer,
> My Lord shall be most welcome, when his pleasure
> Conducts him this way. I will sway mine owne;
> Women with women can worke best alone.
>
> (II.i.268–271)

This speech marks the turning point in Vindici's attitude
toward women. From this moment onward he tends to blame
evil sexuality more on women than on men :

> Wert not for gold and women; there would be no damnation,
> Hell would looke like a Lords Great Kitchin without fire in't;
> But 'twas decreed before the world began,
> That they should be the hookes to catch at man.
>
> (II.i.278–281)

He has wagered his soul on Castiza and Gratiana, and he is
losing it.

In the following scene Vindici reports his success with

Gratiana to Lussurioso. Already he fears Castiza has yielded to her mother's importunities:

> But she is close and good;—yet 'tis a doubt by this time;
> oh the mother, the mother? (II.ii.37–38)

Again he must do evil, compelled by his oath, and again he is keenly aware of his own sin:

> Now must I blister my soule, be forsworne,
> Or shame the woman that receiv'd mee first.
> I will be true, thou liv'st not to proclaime;
> Spoke to a dying man, shame ha's no shame.
> (II.ii.41–44)

But Vindici is wrong; the shame *does* out because of his refusal, shortly afterward, to murder Lussurioso while his back is turned (II.ii.101–103). As a result we have the ironic cross-parallel of Spurio going to trap Lussurioso stealing "Unto *Hippolitoes* sister, whose chast life/ The mother has corrupted for his use" (II.ii.138–139), and Lussurioso going to trap, as he thinks, Spurio in bed with the Duchess.[87]

Vindici's judgment of himself and his mother, his consciousness of moral error, and his gnawing, obsessive fears for his sister are all expressed in his one real soliloquy in this scene:

---

[87] G. K. Hunter, in "A Source for *The Revenger's Tragedy*," *RES*, X (1959), 181–182, suggests that this incident in which Lussurioso, misinformed by Vindici, rushes into his father's bedchamber, is probably derived from Heliodorus' *Æthiopian History* as Englished by Thomas Underdowne, 1587 (London, 1895), pp. 20ff. The stepmother is in love with the son, but he repulses her advances. She gets revenge by sending false information through a servant (female, it seems) that the father is gone and the stepson and the mother are abed. The son rushes in with drawn sword, is amazed at the sight of his father, drops the sword (which the stepmother seizes) and is bound. Hunter notes parallel phrasing in Cnemon's saying "Where is that same villaine" (*cf.* Lussurioso's "Where is that villain"). Also, Cnemon "stood still amased" (Lussurioso is "amazed to death"). Hunter thinks later versions of the story in Sidney's old and new *Arcadia* do not afford parallels so close.

Forgive me heaven, to call my mother wicked,
Oh lessen not my daies upon the earth.
I cannot honor her; by this I feare me
Her tongue has turnd my sister into use.
I was a villaine not to be forsworne
To this our lecherous hope, the Dukes sonne,
For Lawiers, Merchants, some divines and all,
Count beneficiall perjury a sin small.
It shall go hard yet, but ile guard her honor
And keepe the portes sure.

                                        (II.ii.106–115)

Before the end of this scene Vindici retires from the stage in some confusion, and we do not see him again until his despair about "chastity" has led him to offer Gloriana's painted skull to the lustful Duke. Transported by violent joy over the ingenuity of his revenge, Vindici has forgotten his original purpose, to affirm the chastity of Gloriana. Hippolito asks where the Duke's new concubine is, and Vindici replies:

Oh at that word,
I'me lost againe, you cannot finde me yet
I'me in a throng of happy Apprehensions.

                                        (III.v.31–33)

He is indeed lost, and does not perceive that as the procurer of Gloriana his "outward shape, and inward heart/ Are cut out of one peice" (III.v.11–12). When Vindici unmasks the lady, Hippolito sees in an instant the horror of the situation, and can only murmur "Why brother, brother" (III.v.53). The Duke arrives, and Vindici ironically comments on his procurement of Gloriana: "now come and welcome Duke,/ I have her for thee" (III.v.113–114). As he replaces her mask he says "Hide thy face now for shame" (III.v.117). Vindici's revenge is perfect in its ironic retaliation against the Duke, but it destroys the moral value of Gloriana's martyrdom, making a whore and a murderess of her :

> Villaines all three !—the very ragged bone
> Has beene sufficiently revengd.
>
> (III.v.162–163)

Vindici acknowledges himself a villain and a knave, but when the Duke asks "Is there a hell besides this, villaines?" he insists on the *justice* of his villainy : "Villaine?/ Nay heaven is just, scornes are the hire of scornes" (III.v.196–198).

Thus, to suppose Vindici is as cynical about women at the beginning as after his subornation of Gratiana is to miss much of the point of the play. There is no inconsistency and no significant change in his character immediately upon his assuming the role of Piato; the real change comes when, *after* becoming Piato and entering upon a course of action he knows is evil, he is forced to accept the cynical view of women characteristic of the pander, and consequently is driven to perform an act betraying his original goals. The peculiarly "Italianate" aspects of his revenge would, of course, be noted by the audience as confirmation that he has exceeded the bounds of human decency.

The shift in Vindici's attitudes toward Gloriana and in his ideas about the sexuality of women is subtly suggested in parallel speeches delivered before and after his disillusionment. First there are the "skull" speeches—the one opening the play and the one preceding the murder of the Duke. In the first the emphasis is on the tragic contrast between the skull's "ragged imperfections" and the former *natural* glory of his love—"a face/ So farre beyond the artificiall shine/ Of any womans bought complexion/ That the uprightest man" sinned by looking after her (I.i.21–28). *Men* sinned by looking after her, but she was not a coy, painting temptress, and any effort to buy her virtue failed (I.i.29–32). In the second of these speeches, after Vindici has painted Gloriana's skull, he rails against her "prety hanging lip, that has forgot now to dissemble" (III.v. 60). Hippolito reminds him that this is "the forme that living shone so bright," but Vindici chides himself "For doating on her beauty" (III.v.70,73). He can think only of the vanity of sin and of service to women.

In the soliloquy opening the play Vindici has recognized the bare skull as a reality to be contrasted with the dissemblers of the court, but this notion was carefully insulated from his belief in Gloriana's natural, unpainted beauty, so that he did not regard her "glory" as false. In the murder scene, however, the implication is that Gloriana in the flesh was not the reality. Vindici says that women paint and dress and dissemble to tempt men, and the skull of Gloriana herself is become proof that though ladies may deceive men "with false formes," they "cannot deceive wormes" (III.v.87–101).

The distinction between the two skull speeches is slight because in both the *memento mori* theme is dominant. A greater distinction in Vindici's thoughts on the sexuality of women occurs in the parallel "night" speeches, one before and one after his disillusionment. In the first, men are lechers; in the second, women are whores:

> Some father dreads not (gonne to bedde in wine) to slide
> > from the mother,
> And cling the daughter-in-law,
> Some Uncles are adulterous with their Neeces,
> Brothers with brothers wives, O howre of Incest!
> Any kin now next to the Rim ath sister
> Is mans meate in these dayes, and in the morning

When they are up and drest, and their maske on,
Who can perceive this? save that eternall eye
That see's through flesh and all, well :–If any thing be dambd,
It will be twelve a clock at night; that twelve
Will never scape;
It is the *Judas* of the howers; wherein,
Honest salvation is betrayde to sin.

(I.iii.67–79)

Night! thou that lookst like funerall Heraulds fees
Torne downe betimes ith morning, thou hangst fittly
To Grace those sins that have no grace at all.
Now tis full sea a bed over the world;
Theres jugling of all sides; some that were Maides
E'en at Sun set are now perhaps ith Toale-booke;
This woman in immodest thin apparell
Lets in her friend by water, here a Dame
Cunning, nayles lether-hindges to a dore,
To avoide proclamation.
Now Cuckolds are a quoyning, apace, apace, apace, apace.
And carefull sisters spinne that thread ith night,
That does maintaine them and their bawdes ith daie!

(II.ii.149–161)

The "spinning" metaphor in the second of these speeches is used similarly in "you shall have one woman knit more in a hower then any man can Ravell agen in seaven and twenty yeare" (II.ii.77–79). The image is repeated with the same connotations in the famous "silkworm" speech in III,v,75ff.

Despite all his admissions of guilt, it is Vindici's fundamental error to blame Gratiana too much and himself too little for acceding to the designs of Piato. He consistently maintains mental reservations about his identity with Piato, as when Castiza says Gratiana's attempt to subvert her would be better coming from Piato, and he thinks aloud, "Faith bad inough in both,/ Were I in earnest as Ile seeme no lesse" (II.i.200–201). In IV,iv, when Gratiana denies to Vindici what she has conceded to Piato, he may well wonder, "Oh I'me in doubt,/ Whether I'me my selfe, or no" (31–32). He continues to accuse her of being a wicked and unnatural mother, but she will not confess until he reveals that he has played the role of Piato, thinking this will confirm his mother's guilt. But her reply shows him the full extent of his responsibility for all that he has done:

> VIND. In that disguize, I sent from the Dukes sonne,
> Tryed you, and found you base mettell,
> As any villaine might have donne.
> MO. O no, no tongue but yours could have bewitcht me so.
> VIND. O nimble in damnation, quick in tune,
> There is no divill could strike fire so soone:
> I am confuted in a word.
>
> (IV.iv.39–45)

Then repentance "conjures" the "base divill" out of Gratiana, and Vindici believes in the possibility of virtue again:

> VIND. Nay Ile kisse you now: kisse her brother.
> Lets marry her to our soules, wherein's no lust,
> And honorably love her.
> HIP. Let it be.
> VIND. For honest women are so sild and rare,
> Tis good to cherish those poore few that are.
>
> (IV.iv.64–69)

Had he felt this way when he arranged the murder of the Duke, it is hard to believe he would have dishonored the dead Gloriana for the sake of his satanic "justice." In the following

scenes he attempts to purge himself of the character of Piato,
but he has gone too far under the influence of his disillusionment. The danger arising from his earlier error in letting
Lussurioso think he can procure Castiza is compounded when
Lussurioso becomes duke, and it is necessary to murder again
to prevent him from destroying her as the old Duke did
Gloriana. In the perpetration of this murder, by which he is
finally destroyed, Vindici is paralleled with the absurd
Ambitioso and Supervacuo. We are given a glimpse of his
perverted delight in murder when he laments Lussurioso's
escape from "the sweetest occasion, the fittest houre" to have
made his revenge a masterpiece of sadistic torment: "oh I'me
mad to loose such a sweete opportunity" (V.i.15,19).

Although Vindici believes his revenge to be necessary and
just, the play makes clear his ultimate realization that in his
betrayal of chastity he has been "nimble in damnation." His
moral perception is blinded at the moment when disillusion
cuts through to his sexual obsession, and he is driven to seek
sadistic revenges. Then the Duchess' accusation of the judges
who condemn Junior applies as well to Vindici: "Your too
much right, dos do us too much wrong" (I.ii.91).

Vindici is not judged only by his own self-accusations. At
the end of the play he is condemned by Antonio and hustled
off to execution. Some critics regard Antonio as a moral
touchstone and therefore see in his succession to power a
restoration of justice. I find it hard to accept this interpretation of Antonio; his judgment of Vindici seems to me rather
to be in a class with the old Duke's judgment of Junior. Since
the problem is crucial for interpretation of the play and since
there has been little agreement on it among critics, it demands
further consideration.

The critics who see in Antonio the return of justice and
order believe his revenge for the rape of his wife is of the right

sort. He accepts the oaths of Piero and Hippolito to murder
Junior providing they act only if the courts or heaven do not.
Junior is destroyed through a misunderstanding, and at the
end Antonio speaks of this as divine justice.[88] Fredson Bowers
thinks Antonio is a moral touchstone whose "common sense
horror" sends Vindici off to execution and so reveals him to
be a villain.[89] John Peter argues that Antonio's "Ire" of I,iv is
"grief and outraged virtue," and that by the end this ire has
cooled, so that he does not condone treason and murder, and
wants only justice.[90] These critics would agree with Lacy
Lockert that Antonio's condemnation of Vindici represents the
"ultimate restoration of ethical standards."[91]

Lockert goes on to add that Vindici has erred in thinking
Antonio's "chief motive is self-interest," and so has expected
Antonio to thank him for murdering the old Duke.[92] But self-
interest is precisely the motive to which other critics attribute
Antonio's condemnation of Vindici![93] As Lockert himself
points out, Vindici might have defended himself by arguing
that Antonio had already accepted the principle of blood
revenge in the case of the rape of his wife, and that only by
murdering the Duke could he right the wrongs Antonio had
suffered. Nevertheless, Vindici makes no attempt to explain
anything to Antonio.[94] Perhaps this last point is the key here :
Vindici sees Antonio's injustice and knows there is no use protesting. Certainly he has reason to doubt that truth will

---

[88] Adams, "Cyril Tourneur on Revenge," p. 78.
[89] *Elizabethan Revenge Tragedy*, p. 134.
[90] In his note at the end of T. W. Craik's "The Revenger's Tragedy."
[91] *Op. cit.*, p. 125. As Peter Lisca puts it, Vindici's death restores the
"moral balance" of the world. *Op. cit.*, p. 251.
[92] *Op. cit.*, p. 125.
[93] Robert Ornstein, "The Ethical Design of *The Revenger's Tragedy*,"
p. 87, T. W. Craik, "The Revenger's Tragedy," p. 484; Madeleine Doran,
Endeavors of Art, p. 358.
[94] *Op. cit.*, pp. 111–112.

prevail: Antonio has already condemned the nameless "4," accomplice of Supervacuo and Ambitioso, for the treasonous murder of Lussurioso—a crime he did not commit. Antonio has called "4" a "foule monster,/ Dipt in a Princes bloud"— although the illegitimate Spurio, his actual victim, is not in fact a prince (V.iii.105–106). Here, at any rate, Antonio is portrayed as deaf to the truth, as Lussurioso has been in the parallel scene in which he has condemned the gentleman who told the truth about his instructions from the Duke just before his murder. Vindici then has been led to observe: ". . . see what confession doth./ Who would not lie when men are hangd for truth?" (V.i.141 142) This point is confirmed in Antonio's condemnation of "4," and again when Vindici proclaims himself the murderer of the Duke.

Vindici is indeed guilty of treasonous murder, but he seems to have good reason to regard Antonio as the leader of the group of nobles with whom he plots against the life of Lussurioso. Antonio is introduced in I,iv through a stage direction as the *"the discontented Lord* ANTONIO, *whose wife* ~~Oedipal~~ *the Duchesses yongest Sonne ravisht; he Discovering the body of her dead to certaine Lords : and* HIPPOLITO" (I.iv.1–3). Not the "grieving" Antonio, but the "discontented" Antonio. "Discontented" is used elsewhere in this play to connote an *evil* character, or at any rate a character ambitious for advancement at court. Thus Vindici is later introduced to Lussurioso under his own name as a man "full of want and discontent," and Lussurioso immediately rejoices that "There's hope in him, for discontent and want/ Is the best clay to mould a villaine off" (IV.i.56–58).[95]

Throughout I,iv, Antonio does his best to work Hippolito, Piero and the others into a passion for revenge. His opening

---

[95] *Cf.* also IV, i, 80–82. In I, i, 142–143, Vindici says his father died "of discontent: the Noblemans consumption."

speech, with its obviously artificial metaphor describing his wife as "a fayre comely building newly falne,/ Being falsely undermined," is like the artificiality scheming dissemblers speak elsewhere, as when Ambitioso pretends to weep for the supposed death of Lussurioso (III.vi.49–52). Antonio seems to have prearranged the corpse of his wife to suit his purpose, and we are later reminded of his lack of honor for the dead when Vindici likewise "uses" the dead Gloriana to her dishonor. We cannot believe Antonio, who is not freshly discovering his wife's body, when he says "I markt not this before" and points out

> A prayer Booke the pillowe to her cheeke,
> This was her rich confection, and another
> Plac'd in her right hand, with a leafe tuckt up,
> Poynting to these words.
>   *Melius virtute mori, Quam per Dedecus vivere.*
>
>   (I.iv.18–23)

And then, just after Hippolito has said that light griefs speak but heavy ones are silent, Antonio launches into a speech of more than twenty lines about the rape of his lady! Antonio accepts the vow of Hippolito and the others to seek blood revenge— to put the youngest son to death before the court if justice is deferred when he returns from prison for sentencing. It is hard to see how Antonio supposes that this revenge can be accomplished without more bloodshed following.

In V,ii, Vindici meets with the same Piero who has supported Antonio's revenge in I,iv, and—presumably—the same lords who have supported Antonio in that earlier scene, and they prepare to murder Lussurioso, now duke. There is no thought that Antonio might condemn the murder of a duke.

When he proclaims Antonio duke, Vindici makes much of the hope that his "hayre will make the silver age agen,/ When

there was fewer but more honest men" (V.iii. 126–127), for-
getting for the moment the evil connotations built up around
silver hair, not to mention silver itself: the silver hair of the
Duke, that sorted so ill with his lechery, and Lussurioso's evil
implications about gray-beards:

> He that knowes great mens secrets, and proves slight,
> That man nere lives to see his Beard turne white:
>   . . .
> Slaves are but Nayles, to drive out one another.
>
> (IV.i.76–79)

Part of the irony of Vindici's destruction is that although he
has always been aware of his danger in acting as the tool of
the Machiavellian "policy" of Lussurioso, and has managed
to outwit him, he is now shown to have been used as a tool by
one who *has* lived to see his beard turn white, a discontented
"politician" who has used Vindici to destroy those who stand
between him and power. Vindici has praised his silver hair,
and Antonio cleverly turns the words back against him:

> . . . away with 'em; such an ould man as he,
> You that would murder him would murder me.
>
> (V.iii.147–148)

From this speech it is clear that no argument from right and
wrong can save the brothers: it will do Vindici no good to
speak of the crimes of the old Duke; it will do no good to
argue that Antonio himself has accepted blood revenge for
the rape of his wife, and has only a moment before accepted
all the murders as part of that revenge, as evidence of the
justice of the "Lawe above" (V.iii.130–132). Antonio now is
pleased to be classed with the old Duke, and perhaps he is
congratulating himself on his politic cleverness in catching
Vindici when he says "How subtilly was that murder closde!"
(V.iii.170).

But perhaps this is to go too far, and it certainly is to go farther than is necessary. Unfortunately we have no dramatic tradition to help us decide how Antonio was to be played—as a glossing hypocritical Machiavel or as an honest but impercipient old man. In either event the point immediately relevant here is that in the condemnation of "4" he is deaf to the truth and that his condemnation of Vindici and Hippolito is based on a misunderstanding of the situation. Antonio's verdict against Vindici and Hippolito is tainted because he shares their guilt, having accepted the principle of blood revenge. In the world of *The Revenger's Tragedy* human justice fails partly because any man who has lived long enough to understand life is bound to be too corrupted himself to judge others. Those who seek justice are no less corrupted than those who seek sensual pleasure or power. Analysis of the play's moral allegory will demonstrate that only those who accept divine grace can be transformed to the good; that the "salvation" possible through the means the world offers is not a salvation from hell-fire.

4   THE MORAL ALLEGORY

Through a fusion of Italianate revenge tragedy with medieval dramatic and ritual forms, *The Revenger's Tragedy* dramatizes the conflict of Italianate decadence with medieval values. There is on the one hand the influence of Italian *novelle* and their offspring in English Palaces of Pleasure and popular drama; on the other, there are the morality play, the sermon, the *memento mori,* and the Dance of Death. The observance of decorum in this fusion of material, and the art of the carefully constructed moral allegory are both evidence that aesthetic purposes and moral insight, not neurosis, dominate the author's work.

The relation of the play to the morality tradition has been described in some detail.[96] As L. G. Salingar notes, *"The Revenger's Tragedy* is the last, as well as the most brilliant, attempt to present the emotional conflicts of Renaissance society within the framework of moral allegory."[97] The influence of the moralities came from such plays as George Wapull's *The Tyde Taryeth no Man*[98] and Thomas Lupton's *All for Money,*[99] from Marlowe's *Doctor Faustus* and, most importantly, from the plays of Ben Jonson, especially *Volpone.*[100] The procession of the ducal family at the beginning of *The Revenger's Tragedy* is akin to medieval dramatizations of the Seven Deadly Sins.[101] As in moralities, the characters are personified abstractions subordinated to the symbolic and allegorical action,[102] Metaphors treat the physical world "as emblematic of the moral order."[103]

Implicit or explicit moral evaluation occurs everywhere in the play—in the names of characters and in other symbols, in the lines themselves, and in the punishment of evil-doers. The condemnation of luxury and avarice, of lawyers and usurers, of cosmetics and, in general, the preoccupation with "sin" and "damnation" as alternatives to "heaven" are typically

[96] L. G. Salingar, " 'The Revenger's Tragedy' and the Morality Tradition." *Cf.* his discussion in "Tourneur and the Tragedy of Revenge." See also Inga-Stina Ekeblad, "On the Authorship of *The Revenger's Tragedy.*"

[97] In "Tourneur and the Tragedy of Revenge," p. 348.

[98] (London, 1576), reprinted in *Shakespeare Jahrbuch,* XLIII (1907), 12–52.

[99] (London, 1578), reprinted in *Shakespeare Jahrbuch,* XL (1904), 145–186.

[100] L. G. Salingar, in " 'The Revenger's Tragedy' and the Morality Tradition," pp. 403, 415.

[101] Schoenbaum, *Middleton's Tragedies,* p. 28.

[102] Salingar, " 'The Revenger's Tragedy' and the Morality Tradition," pp. 403–404.

[103] *Ibid.,* p. 406.

medieval, and they are expressed in the medieval manner.[104]
The "silkworm" speech in III, v, 58–101, is close to being a
true *memento mori*.[105] Vindici seems to address some of the
lines on the skull directly to the audience. He is then like the
medieval homilist, who combines moralizing with realistic,
often satirical detail:

> A little later he will point his audience to the skulls and bones
> of the departed, bidding them reflect how through the mouth
> once so delectable to kiss, so delicate in its eating and its
> drinking, through eyes but a short while before so fair to see,
> worms now crawl in and out. The body or the head, once so
> richly attired, so proudly displayed, now boasts no covering
> but the soil, no bed of softness, no proud retinue save worms
> for the flesh, and, if its life was evil, demons for the soul.
> Therefore let all going forth to God's eternal banquet prepare
> themselves beforehand—by looking into the mirror of the
> Dead.[106]

Samuel Schoenbaum has discussed the relation of *The
Revenger's Tragedy* to the Dance of Death.[107] The spirit and
something of the form of the Dance are to be seen in the
depiction of worldly life as a "terribla dansa" in which men
lose sight of true values and are objects of sport for Death.[108]
There are elements of the Dance in the use of the skull, the

---

[104] John Peter, *Complaint and Satire*, pp. 60ff; Ekeblad, "On the
Authorship of *The Revenger's Tragedy*," pp. 230–231.

[105] Schoenbaum, *Middleton's Tragedies*, pp. 28–29. John Peter agrees
in "*The Revenger's Tragedy* Reconsidered," p. 140, but Theodore Spencer, his eye on Vindici's worldly drive for revenge, sees that Vindici
"does not turn for refuge to the other world" as he would in a conventional *memento mori*. *Death and Elizabethan Tragedy* (Cambridge,
Mass., 1936), p. 240. *Cf.* pp. 253, 262–263.

[106] Gerald R. Owst, *Preaching in Medieval England* (Cambridge, 1926),
p. 344.

[107] "*The Revenger's Tragedy*: Jacobean Dance of Death," *MLQ*, XV
(1954), 201–207.

[108] Leonard P. Kurtz, *The Dance of Death and the Macabre Spirit in
European Literature* (New York, 1934), p. 87.

literal death-dance ending the play, and the role of Vindici,
who "may be regarded as a sort of 'Docteur,' pointing out the
moral and warning all potential sinners."[109]

The chief example of the Dance of Death in English poetry
is John Lydgate's *Dance Macabre,* a processional of all estates
to death, with dialogue in alternating stanzas between death
and his victims, from pope and emperor through beggars and
children.[110] In this, and in almost all representations of the
Dance of Death, the theme is not only the frailty of life but
the equality of all men in the grave.[111] In *The Revenger's
Tragedy* all the victims of death are nobles and gentlemen,
but the social concern of the Dance and of the *memento mori*
literature from which it developed[112] is reflected in the social
contrasts of the "silkworm" speech[113] and elsewhere in the
satire of the play.

The morality tradition and the medieval heritage in general
give us a valuable perspective on the character of Vindici and
his role in the moral allegory of the play.[114] From this point of
view we can see how fully Vindici is a product of literary and
popular tradition, and thus how unnecessary it is to postulate a
mental illness for his creator. The primary moral connotation
of *disguise* was evil, for the Elizabethans associated the term
not only with "strange apparel" but with drunkenness,
deformity, dissimulation and the devil.[115] Satan, the Gospel's

---

[109] Schoenbaum, *"The Revenger's Tragedy* : Jacobean Dance of Death,"
pp. 206–207.

[110] Eleanor Prescott Hammond, *English Verse between Chaucer and
Surrey* (Durham, 1927), p. 126.

[111] Hammond, *ibid.* See also J. Huizinga, *The Waning of the Middle
Ages* (London, 1924), p. 131.

[112] Kurtz, *op. cit.,* pp. 10–17.

[113] Salingar, "Tourneur and the Tragedy of Revenge," p. 347.

[114] Sidney Thomas, *The Antic Hamlet and Richard III,* has a brief
mention of this aspect of the play.

[115] Muriel C. Bradbrook, "Shakespeare and the Use of Disguise in
Elizabethan Drama," *EIC,* II (1952), 160.

"envious man" and for Elizabethans the archetypal "mal-content,"[116] is "nimble and sodaine . . . in shifting his habit, his forme he can change and cogge as quicke as thought."[117] The devil appears in the morality as the Vice, who rails cynically and disguises himself as a Virtue in order to lead men to damnation.[118] The later Vice is a sophisticated rhetorician, like Vindici-Piato, using his demonic wit to invent ambiguities for brilliant ironic effects.[119]

Although personifications of divine vengeance appear in some early sixteenth-century plays influenced by the moral-ities,[120] the *Vice* calls himself "revenge" in John Pikeryng's *Horestes,* a morality-revenge play of 1567.[121] Here "Nature" argues against matricide on the basis of natural law, but when Clytemnestra is captured, wicked Revenge argues against mercy on the ground that the captive refused mercy to Agamemnon. It is "wicked" Revenge, significantly, who insists on the justice of the *lex talionis.*[122]

---

[116] See, for example, Heydon, *A Defence of Judiciall Astrologie,* p. 90.

[117] Thomas Nashe, *The Terrors of the Night* (London, 1594), ed. McKerrow, I, 349.

[118] The Vice in Wapull's *The Tyde Taryeth no Man, ed. cit.,* p. 27, says, "For I of kind, am alwayes various, / And chaunge, as to my mind seemeth best." He is assisted in damning men by "Hurtfull help," who calls himself "Help," and so on.

[119] Thomas, *op. cit.,* pp. 26–52, traces this later development from such plays as Robert Wilson's *The Three Ladies of London* (published 1584) and *Three Lords and Three Ladies of London* (publ. 1590) through *Richard III* and *Hamlet* to Vindici.

[120] Howard Baker, *Induction to Tragedy,* p. 124.

[121] Published at London. Included in *Illustrations of Old English Liter-ature,* ed. J. Payne Collier (London, 1866), II.

[122] After executing Clytemnestra, the Vice says "Horestes now doth rew. . . . And was it not yll/ His mother to kyll?" (p. 37). At the end of the play Horestes marries Menelaus' daughter with Truth, Duty, etc., at hand, and Revenge, solus, bids us farewell: he cannot succeed where Truth and Duty reign. In his parting speech he rails wittily against women, who he thinks are very vengeful. He laments that

Eache knave, nowe a dayes, would make me his man.
But chyll master them, I, be his Oundes, and I can.
A begginge, a begginge, nay now must I go. (p. 45)

Miss Bradbrook writes that *The Revenger's Tragedy* "might almost be called a *drame à thèse* on the contrasts between earthly and heavenly vengeance, and earthly and heavenly justice."[123] "The vengeance of the skull is . . ., in a sense, Heaven's vengeance. Measure for measure is meted out."[124] Samuel Schoenbaum says that "irony . . . constitutes the framework of the dramatist's morality," and I take it Robert Ornstein would agree with him.[125] Perhaps these critics are right, but I think it necessary to clarify their terms in order to avoid confusion. The author does not regard ironic "measure for measure" as an *ideal* standard. It is not God who argues for and deals out the ghastly reprisals of the *lex talionis*, but Satan. Miss Lily Bess Campbell regards as basic to Elizabethan tragedy the understanding of divine vengeance in which the punishment is made to fit the crime.[126] But she immediately proves *my* point by citing *Iago* as an authority for her position :

Do it not with poison; strangle her in her bed, even the bed she hath contaminated.   (IV.i.204-205)

God may use Satan to achieve some of His ends as Calvin argues,[127] but He would rather deal with men through love and grace, and the description of the death of the Duke in *The Revenger's Tragedy* as "heavenly vengeance," though it may be good Calvinist theology, is, I think, not quite applicable to the play itself. We have already seen that in the perpetration of this murder Vindici is perfectly willing to acknowledge his vil-

[123] *Themes and Conventions of Elizabethan Tragedy,* pp. 165–166.
[124] *Ibid.,* p. 170.
[125] Schoenbaum, *"The Revenger's Tragedy*: Jacobean Dance of Death," p. 207; Ornstein, "The Ethical Design of *The Revenger's Tragedy,"* p. 91.
[126] *Tudor Conceptions of History and Tragedy in "A Mirror for Magistrates,"* (Berkeley, 1936), pp. 19, 21.
[127] See Michael H. Higgins, "The Influence of Calvinistic Thought in Tourneur's *Atheist's Tragedy,"* p. 258.

lainy, and insists only on the justice of his revenge; but he, and likewise the critics I have quoted, regards it as the justice and vengeance of Heaven (III.v.198). We have also seen that this perfect revenge against the Duke is an ironic perversion of the very value it is to affirm—the purity of Vindici's murdered love —and is therefore morally flawed. Let us here ask what the controlling principles and essential ingredients of the revenge itself are, and whether they are heavenly or demonic.

The consideration that transports Vindici to the midst of "a throng of happy Apprehensions" is the poetic justice or "fitting irony" of the revenge he has planned (III.v.33, 105– 109). The Duke poisoned Gloriana because she would not submit to his lust, and now through his lust Gloriana shall poison him! She is a fit object now for his lust: "age and bare bone/ Are ere allied in action" (III.v.57–58). Everything is made perfect "unto the torturing of his soule" (III.v.22). The Duke will suffer a "delectably" ironic death—even to the disfigurement of his face by the corrosive poison, a disfigurement like that caused by the diseases of lechery.[128] His murderers will stick his soul with ulcers by making him watch his bastard embrace the Duchess (III.v.186). And the revengers will reveal their true identity in order to gloat over him.

This revenge is absolutely just and absolutely demonic; it is the epitome of the "divillish" Italianate and of the traditional conception of the torments imposed by demons. Well may the dying Duke ask "Is there a hell besides this, villaines?" (III.v. 196). In the hour of death,

> . . . when the lyf sal pas fra a man
> Devels sal gadir obout hym than,
> To ravissche the saul with tham away
> Tyl pyne of helle, if thai may.[129]

---

[128] Bradbrook, *Themes and Conventions*, p. 170.
[129] *The Pricke of Conscience* (c. 1340), quoted from Theodore Spencer, *Death and Elizabethan Tragedy*, p. 10.

These devils make frightful grimaces and noises in order to bring the dying to despair of the salvation of their souls.[130] In the late medieval phase of the Dance Macabre, Death came to be a demonic figure moving among men and inventing ingeniously fitting ways to kill, "forceably pouring liquor down the throat of the drunkard."[131] Indeed, *hell* is the place where punishments are made to fit the crime. In medieval mystery plays demons sometimes torture the damned : "Innkeepers who cheat on a measure of beer are certain to receive in hell a hot drink composed of oil, molten lead, pitch and sulfur."[132]

Ironic justice is, then, *demonic*. It is "heavenly" only in that by disobeying God men put themselves in the power of demons. And this distinction is, I think, the key to the moral allegory of *The Revenger's Tragedy*. It is a *drame à thèse* not so much on the contrast between earthly and heavenly justice as—quite as one would expect in a morality play—between the courses that lead to salvation and to damnation. And among the courses leading to damnation is that of seeking *justice* in any way, for men are saved not by their merit but by God's grace.

Much of the revenge action and the parallel action motivated by ambition and lust suggests that *The Revenger's Tragedy* is not "the war of good with evil, nor the self-division of good, but rather the intestinal division of evil itself,"[133] and the play *is*, in part, an "Anatomy of Evil."[134] The author does not stop, however, with showing the various ways a man may damn himself, or with showing conflicts of evil persons with one another. He also dramatizes the conflict between good and evil in the temptation of Castiza and Gratiana, which is

---

[130] Spencer, *Death and Elizabethan Tragedy,* p. 11.
[131] Kurtz, *op. cit.,* p. 194.
[132] *Ibid.,* p. 221.
[133] Peter Lisca, *op. cit.,* p. 245, *Cf.* Bowers, *op. cit.,* pp. 136–137.
[134] See the title of Rosenberg's dissertation on Tourneur.

resolved in their salvation through the divine grace that re-transforms Gratiana from a bawd into a true mother. If we arbitrarily classify Vindici as "evil," it is true that only a small portion of the play's on-stage time consists of incidents in which "good" characters are active, but the conflict between good and evil is always active in ambivalent words, in the tension of the imagery, and in the speeches of Vindici.

The fundamental conflict is between the decadent Italianate court with its associated "usury," and the old "country" virtues of the feudal society. There is on the one hand the home of chastity—here standing for purity of all sorts—and on the other hand the ducal palace and its many sins. Those in the palace of sin have abandoned all hope for their souls. Theirs is "a world of virtually unmixed evil, every line dyed in the consciousness of sin. . . . Such a community of the damned" as the play presents "could exist only in hell; in the state of nature its constituent parts would immediately destroy one another."[135] Precisely! The author has pictured the world of the palace and the society it has corrupted as a hell—in its notions of justice as in its overt sins—whose constituent parts *do* immediately (are two hours too long?) destroy each other.

The moral perversion of the court goes deeper than any carnal appetite. The viper and her brood are satisified only if their fornications are secret and sinful : only incest and rape truly gratify.[136]

DUTCH.   . . . there's no pleasure sweet but it is sinfull.
SPU.   True, such a bitter sweetnesse fate hath given;
          Best side to us, is the worst side to heaven.
                                        (III.v.220–222)

---

[135] Henry W. Wells, *Elizabethan and Jacobean Playwrights*, p. 34.
[136] *Cf.* Noel Annan, "Books in General," *The New Statesman and Nation*, XXVII (1944), 423.

Vindici, as we have seen, enters the court and yields to this same sort of unnatural pleasure, enjoying the sadistic ingenuity of his crimes, proud of his brilliance disguised as Piato[137] (e.g., IV.iv.98). His perversion brings him to the same fate as the others who live in the ducal palace, even though his origin is in the opposed world, where chastity is valued. He is the ambivalent link between these two worlds, the one rounded figure set against a background of flat symbols. He moves back and forth between the palace and the country, revealing the basic weakness of each : the virtuous poor are corrupted by gold and the sinful rich are destroyed by their perversion of sensuality.

The ambivalence of Vindici is best epitomized in lines from the two scenes with Castiza and Gratiana. In the first of these, after Gratiana has been bought for the devil's party, she and Vindici try to persuade Castiza to go to the palace :

> [VIND.] Nine Coaches waiting—hurry, hurry, hurry.
> CAST. I to the Divill.
> VIND. I to the Divill, to th' Duke by my faith.
> MOTH. I to the Duke.
>
> (II.i.228–231)

In his aside Vindici acknowledges the voice of Chastity, but aloud he is on the "Mother's" side. Later, after he has admitted his double role in the earlier scene, Gratiana pays a tribute to his brilliance as an ambivalent Vice :

> MOTHER. Ile give you this, that one I never knew
>   Plead better, for, and gainst the Divill, then you.
>
> (IV.iv.96–97)

One meaning of "Piato" is "a plea, a suite in law, a controversie, a processe, a pleading."[138] Vindici as pander is to be

---

[137] Cf. Fluchère's discussion of some of these points, op. cit., pp. 131–134.
[138] Florio, A Worlde of Wordes, p. 275.

Lussurioso's "sinnes Atturney" (II.i.42), to go "and with a smooth enchaunting tongue/Bewitch her eares, and Couzen" Castiza "of all Grace" (I.iii.125–126).

On one side of the morality play, legalistic pleading for justice or sensual pleasure; on the other, the gift of divine grace. Contrasting with the evil effects wrought by worldly pleading and the many souls that are damned, is a single but important instance of redemption: the purgation of Gratiana's soul in IV, iv. When confronted with the truth, that Vindici and Piato had been one, she repents and confesses her guilt. Then come tears:

VIN.   Yfaith tis a sweete shower, it dos much good.
         The fruitfull grounds, and meadowes of her soule,
         Has beene long dry: powre downe thou blessed dew;
         Rise Mother, troth this shower has made you higher.
MOT.   O you heavens! take this infectious spot out of my soule,
         Ile rence it in seaven waters of mine eyes.
         Make my teares salt ynough to tast of grace.
         To weepe, is to our sexe naturally given:
         But to weepe truely thats a gift from heaven.
                                        (IV.iv.55–63)

The sacramental pattern of grace, repentance, and confession is made even more explicit a few lines later, when Vindici refers to Gratiana's tears as "holy water" (IV.iv.94). At the end of the play this is the single beneficent transformation Vindici can look to with hope: "Yfaith, we're well, our Mother turnd, our Sister true" (V.iii.168).

Fluchère, while noting the significance of Gratiana's conversion, thinks it is inadequate as an affirmation of the possibility of good in the world because it does not seem to him to occupy a large enough place in the drama.[139] But "Grace,"

---

[139] *Op. cit.*, pp. 78–79, 131–134.

like Vindici, stands at the morally ambivalent center of the play. This is dramatized in the fall and reconversion of "Gratiana" and symbolized in the various meanings of the word *grace*. Divine grace is everywhere implicitly contrasted with human grace that must be pled for. Early in the play Vindici says "Save *Grace* the bawde I seldome heare *Grace* nam'd!" (I.iii.18). But that is only because he was not on stage in the second scene, when we witness the trial of Junior for the rape of Antonio's wife The Duchess pleads with the Duke to save her son: "My gratious Lord I pray be mercifull" and "temper his fault with pitty" (I.ii.24,29). She prays for purely human "grace" and, ironically, Junior is denied true grace:

> [Luss.] I love thee so far, play not with thy Death.
> Juni.   I thanke you troth, good admonitions faith,
>   If ide the grace now to make use of them.
>   (I.ii.60–62)

And when Junior dies he can only curse, and will not be tricked into looking up to heaven (III.iv.75–84). He and the other evil figures of the play are lost because, recognizing their own sin, they have despaired of salvation and in so doing denied the possibility of grace.

There are other notable ironic exploitations of the contrast between the Duke's grace and divine grace, revealing that the play's great criminals think that grace must be pled for, that grace is unforgiving. Lussurioso unintentionally attacks his father in his bed, and the old Duke pleads that much time will be necessary to achieve his salvation; he must have time for prayer and pleading, and he does not seem to anticipate an influx of divine grace. Ironically, a moment later this graceless being is addressed as "your Grace" (II.ii.216–226). Then follows the false pleading of Ambitioso and Supervacuo for the life of Lussurioso:

AMBI. My gratious Lord, take pitty,—
DUKE. Pitty boyes?
AMB.   Nay weed be loth to moove your Grace too much,
       Wee knowe the trespasse is unpardonable,
       Black, wicked, and unnaturall.

                                        (II.ii.284–288)

Not one of the characters who plead before any bar of justice is successful. The Duchess, Ambitioso and Supervacuo merely bring about the despairing death of Junior, whom they would have saved. The "gentleman" who has done the Duke's bidding and lied about his whereabouts is not saved from execution by the truth, and neither is "4." Vindici hardly bothers to plead for his life at the end : he, alone among them all, has seen that legalistic pleading is a perversion of the true way to salvation. As he has said to Lussurioso :

> There are old men at the present, that are so poysoned with the affectation of law-words, (having had many suites canvast), that their common talke is nothing but Barbery lattin : they cannot so much as pray, but in law, that their sinnes may be remov'd, with a writ of Error, and their soules fetcht up to heaven, with a sasarara.   (IV.ii.63–68)

Those who plead with the intent of corrupting one another are somewhat more successful : Piato conquers Gratiana, and the Duchess overcomes Spurio. Contrasting with these is the incorruptible Castiza. She realizes that "To deale with my Lords Grace" will be indeed to lose her soul when the "grace" is that of Lussurioso (II.i.217–218).

The virtue of chastity comes to stand for the spiritual values that must be preserved or restored. This is made clearest in the important speech of Lussurioso commissioning Vindici to seduce Castiza, part of which I have quoted before :

Go thou, and with a smooth enchaunting tongue
Bewitch her eares, and Couzen her of all Grace.
Enter upon the portion of her soule,
Her honor, which she calls her chastity
And bring it into expence . . .

(I.iii.125–129)

There is no avoiding the sexual implications of "enter" here,
for almost immediately Vindici and Lussurioso make obscene
jokes about what will "put a man in" (I.iii.143). The use of
"enter" to suggest a corrupting intercourse immediately relates
this passage to lines nearer the beginning of the scene, when
Lussurioso pays Vindici to become his servant :

    LUSS.   So, thou'rt confirmed in mee
              And thus I enter thee.
    VIND.   This Indian divill,
              Will quickly enter any man . . .

(I.iii.96–99)

In both these passages corruption is represented as "entrance"
by the devil or one of his agents. So later, when he is about
to overcome Gratiana, Vindici-Piato says aside "I feare me
she's unmotherd, yet ile venture,/ 'That woman is all male
whome none can Enter' " (II.i.123–124). Gratiana immediately "forgets heaven" for Lussurioso's gold, and her transformed state is regarded as possession by the devil. Castiza says
that there is a "poysonous woman" who is "too inward" with
her mother (II.i.260, 262). The theme of "entering" is linked
to the use of daggers and especially of poison as agents of the
devil. The corrupting effect of evil pleading on the pleader is
best described in Gratiana's remark in IV, iv, after her conversion : "O see, I spoke those words, and now they poyson
me" (IV.iv.150).

The entrance of Lussurio's gold into Vindici symbolizes the beginning of his evil transformation, and it also is the moment when Vindici, like Richard II's antic death, "Comes at the last and with a little pin/ Bores through" the ducal "castle wall." [140] The theme of "entering" is thus related to the structure of the play, for this penetration of his enemy's stronghold is only through the outermost wall, and Vindici must yet penetrate further, beyond Lussurioso to the Duke himself—a penetration consummated at the inmost part of the play, its very center in the murder scene at III,v.

In his temptation of Gratiana and Castiza, Vindici insists that their choice is absolute : they can enjoy riches only if they become corrupt. Thus what L. G. Salingar calls the play's "social dilemma" is presented in essentially moral terms of "pollution on entry into 'the world.' " [141] If Gratiana can "forget heaven" she can be rich (II.i.134). Worldly salvation is contrasted with heavenly salvation, [142] and "angells," like Vindici, are active agents of both good and evil, the contrasting significances of the word as heavenly beings and as coins ironically emphasizing the abyss between the moral poles of the play :

> MOTH. O fie, fie, the riches of the world cannot hire a
> mother to such a most unnaturall taske.
> VIND. No, but a thousand Angells can;
> Men have no power, Angells must worke you too't,
> The world descends into such base-borne evills
> That forty Angells can make fourscore divills.
> (II.i.96–101)

---

[140] *Richard II,* III, ii, 169–170.
[141] "Tourneur and the Tragedy of Revenge," p. 348.
[142] *Cf.* IV, iv, 117, 168 with II, i, 113–115 and the use of "salvation" in the usual religious sense elsewhere in the play; *e.g.,* II, ii, 25–26.

But at the end of the scene, when "celestiall Soldiers" have successfully defended the heart of Castiza, Vindici calls on "Angels" to "give this Virgin Christall plaudities" (II.i.157, 266–267). The world is so evilly transformed that even the agents which should serve good ends—Vindici and the angels—are alike corrupted, "plated" with gold masks.

"Time hath several falls" in the structure of *The Revenger's Tragedy*.[143] The action is rapid; the old virtues are contrasted with the decadence of this transformed age; moral transformations occur in a "minute" despite the sinners' despairing belief that repentance requires a long time, and the vanity of transitory worldly pleasure is exposed through contrast with the eternity that lies beyond life. In the transformed world of the play Vindici becomes Piato, of whom Hippolito says "This our age swims within him : and if Time/ Had so much hayre, I should take him for Time,/ He is so neere kinne to this present minute" (I.iii.27–29). By torchlight night becomes day and age becomes unnaturally youthful in its lusts. Vindici rails against this unnatural lust in his opening speech, and the Duke himself admits later that "Age hot, is like a Monster to be seene : / My haires are white, and yet my sinnes are Greene" (II.ii.359–360). Similarly, when Lussurioso asks Vindici "Ist possible that in this/ The Mother should be dambd before the daughter?" the witty reply is "Oh, that's good manners my Lord, the Mother for her age must goe formost you know" (II.ii.55–58).

People *rush* to death and damnation : the "Indian divill" of Lussurioso's gold "quickly" enters Vindici, and Vindici sets "golden spurs" to Gratiana, which "put her to a false gallop in a trice" (II.ii.53–54). "Cuckolds are a quoyning, apace, apace, apace, apace," and Vindici-Piato urges Castiza to go

---

[143] Salingar discusses some of these points in "Tourneur and the Tragedy of Revenge," pp. 343, 348, and Bradbrook touches on some in *Themes and Conventions*, p. 169. See also Irving Ribner, *Jacobean Tragedy* (London, 1962), pp. 75–86.

to the court : "Nine Coaches waiting—hurry, hurry hurry"—
to which Castiza replies, "I to the Divill" (II.ii.159; II.i.228–
229). The first gentleman is sent "straight" to execution, and
at the end, when Vindici is made to bring himself forward as
a murderer by "time" (Piato?), he is borne to "speedy execution" (V.i.135; V.iii.160,145).

The emphasis on speedy damnation and death is greatest in
the bizarre execution of the Duchess' youngest son. Ambitioso
and Supervacuo pretend to plead for Lussurioso's life, but
actually want the Duke to execute him. The Duke, to test
them, says "he shall dye/ Ere many dayes, make hast"—to
which Ambitioso replies, "All speed that may be," and off
Ambitioso and Supervacuo rush with the Duke's signet to have
Lussurioso executed (II.ii.325–327). The Duke releases Lussurioso, and the order for execution is applied to the Youngest
Son, while Ambitioso congratulates himself that he shall be
"Duke in a minute" (III.i.16). The officers tell the treacherous
brothers "weele not delay/ The third part of a minute" in
executing their victim (III.iii.19–20). The whole of Act III,
scene iv is an ironic "knavish exposition" upon the letter the
Youngest Son has received from his brothers :

> *Brother be of good cheere . . .*
> *Thou shalt not be long a prisoner . . .*
> *We have thought upon a device to get thee out by a tricke! . . .*
> *And so rest comforted, be merry and expect it suddaynely.*
>
> (III.iv.11, 13, 15, 17)

The joke plays back and forth over not *long* a prisoner and
suddaynely : Junior "must straight suffer"; he is to be granted
"no delaying time" (III.iv.30,49).

> [JUNIOR] Looke you officious whoresons words of comfort,
>   *Not long a Prisoner.*
> 1. OFF.   It sayes true in that sir, for you must suffer presently.
>
> (III.iv.66–68)

Damnation can come in a single minute, often associated with midnight at noon or noon at midnight. Midnight is the "*Judas* of the howers; wherein,/ Honest salvation is betrayde to sin," the "howre of Incest" (I.iii.78–79,70). In revels, "When Torch-light made an artificiall noone," occurred the "Vitious minute" of the rape of Antonio's wife and the damning conception of Spurio, "By one false minute disinherited" (I.iv.33, 45; I.ii.183,188). At the beginning of the play Vindici calls upon vengeance to keep its "day, houre, minute," and in the "un-sunned lodge,/ Where-in tis night at noone" he damns himself as he crowds "9. years vengeance . . . into a minute" (I.i 44; III.v.20–21, 126). Recapitulating these fatal minutes and the mad, whirling pace of the play and all its revels, disguises and murders, is the microcosmic Dance of Death in the masque that closes the action. Pleasure-seeking permits enemies to penetrate the court in disguise, and "Within a straine or two" of music Vindici and his accomplices turn the hopes of Lussurioso that he "shall nere die" into blood (V.ii.21; V.iii.45).

Although the evil characters believe death and damnation can be crowded into a minute, they think the processes of salvation are slow. Supervacuo and Ambitioso fear the Duchess and Spurio will "sinne faster then weele repent" (IV.iii.25), and the Duke speaks of his need for days and months to clear his soul of sin. The author, of course, believes in the efficacy of instantaneous grace, as it is dramatized in the re-conversion of Gratiana.

The most thoroughly evil of the characters never sincerely think of repentance, and though they believe in damnation, they usually do not think sin has long-lasting evil effects while one is living. Thus the Duke has no real desire to repent—he only wants Lussurioso to spare his life—and Ambitioso and Supervacuo speak of repentance in a merely figurative manner.

Ambitioso thinks that now Antonio's wife is dead, "peoples thoughts will soone be buried"; but we know such crimes are not soon forgotten, that Vindici has spent nine years brooding over his dead lady (III.i.23–24; I.i.54). Vindici, Hippolito and Gratiana after her re-conversion are the characters most aware of the enduring consequences of sin. Hippolito speaks of being "eternally wretched" as a consequence of riches, and Gratiana finally sees that "when woemen are yong Courtiers, they are sure to be old beggars,/ To know the miseries most harlots taste" (IV.iv.82,156–157). Vindici, who sees these evil consequences from a somewhat different angle, is perhaps alluding to the relationship between the Duke and Spurio when he says: "You shall have one woman knit more in a hower then any man can Ravell agen in seaven and twenty yeare" (II.ii.77–79).

The climactic and morally the most significant expression of the vanity of sin is Vindici's *memento mori* sermon in III,v. Here the "bewitching minute" of sin is directly opposed to the skull and its moral:

> . . . it were fine me thinkes,
> To have thee seene at Revells, forgetfull feasts,
> And uncleane Brothells; sure twould fright the sinner
> And make him a good coward . . .
>
> (III.v.93–96)

These dramatic and symbolic structures develop and support the central moral dialectic of the play—the struggle between the powers and the ways of life working toward salvation and those working toward damnation. The drama is now external—as in the transformations brought about through seduction and revenge—and now internal—within the character of Vindici or between opposed meanings of a single word. The author's approach to man in *The Revenger's Tragedy* is primarily moral, but in one instance at least it is also psychological. Most of his characters are intellectually conceived as allegorically "good" or "evil" abstractions. Vindici, however, develops as a living person who changes in response to experience. He may have begun in his creator's mind as one more allegorical character, ambivalent only in being "polluted," one thing "entered" by another, but he has also been provided with complex emotions and allowed the freedom to act as these dictate. The result is one of the most believable portraits of neurotic perversion in all the Jacobean drama.

The Revenger's Tragedy dramatizes the traditional Christian doctrine of fallen man and the traditional pattern of sin and redemption. The world of the play is the *fallen* world, a world transformed by the loss of its innocence into an Italianate hell which caricatures the depravity caused by the Fall, and at the same time depicts the terrible consequences of man's refusal of God's grace: "Is there a hell besides this, villaines?" Dramatically contrasting with the exaggerated corruption of "the world" is the comparative innocence of the home of "Chastity" and her mother, "Grace." But the devil enters even the havens of innocence, and man is corrupted and falls. Gratiana's later redemption suggests the restoration that is possible through divine aid.

All of the play's impure characters conform to the traditional conception of the fallen state of man. They are corrupted in will, and although they can still dimly distinguish right from wrong, their reason has been so weakened and subverted by their appetites that it is unable to move the will toward good. In critical moments these characters are blinded by passion and lack insight into the truth of their situation. Caught up in the traditional Christian warfare with the World, the Flesh and the Devil, they are overcome; the ducal family by the temptations of the Flesh, Gratiana by the World, and Vindici by the Devil of malice. In this unequal conflict, Elizabethans believed, man has only one great hope; he may be saved by the direct intervention of the grace of God, the greatest of all agents of transformation :

> . . . grace, no matter how it came, was by all churches thought of as irradiating the entire character. It calmed and assuaged the passions, rectified the will, opened the eye of reason to spiritual truths, and by cleansing the motives enabled men to practice true Christian charity in their daily lives. So incredible was the change that a person having a justifying grace might be said to be reborn, "a new creature . . . endued with a new nature or disposition."[144]

5   THE PLAY AND ITS AUTHOR IN PERSPECTIVE

The Revenger's Tragedy has sometimes been misunderstood because it has not been seen in its proper relation to the plays that preceded and influenced it. Compared with earlier tragedies of revenge, it appears confused in structure, for in much of the conflict the protagonist seems as much a spectator as a participant.[145] Readers who approach the play as dramatic satire, on the other hand, tend to detach Vindici's railing and moralizing from the play as a whole, leaving the way open for charges of cynicism and a horror of life on the part of the author himself.

Inga-Stina Ekeblad discusses the necessity of seeing the play as a fusion of elements drawn from the Senecan-Kydian revenge play, from the dramatic "humours" satire which developed at the end of the sixteenth century, and from the

---

[144] Paul H. Kocher, *Science and Religion in Elizabethan England*, p. 311.
[145] Bowers, *op. cit.*, pp. 136–137.

morality and homiletic tradition.[146] These elements work
together to give the play unity. Satiric realism prevents excessive melodrama, moral allegory gives greater significance to
the satire, and the satire and the revenge plot give body to the
morality framework.[147]

Although there are reminiscences of *Hamlet* and of
Chettle's *Hoffman* in the situation and in some details of its
treatment, the writer in the revenge *genre* to whose plays *The
Revenger's Tragedy* is most nearly related is Marston. His is
the first full dramatization of Italianate revenge, and the
dramatic condemnation of the Italianate revenge of Vindici
against the Duke may be regarded as a comment on Marston's
apparent attitude toward the torture of Piero by Antonio,
who remains the hero at the end of *Antonio's Revenge*.

The Revenger's Tragedy is even more clearly a dramatic
comment on Marston's satiric revenge play, *The Malcontent*,
1604, which it imitates very closely. The setting of *The Malcontent* is an Italian ducal court populated by monsters of
lust and ambition. The central figure, the revenger-satirist
Malevole, seeks justice by going into the court disguised as a
railing malcontent, and is hired by his enemy. Among other
duties, he is sent as pander to his own wife. He manages to set
his enemies against one another by betraying their secret
adulteries. The play ends with revels in which masked members of the malcontent's party seize power from the usurper.
But unlike Vindici, Marston's moralizing malcontent is able
to return to his original identity at the end, to resume his rightful place in society, accepted by all. His extreme cynicism has
been purged by his rediscovery of virtue, and there is no
suggestion that cynicism has tainted him, that by entering into
the employ of villainy and assuming the pander he has irre-

---

[146] "On The Authorship of *The Revenger's Tragedy*," p. 227.
[147] *Ibid.*, p. 233.

vocably corrupted himself. The mask of the bitter, satirical
malcontent is in the last analysis only a mask, and it can be
as easily removed as put on. The author of *The Revenger's
Tragedy* seems implicitly critical of Marston's work : he relates
every term of the satire to the obsessions of the satirist, Vindici,
and shows what happens to the *real* malcontent.

The moralist who put on the mask of the satirist was
developed to provide the dramatic equivalent of the speaker's
point of view in formal Juvenalian verse satire.[148] In Jonson's
Every Man Out of His Humour the moralist Asper, disguised
as Macilente, stands aside from the action and ironically
reveals the folly of his satiric targets. He refrains from criminal
action and makes it clear that his cynicism and prurience as
Macilente are only *pretended*. At the end he steps back into
his true identity as Asper. Some critics argue that once we
accept the mask as a symbol of Jonson's recognition that the
satirist's view is partial and distorted, we can regard the
ironical Macilente's comments as essentially authorial. The
conclusion is that "it is still from [the author] that the Satire
emanates," though we are cautioned that we must not see
dramatic speeches as "word for word" the author's "own
ideas."[149]

When we apply this formula too simply to *The Revenger's
Tragedy,* we feel that it is impossible to regard Vindici's
bitterness as conventional "satiric exaggeration." His prurient
obsession with sex and vice, and his spiritual despair, are so
extreme that if we believe his point of view is ultimately that
of the author, we must attribute some of his perversion to the
dramatist. This interpretation of the play found final expres-

---

[148] O. J. Campbell, *Comicall Satyre and Shakespeare's Troilus and
Cressida* (San Marino, 1938), pp. 48–57. *Cf.* John Peter, *Complaint and
Satire*, pp. 198–205.

[149] John Peter, *Complaint and Satire*, p. 206. *Cf.* O. J. Campbell, *op.
cit.,* p. 79.

sion in an essay by Padraic Fallon, who imagines that Tourneur, whom he takes to be the author of *The Revenger's
Tragedy,* must have come from the family of a "high-graded
servant" of neither the upper nor the lower class. Tourneur
must thus have been out of place in his society, and the result
was a neurotic "withdrawal into the self."[150] This is, of course,
an excellent description of the sort of man Lussurioso wants
for his pander : "some strange digested fellow . . ./ Of ill-
contented nature, either disgracst,/ In former times, or by
new groomes displacst,/ Since his Stepmothers nuptialls"
(I.i.84–87).

Fallon and others who would go most of the way with him
read *The Revenger's Tragedy* too narrowly as authorial self-
expression. The playwright has made Vindici-Piato a much
more fully *dramatic* character than were Macilente and
Malevole. Vindici's every word defines his character and is
integrated into the complex dramatic structure. As we have
seen, the playwright holds that Vindici's is a partial view,
that his quest for justice is a journey to damnation, and that
his action places him on a level with the super-vacuous. And
note that the author further detaches himself from Vindici's
attitudes by giving Hippolito lines pointing a finger at the
ludicrous elements in the railing satirist, Macilente–Malevole–
Vindici–Piato. After Vindici's cynical appeal to Impudence
to transform him into the scheming Piato, in which he rails
against the loss of "Grace" in his society, Hippolito responds
"Nay brother you reach out a'th Verge now" (I.iii.19). And
after Vindici's "Cuckolds are a quoyning, apace, apace, apace,
apace" speech, Hippolito joshes him with "You flow well
brother" (II.ii.159, 162). In the skull speech in III,v, when
Vindici says that mad people are mad only in clothes, and
he and his brother are the ones mad in sense, Hippolito inter-

---

[150] "The Unique Genius," *The Dublin Magazine,* XII, No. 3 (1937), 65.

rupts with the comical "Faith and in clothes too we, give us our due" (III.v.86).

I think Alvin Kernan is right in saying that in Renaissance satire the adoption of the satiric persona may be in many instances entirely dramatic : the author may be fully aware of the tensions inherent in the satiric character—the cruel lasher of cruelty—and may give these tensions full development, regarding the persona ironically and exposing either directly or indirectly the contradictions of the character he has created. But Kernan misinterprets *The Revenger's Tragedy* by regarding too much of the revenge action as satire. He contends that because Vindici perceives that "lust is death," "his satiric business of cutting away pretense can be realized only by cutting away the bodies of his enemies and reducing them to the reality of the skeleton."[151] If the murder of the old Duke is a *satiric* act, however, then the satire must emanate directly from the author, and Kernan's posited relation of the author to his satire through the persona breaks down. *Vindici* has no satiric business, no satiric aim in mind when he murders. When he calls out "Brother—place the Torch here, that his affrighted eyeballs/ May start into those hollowes," it is not to exhort the duke to consider the "reality" of the skull and the vanity of a life of sin, but to *recognize* the skull "Of *Gloriana*, whom thou poysonedst last," for "the very ragged bone/ Has beene sufficiently revengd" (III.v.155–158, 162–163).

Other critics find *The Revenger's Tragedy* so obsessed with evil as to seem neurotic even without identifying the author's point of view with that of Vindici. Una Ellis-Fermor writes that the author's "detachment from his characters is nearly as complete as Middleton's in tragedy, but they are produced upon a background of horror and evil fraught with emotional implications from which Middleton's are free . . . His definite

---

[151] *The Cankered Muse*, p. 227.

affirmation of evil stands inflexible and positive."[152] Fluchère says that the author of *The Revenger's Tragedy* thinks man is trapped by evil in a world where there can be no hope.[153] And T. B. Tomlinson believes that the dramatist is drawn toward decadence, and can only precariously maintain his balance on the verge of "the pit he is contemplating."[154]

T. S. Eliot's is still the classic statement of this general view of the play. Although in part he seems to make the error of equating the point of view of the author with that of Vindici, his statement transcends that error :

> The cynicism, the loathing and disgust of humanity, expressed consummately in *The Revenger's Tragedy,* are immature in the respect that they exceed the object. Their objective equivalents are characters practising the grossest vices; characters which seem merely to be spectres projected from the poet's inner world of nightmare, some horror beyond words. So the play is a document on humanity chiefly because it is a document on one human being, Tourneur; its motive is truly the death-motive, for it is the loathing and horror of life itself.[155]

But the characters are not projected from the dramatist's nightmare world. They are part of the popular conception of the "Italianate" which he was epitomizing. If Eliot means that the play fails as great drama because most of the characters are not sufficiently realized as human beings, he is criticizing its art, and he may have a point, but he should not read an author's *attitudes* thus directly out of his *failures.*

More important, Eliot and the other critics who see no

---

[152] *The Jacobean Drama,* p. 153.

[153] *Op. cit.,* p. 132.

[154] "The Morality of Revenge: *Tourneur's Critics,*" EIC, X (1960), 136, 143.

[155] "Cyril Tourneur," *Selected Essays 1917–1932* (New York, 1950), p. 166.

assertion of hope in the play ignore the re-conversion of
Gratiana : it may not come off artistically, and it may be
isolated in a welter of evil conversions, since there be few that
find the narrow way to life, but it is essential to the structure
of the work, and should therefore not be written off as a bit
of piety added to an otherwise pessimistic work merely for the
sake of appealing to the orthodox. Skeptical modern readers
have great difficulty accepting the orthodox seventeenth-century Christian doctrine of salvation. Many of us tend no
longer to believe in divine grace, and as a consequence we
impute our own despair to the dramatist who shows that only
grace can save us from the World, the Flesh and the Devil.
The *world* of *The Revenger's Tragedy* is "vibrant with imaginative horror," but it is not "a universe denuded of spiritual
significance,"[156] not "un monde irrémédiablement perdu" in
which there is no hope,[157] for in the early seventeenth century
God was not yet dead; man had not yet envisioned his own
salvation in the myth of scientific and social progress, but
rather still "remembered death" and prayed for grace. Vindici, Junior, Lussurioso and the Duke truly despair; their
creator's despair is only the hope of orthodox Christians seen
through the distorting perspective-glass of the centuries.

It seems to me that the author's careful artistry, and the
fact that "his ironic intellect is always in control"[158] also argue
for his detachment from the "horror" of the world he portrays
and from Vindici's death-motive. The structure of the play,
though complex, is wonderfully coherent. I think the analysis
of the play in the earlier sections of this chapter has demon-
strated this coherence sufficiently, but here I should like to
add the testimony of Una Ellis-Fermor, who elsewhere argues
in such strong terms that the author lacks detachment from

[156] Una Ellis-Fermor, *The Jacobean Drama*, pp. 155–156.
[157] Fluchère, *op. cit.*, pp. 131–132.
[158] Ornstein, *The Moral Vision*, p. 110.

his play. She writes that "it is this very quality of control, this steady, cool handling (even in the tempest of passion) of the forces he has set going that distinguishes most notably Tourneur's conduct of a play, extending from his handling of imagery and metre . . . to the revelation and manipulation of the characters and even to the narrative itself. . . . There is, in his use of imagery, a sensitiveness to the underlying harmony of image and character, image and setting, or image and situation which deserves no less a term than the much-loved Elizabethan 'decorum.' "[159]

The dramatist's ironic detachment from the passionate fury of Vindici and of the play as a whole can also be seen in his burlesque of the revenge tradition. Throughout the play there are lines and incidents so grotesque or exaggerated as to parody the stock devices of conventional revenge melodrama.[160] This absurd exaggeration is, of course, often felt in the satirical lines of Piato, who has witnessed the surrenders of "a thousand" virgins (I iii.54–55), who tells Gratiana she can take coach upon her daughter's lip, and so on (II.i.110). There is farcical grotesquerie in the macabre and demonic jesting and in the melodramatic excesses of the scene in which the old Duke is murdered: in such lines as Vindici's "T'is I, 'tis *Vindici*, tis I," and "make his eyes like Comets shine through bloud;/ When the bad bleedes, then is the Tragedie good," and in Vindici's punning rejoinder to the Duke's dying "I cannot brooke—" : "The Brooke is turnd to bloud" (III.v.179, 215–216, 234–235). Among other obviously farcical elements are Junior's blasphemous good cheer in the face of death, Supervacuo's threat to "braine" the Officer with Junior's

<hr/>

[159] *The Jacobean Drama,* pp. 160–161. See also Moody E. Prior, *The Language of Tragedy* (New York, 1947), pp. 139–144, and L. G. Salingar, "Tourneur and the Tragedy of Revenge," p. 344.

[160] See Salingar, "*The Revenger's Tragedy* and the Morality Tradition," p. 415; Schoenbaum, *Middleton's Tragedies,* pp. 23 and 29; and Ekeblad, "On the Authorship of *The Revenger's Tragedy,*" p. 232.

detached head, and the stabbing of the dead body of the Duke (III.iv; III.vi; V.i).

In *The Old Drama and the New,* his impatient attack on the *Old,* William Archer perhaps wrote truer than he meant when he concluded from these grotesque farcical elements that the play is "a mere farrago of sanguinary absurdities," and berated modern criticism for taking seriously what its author might have intended as a burlesque of revenge melodrama.[161] Actually, if the author had *not* been in part parodying the genre of revenge melodrama he would have been breaking with the tradition he was attempting to epitomize. That is to say, the two earlier tragedies of bloody revenge to which *The Revenger's Tragedy* is most closely akin both parodied revenge melodrama. Chettle's *Hoffman* contains an absurd subplot in which the feeble-minded Jerome seeks revenge, his lines burlesquing those of Hoffman himself or of old Hieronimo and other figures in the revenge tradition. In *Hamlet* the clowning and the parody of bombastic drama and ranting actors achieve much the same effect as one of their functions.[162]

Archer's error, it would seem, was to assume that an author cannot be serious in a play that burlesques the "prevailing style of tragedy." In *The Revenger's Tragedy,* Renaissance unity gives way to the ironies of medieval drama and art, which had attempted to reach equilibrium by balancing yes against no, reverence against mockery.[163] The parody, and the

---

[161] *The Old Drama and the New* (Boston, 1923), p. 76.

[162] See Allan Gilbert, *The Principles and Practice of Criticism* (Detroit, 1959), pp. 141–145.

[163] Willard Farnham, "The Mediaeval Comic Spirit in the English Renaissance," *Joseph Quincy Adams Memorial Studies,* ed. James G. McManaway, Giles E. Dawson and Edwin E. Willoughby (Washington, 1948), pp. 429–437; A. P. Rossiter, *English Drama from Early Times to the Elizabethans,* p. 72; and Wylie Sypher, *Four Stages of Renaissance Style* (New York, 1955), pp. 36–37. Sypher relates Jacobean ambiguities to Mannerism, not to the Gothic; pp. 116–117 *et passim.*

subplot paralleling the absurd Ambitioso and Supervacuo with Vindici and Hippolito, provide comic perspectives on the action—distorted reflections which, like the gargoyles on heaven-aspiring Gothic cathedrals, frighten off the evil demons of obsessive passion.

V

Conclusions on Cyril Tourneur

As critical fashions have changed over the past century, we have moved away from prim Victorian disgust at the "sewer-windings" of Tourneur's works to the late romantic readings of Swinburne, Collins, Eliot and Una Ellis-Fermor, in which the emphasis is on Tourneur's "horror of life." Not only is *The Revenger's Tragedy* taken for evidence of its author's prurient obsession with vice, but under its influence *The Transformed Metamorphosis* is read as a testament of spiritual despair, and even the world of *The Atheist's Tragedy* is "denuded of spiritual significance."

These views misread the works, and they are, of course, chiefly dependent on the critics' identification of Vindici with Tourneur—a misreading of a play Tourneur probably did not write. *The Revenger's Tragedy* in concatenation with the apocalyptic *Transformed Metamorphosis* and the grim *Atheist's Tragedy* was too much for critical sanity; placed in the context of Middleton's work it does not seem to evoke hysteria.[1]

---

[1] See Schoenbaum, *Middleton's Tragedies*, pp. 3–35; Barker, *Thomas Middleton*, pp. 64–75.

Once it is insulated from the works of Tourneur, *The Revenger's Tragedy* clearly need no longer be the product of a diseased mind, and we can begin to see its true relation to *The Transformed Metamorphosis* and *The Atheist's Tragedy*. The three works, like most Jacobean literature, support the Anglican center against attack from all extremes, expressing the traditional Christian view that man cannot save himself, but must have the help of God—a view, it must be granted, that many modern readers find pessimistic.

The difference between the writers becomes definable only when we consider the works as art, and not as statement. The author of *The Revenger's Tragedy* would appear to have been chiefly interested in the psychological development of his central character in response to experience. Any symbolism or morality play structure he may employ are secondary to this interest. Tourneur, on the other hand, is dominated by interest in the ritual structure of his fable, and the development of character is secondary. In *The Atheist's Tragedy* the characters are sharply drawn but not complex, and so the play does not affect us as a profound *exploration* of the human condition. Instead we have an *assertion* about the human condition, an assertion brilliantly worked out through an artful and complex structure of action, character and symbol.

In this *The Atheist's Tragedy* follows *The Transformed Metamorphosis,* which is even more fully dominated by a mythic structure. To insert the more psychological *Revenger's Tragedy* between these two would be to suggest a break in the continuity of Tourneur's art, a continuity that is otherwise straightforward. His domination by his fable readily explains the progression from apparent pessimism in *The Transformed Metamorphosis* to relative optimism in *The Atheist's Tragedy,* for the assertion that man can be saved only by God must take a darker form in an apocalyptic myth than in a *de casibus* legend. The fable of *The Atheist's Tragedy* makes central and dominant the affirmation of the power of God to save that is forced into a secondary position by the myth dealt with in *The Transformed Metamorphosis*. In the earlier work our attention is primarily directed to the action that ensues when men turn away from God. Only in the last few lines of the poem does the power of God break through the clouds of evil to lighten and transfigure the world, and in that transfiguration God is shown as remote and impersonal, completely bound up within the apocalyptic convention and the mythic metaphor of the sunrise.

In *The Atheist's Tragedy,* however—even though there is, if anything, an even fuller exposition of Tourneur's "pessimistic" view that man cannot save himself—something approximating a balance is struck between salvation and damnation. God is not a remote figure in the manorial world, and man begins to emerge from his entrapment within the archetypal forms of monster and hero. God becomes an immediate and dramatically active agent, and we find that some men, at least, are capable of vital responses to His word.

Neither *The Transformed Metamorphosis* nor *The Atheist's Tragedy* depends on merely arbitrary allegory, for in both works the symbols used to express the relation of the individual to higher orders are great natural metaphors that have always been meaningful to men. In its imaginative fusion of dramatic realism with symbol allegory, *The Atheist's Tragedy* is of course a greater work than *The Transformed Metamorphosis*. Through this fusion Tourneur can achieve his larger purpose, which is to bring the light of the Christian world-view to bear on even the darkest reaches of reality. The little world of men is realistically created on the stage, and the symbolism enables us to interpret each word and incident as part of an ordered pattern, a pattern revealing the world to be truly a poem of God.

Bibliography

ADAMS, HENRY HITCH. "Cyril Tourneur on Revenge," *JEGP,* XLVIII (1949), 72–87.

ALDEN, RAYMOND MACDONALD. *The Rise of Formal Satire in England under Classical Influence.* Philadelphia, 1899.

ALLEN, DON CAMERON. *The Star-Crossed Renaissance: The Quarrel about Astrology and Its Influence in England.* Durham, 1941.

ANNAN, NOEL. "Books in General," *The New Statesman and Nation,* XXVII (1944), 423.

ANONYMOUS. *The Revengers Tragaedie.* London, 1607.

———, *La Tragédie du Vengeur.* Translated and edited by Henri Fluchère. Paris, 1958.

ARBER, EDWARD. *A Transcript of the Registers of the Company of Stationers of London, 1554–1640.* 5 vols. London, 1875–77.

ARCHER, WILLIAM. *The Old Drama and the New.* Boston, 1923.

BAKER, HOWARD. *Induction to Tragedy.* University, La., 1939.

BARBER, CHARLES. "A Rare Use of the Word *Honour* as a Criterion of Middleton's Authorship," *ES,* XXXVIII (1957), 161–168.

BARKER, RICHARD HINDRY. "The Authorship of the *Second Maiden's Tragedy* and *The Revenger's Tragedy,*" *SAB,* XX (1945), 51–62, 121–133.

———. *Thomas Middleton.* New York, 1958.

BARNES, BARNABE. *The Devil's Charter.* London, 1607. In Student's Facsimile Edition, 1913, part 8.

261

BAWCUTT, N. W. " 'The Revenger's Tragedy' and the Medici Family," *NQ*, 202 (1957), 192–193.

BAYLEY, HAROLD. *A New Light on the Renaissance Displayed in Contemporary Emblems*. London, 1909.

BEARD, THOMAS, and THOMAS TAYLOR. *The Theatre of Gods Judgements*. 4th edition. London, 1648.

BERRY, FRANCIS. *Poets' Grammar*. London, 1958.

BLACK, JOHN B. *The Reign of Elizabeth: 1558–1603*. 2nd edition. Oxford, 1959.

BOWERS, FREDSON THAYER. *Elizabethan Revenge Tragedy, 1587–1642.* Princeton, 1940.

BOYER, CLARENCE VALENTINE. *The Villain as Hero in Elizabethan Tragedy*. New York, 1914.

BRADBROOK, MURIEL C. *The School of Night*. Cambridge, 1936.

———. "Shakespeare and the Use of Disguise in Elizabethan Drama," *EIC*, II (1952), 159–168.

———. *Themes and Conventions of Elizabethan Tragedy*. Cambridge, 1935.

BREWER, EBENEZER COBHAM. *Brewer's Dictionary of Phrase and Fable*. New York, 1952.

BURCKHARDT, JACOB. *The Civilization of the Renaissance in Italy*. Translated by S. G. C. Middlemore. New York, 1904.

BUSH, DOUGLAS. *Mythology and the Renaissance Tradition in English Poetry*. Minneapolis, 1932.

Butler's Lives of the Saints. Edited by Herbert Thurston and Donald Attwater. 4 vols. New York, 1956.

CAMERON, KENNETH N. "Cyril Tourneur and *The Transformed Metamorphosis*," *RES*, XVI (1940), 18–24.

CAMPBELL, JOSEPH. *The Hero with a Thousand Faces*. New York, 1949.

CAMPBELL, LILY BESS. *Shakespeare's Tragic Heroes: Slaves of Passion*. Cambridge, 1930.

———. "Theories of Revenge in Renaissance England," *MP*, XXVIII (1931), 281–296.

———. *Tudor Conceptions of History and Tragedy in "A Mirror for Magistrates."* Berkeley, 1936.

CAMPBELL, OSCAR JAMES. *Comicall Satyre and Shakespeare's Troilus and Cressida.* San Marino, 1938.

The Catholic Encyclopedia. Edited by Charles G. Herbermann et al. 15 vols. New York, 1907–1912.

CAXTON, WILLIAM. *The Lyfe of Saynt Wenefryde.* Westminster, 1485.

CHAMBERS, E. K. *The Elizabethan Stage, 1558–1616.* 4 vols. Oxford, 1923.

CHAPMAN, GEORGE. *Conspiracy and Tragedy of Charles Duke of Byron.* London, 1608.

————. *The Poems of George Chapman.* Edited by Phyllis Brooks Bartlett. New York, 1941.

CHICKERA, ERNST DE. "Palaces of Pleasure : The Theme of Revenge in Elizabethan Translations of Novelle," *RES,* XI (1960), 1–7.

CLARKSON, PAUL S., and CLYDE T. WARREN. *The Law of Property in Shakespeare and the Elizabethan Drama.* Baltimore, 1942.

COPE, JACKSON I. "Tourneur's *Atheist's Tragedy* and the Jig of 'Singing Simpkin,'" *MLN,* LXX (1955), 571–573.

CRAIK, T. W. "The Revenger's Tragedy," *EIC,* VI (1956), 482–485.

DABORNE, ROBERT. A letter to Philip Henslowe in *The Alleyn Papers.* Edited by John P. Collier. *Shakespeare Society,* IX (London, 1843), 58.

DEKKER, THOMAS. *The Dramatic Works of Thomas Dekker.* Edited by Fredson T. Bowers. 4 vols. Cambridge, 1955–61.

DELONEY, THOMAS. *The Novels of Thomas Deloney.* Edited by Merritt E. Lawlis. Bloomington, 1961.

DORAN, MADELEINE. *Endeavors of Art.* Madison, 1954.

DUNBAR, HELEN FLANDERS. *Symbolism in Medieval Thought and its Consummation in the Divine Comedy.* New Haven, 1929.

DUNKEL, WILBUR D. "The Authorship of *The Revenger's Tragedy,*" *PMLA,* XLVI (1931), 781–785.

EINSTEIN, LEWIS. *The Italian Renaissance in England*. New York, 1902.

EKEBLAD, INGA-STINA. "An Approach to Tourneur's Imagery," *MLR*, LIV (1959), 489–498.

———. "On the Authorship of *The Revenger's Tragedy*," *ES*, XLI (1960), 225–240.

ELIOT, T. S. "Cyril Tourneur." *Selected Essays, 1917–1932*. New York, 1950.

ELLIS-FERMOR, UNA. *The Frontiers of Drama*. London, 1945.

———. "The Imagery of 'The Revengers Tragedie' and 'The Atheists Tragedie,'" *MLR*, XXX (1935), 289–301.

———. *The Jacobean Drama*. 4th edition. London, 1958.

EMPSON, WILLIAM. *Some Versions of Pastoral*. London, 1938.

FALLON, PADRAIC. "The Unique Genius," *The Dublin Magazine*, XII, No. 3 (1937), 62–69.

FARNHAM, WILLARD. "The Mediaeval Comic Spirit in the English Renaissance." *Joseph Quincy Adams Memorial Studies*. Edited by James G. McManaway, Giles E. Dawson and Edwin E. Willoughby. Washington, 1948.

———. *The Medieval Heritage of Elizabethan Tragedy*. Berkeley, 1936.

FERGUSSON, FRANCIS. *The Idea of a Theater*. Princeton, 1949.

FLETCHER, JOHN, et al. *The Honest Mans Fortune*, Edited by J. Gerritsen. Groningen Studies in English, Number 3. Djakarta, 1952.

FLORIO, JOHN. *Queen Anna's New World of Words*. London, 1611.

———. *A Worlde of Wordes*. London, 1598.

FLUCHÈRE, HENRI. *See* Anonymous.

FOAKES, R. A. "On the Authorship of 'The Revenger's Tragedy,'" *MLR*, XLVIII (1953), 129–138.

FRAUNCE, ABRAHAM. *The Third Part of The Countesse of Pembrokes Yvychurch, Entituled, Amintas Dale*. London, 1592.

GILBERT, ALLAN. *The Principles and Practice of Criticism*. Detroit, 1959.

GREEN, HENRY. *Shakespeare and the Emblem Writers.* London, 1870.

GREG, WALTER WILSON. *A List of English Plays Written Before 1643 and Printed Before 1700.* London, 1900.

HALL, JOSEPH. *The Collected Poems of Joseph Hall.* Edited by Arnold Davenport. Liverpool, 1949.

HALL, MANLY P. *An Encyclopedic Outline of Masonic, Hermetic, qabbalistic and Rosicrucian symbolical Philosophy.* San Francisco, 1928.

HAMILTON, A. C. "Spenser and Tourneur's *Transformed Metamorphosis,*" *RES,* VIII (1957), 127–136.

HAMMOND, ELEANOR PRESCOTT. *English Verse between Chaucer and Surrey.* Durham, 1927.

HARRISON, G. B. *The Elizabethan Journals,* 3 vols. in 1. New York, 1939.

HEFFNER, RAY. "Spenser's Allegory in Book I of the *Faerie Queene,*" *SP,* XXVII (1930), 142–161.

HEXHAM, HENRY. *Account of the Assault on Ostend, 7th January, 1602.* In *An English Garner,* edited by Edward Arber. Birmingham, 1883. VII, 171–183.

HEYDON, SIR CHRISTOPHER. *A Defence of Judiciall Astrologie, In Answer to a Treatise lately published by M. John Chamber.* Cambridge, 1603.

——. *The New Astrology.* 2nd edition. London, 1786. A later edition of *An Astrological Discourse,* 1650.

HIGGINS, MICHAEL H. "The Influence of Calvinistic Thought in Tourneur's *Atheist's Tragedy,*" *RES,* XIX (1943), 255–262.

HILLEBRAND, HAROLD N. "Thomas Middleton's *The Viper's Brood,*" *MLN,* XLII (1927), 35–38.

THE HOLIE BIBLE. London, 1572.

HOY, CYRUS. "The Shares of Fletcher and his Collaborators in the Beaumont and Fletcher Canon (I)," *SB,* VIII (1956), 129–146.

HUIZINGA, J. *The Waning of the Middle Ages.* London, 1924.

HUNTER, G. K., "A Source for *The Revenger's Tragedy,*" *RES,* X (1959), 181–182.

JENKINS, HAROLD. "Cyril Tourneur," *RES*, XVII (1941), 21–36.

JONES, FRED L. "Cyril Tourneur," *TLS*, June 18, 1931, p. 487.

JONSON, BEN. *Ben Jonson*. Edited by C. H. Herford and Percy Simpson. 11 vols. Oxford, 1925–52.

———. *The Alchemist*. London, 1612. English Replica Series. London, 1927.

JORDAN, WILBUR K. *Philanthropy in England, 1480–1660*. New York, 1959.

JUMP, JOHN D. "Middleton's Tragedies." *The Age of Shakespeare*. Vol. II of *A Guide to English Literature*. Edited by Boris Ford. London, 1956.

KERNAN, ALVIN. *The Cankered Muse: Satire of the English Renaissance*. New Haven, 1959.

KOCHER, PAUL H. *Science and Religion in Elizabethan England*. San Marino, 1953.

KURTZ, LEONARD P. *The Dance of Death and the Macabre Spirit in European Literature*. New York, 1934.

LANGBAINE, GERARD. *The Lives and Characters of the English Dramatick Poets*. Edited and revised by Charles Gildon. London [1699?].

LEECH, CLIFFORD. "*The Atheist's Tragedy* as a Dramatic Comment on Chapman's *Bussy* Plays," *JEGP*, LII (1953), 525–530.

———. "A Speech-Heading in *The Revengers Tragaedie*," *RES*, XVII (1941), 335–336.

LEGOUIS, PIERRE. "Réflexions Sur la Recherche des Sources à Propos de la 'Tragédie du Vengeur,'" *Études Anglaises*, XII (1959), 47–55.

LEWIS, C. S. *English Literature in the Sixteenth Century*. Oxford, 1954.

LISCA, PETER. "*The Revenger's Tragedy*: A Study in Irony," *PQ*, XXXVIII (1959), 242–251.

LOCKERT, LACY. "The Greatest of Elizabethan Melodramas." *Parrott Presentation Volume*. Edited by Hardin Craig. Princeton, 1935.

LUPTON, THOMAS. *All For Money*. London, 1578. In *Shakespeare Jahrbuch*, XL (1904), 145–186.

MARSTON, JOHN. *The Plays of John Marston*. Edited by H. Harvey Wood. 3 vols. Edinburgh, 1934–39.

McKENZIE, D. F. "A List of Printers' Apprentices, 1605–1640," *SB*, XIII (1960), 109–141.

MIDDLETON, THOMAS. *A Game at Chesse*. Edited by R. C. Bald. Cambridge, 1929.

———. *A Mad World, My Masters*. London, 1608.

———. *The Phoenix*. London, 1607.

———. *A Tricke to Catch the Old-one*. London, 1608.

———. *The Works of Thomas Middleton*. Edited by A. H. Bullen. 8 vols. London, 1885–86.

———. *Your five Gallants*. London, 1607.

MINCOFF, MARCO K. "The Authorship of 'The Revenger's Tragedy,'" *Studia Historico-Philologica Serdicensia*, II (1940), 1–87.

MORYSON, FYNES. In *Shakespeare's Europe*. Edited by Charles Hughes. London, 1903.

MROZ, SISTER MARY BONAVENTURE. *Divine Vengeance*. Washington, D.C., 1941.

MYERS, AARON MICHAEL. *Representation and Misrepresentation of the Puritan in Elizabethan Drama*. A dissertation at the University of Pennsylvania, 1931.

NAPIER, C. S. "The Revenger's Tragedy," *TLS*, March 13, 1937, p. 188.

NASHE, THOMAS. *The Works of Thomas Nashe*. Edited by R. B. McKerrow. 5 vols. Oxford, 1958.

NORDEN, JOHN. *Vicissitudo Rerum*. London, 1600. Edited by D. C. Collins. Shakespeare Association Facsimiles, Number 4. Oxford, 1931.

OLIPHANT, E. H. C. "The Authorship of *The Revenger's Tragedy*," *SP*, XXIII (1926), 157–168.

———. *The Plays of Beaumont and Fletcher*. New Haven, 1927.

———. "Tourneur and 'The Revenger's Tragedy,'" *TLS* December 18, 1930, p. 1087.

ORNSTEIN, ROBERT. " 'The Atheist's Tragedy,' " *NQ*, 200 (1955), 284–285.

──────. *"The Atheist's Tragedy* and Renaissance Naturalism," *SP*, LI (1954), 194–207.

──────. "The Ethical Design of *The Revenger's Tragedy*," *ELH*, XXI (1954), 81–93.

──────. *The Moral Vision of Jacobean Tragedy*. Madison, 1960.

OWST, GERALD R. *Preaching in Medieval England*. Cambridge, 1926.

PAINTER, WILLIAM. *The Palace of Pleasure*. London, 1566–67. Edited by Joseph Jacobs. 3 vols. London, 1890.

PARR, JOHNSTONE. *Tamburlaine's Malady and Other Essays on Astrology in Elizabethan Drama*. Univ. of Alabama, 1953.

PARROTT, THOMAS MARC, and ROBERT H. BALL. *A Short View of Elizabethan Drama*. New York, 1943.

PETER, JOHN D. *Complaint and Satire in Early English Literature*. Oxford, 1956.

──────. "The Identity of Mavortio in Tourneur's 'Transformed Metamorphosis,' " *NQ*, 193 (1948), 408–412.

──────. *"The Revenger's Tragedy* Reconsidered," *EIC*, VI (1956), 131–143, and a note on pp. 485–486.

PIKERYNG, JOHN. *Horestes*. London, 1567. In *Illustrations of Old English Literature*, edited by John Payne Collier, vol. II. London, 1866.

POWER, WILLIAM L. *The Ethical Pattern in the Plays of Thomas Middleton*. A dissertation at Vanderbilt University. *DA*, XV, 9 (1955), 1615.

PRICE, GEORGE R. "The Authorship and the Bibliography of *The Revenger's Tragedy*," *The Library*, 5th series, XV (1960), 262–277.

PRIOR, MOODY. *The Language of Tragedy*. New York, 1947.

PYM, DOROTHY. "A Theory on the Identification of Cyril Tourneur's 'Mavortio,' " *NQ*, 174 (1938), 201–204.

QUARLES, FRANCIS. *Emblems, Divine and Moral*. Edited by Augustus Toplady and John Ryland. London, 1839.

REYNOLDS, JOHN. *The Triumphs of Gods Revenge Against The Crying and Execrable Sinne of (Wilful and Premeditated) Murther.* 5th edition. London, 1670.

RIBNER, IRVING. *Jacobean Tragedy.* London, 1962.

ROBERTSON, D. W., JR. "Chaucerian Tragedy," *ELH*, XIX (1952), 1–37.

ROEDER, HELEN. *Saints and their Attributes.* Chicago, 1956.

ROSENBERG, JAMES L. *Cyril Tourneur: The Anatomy of Evil.* A dissertation at the University of Denver, 1954.

ROSSITER, A. P. *English Drama from Early Times to the Elizabethans.* London, 1950.

SALINGAR, L. G. " 'The Revenger's Tragedy' and the Morality Tradition," *Scrutiny*, VI (1938), 402–424.

———. "Tourneur and the Tragedy of Revenge." *The Age of Shakespeare.* Vol. II of *A Guide to English Literature.* Edited by Boris Ford. London, 1956.

SCHOENBAUM, SAMUEL. "Internal Evidence and the Attribution of Elizabethan Plays," *NYPLB*, LXV (1961), 102–124.

———. *Middleton's Tragedies: A Critical Study.* New York, 1955.

———. "*The Revenger's Tragedy:* Jacobean Dance of Death," *MLQ*, XV (1954), 201–207.

———. " 'The Revenger's Tragedy' and Middleton's Moral Outlook," *NQ*, 196 (1951), 8–10.

———. " 'The Revenger's Tragedy' : A Neglected Source," *NQ*, 195 (1950), 338.

SEGAR, SIR WILLIAM. *The Booke of Honor and Armes.* London, 1590.

SIBLEY, E. *A New and Complete Illustration of the Occult Sciences.* London, n.d.

SMITH, HALLETT. *Elizabethan Poetry: A Study in Conventions, Meaning, and Expression.* Cambridge, Mass., 1952.

SPENCER, THEODORE. *Death and Elizabethan Tragedy.* Cambridge, Mass., 1936.

———. *Shakespeare and the Nature of Man.* New York, 1942.

SPENSER, EDMUND. *The Works of Edmund Spenser.* Edited by

Edwin Greenlaw, Charles G. Osgood and Frederick M. Padelford. 9 vols. Baltimore, 1932–49.

STENGER, HAROLD. *The Second Maiden's Tragedy*. A dissertation at the University of Pennsylvania, 1954.

STOLL, ELMER E. *John Webster*. Boston, 1905.

STRATHMANN, ERNEST A. *Sir Walter Ralegh: A Study in Elizabethan Skepticism*. New York, 1951.

SUTHERLAND, JAMES R. "Cyril Tourneur," *TLS*, April 16, 1931, p. 307.

SYKES, H. DUGDALE. "Cyril Tourneur : 'The Revenger's Tragedy' : 'The Second Maiden's Tragedy,' " *NQ*, V (1919), 225–229.

SYPHER, WYLIE. *Four Stages of Renaissance Style*. New York, 1955.

TANNENBAUM, SAMUEL A. "A Tourneur Mystification," *MLN*, XLVII (1932), 141–143.

THOMAS, SIDNEY. *The Antic Hamlet and Richard III*. New York, 1943.

THORNDIKE, ASHLEY H. "The Relations of *Hamlet* to Contemporary Revenge Plays," *PMLA*, XVII (1902), 125–220.

THORNDIKE, LYNN. *A History of Magic and Experimental Science*. Vols. V and VI, *The Sixteenth Century*. New York, 1941.

THORP, WILLARD. *The Triumph of Realism in Elizabethan Drama, 1558–1612*. Princeton Studies in English, Number 3, 1928.

TILLYARD, E. M. W. *The Elizabethan World Picture*. London, 1943.

TOMLINSON, T. B. "The Morality of Revenge : Tourneur's Critics," *EIC*, X (1960), 134–147.

TOMPKINS, J. M. S. "Tourneur and the Stars," *RES*, XXII (1946), 315–319.

TOURNEUR, CYRIL. *The Atheist's Tragedie: Or The honest Man's Revenge*. London, 1611.

———. *The Plays and Poems of Cyril Tourneur*. Edited by John Churton Collins. 2 vols. London, 1878.

————. *The Works of Cyril Tourneur.* Edited by Allardyce Nicoll. London, 1929.

TUVE, ROSEMOND. *Elizabethan and Metaphysical Imagery.* Chicago, 1947.

WAGNER, BERNARD M. "Cyril Tourneur," *TLS,* April 23, 1931, p. 327.

WAITH, EUGENE M. "The Ascription of Speeches in *The Revenger's Tragedy," MLN,* LVII (1942), 119–121.

WALLERSTEIN, RUTH. *Studies in Seventeenth-Century Poetic.* Madison, 1950.

WAPULL, GEORGE. *The Tyde Taryeth no Man.* London, 1576. In *Shakespeare Jahrbuch,* XLIII (1907), 12–52.

WELLS, HENRY W. *Elizabethan and Jacobean Playwrights.* New York, 1939.

WEST, ROBERT HUNTER. *The Invisible World.* Athens, Ga., 1939.

WHITNEY, GEFFREY. *A Choice of Emblemes.* Leyden, 1586 In the facsimile edition by Henry Green. London, 1866.

YATES, FRANCES A. "Queen Elizabeth as Astraea," *Journal of the Warburg and Courtauld Institutes,* X (1947), 27–82.

YOUNG, G. F. *The Medici.* 3rd edition. 2 vols. New York, 1913.

Index

273